S0-BEJ-434

# VOICES
## *of the*
# PAST

VOICES OF THE PAST

*Readings in Ancient History*
*Readings in Medieval and Early Modern History*
*Readings in Modern History*

# VOICES of the PAST

## Readings in

## MEDIEVAL and EARLY MODERN HISTORY

James Hanscom
Leon Hellerman
Ronald Posner

THE MACMILLAN COMPANY, NEW YORK
COLLIER-MACMILLAN, LIMITED, LONDON

© COPYRIGHT THE MACMILLAN COMPANY 1967

1-O

All rights reserved. No part of this book may be reproduced or utilized in any form or by any means, electronic or mechanical, including photocopying, recording or by any information storage and retrieval system, without permission in writing from the Publisher.

Cover Illustrations: *top left,* from *The Bayeux Tapestry,* edited by Sir Frank Stenton, published by Phaidon Press, London; distributed in the U.S.A. by New York Graphic Society; *top right* and *bottom left,* The Granger Collection.

THE MACMILLAN COMPANY, NEW YORK
COLLIER-MACMILLAN CANADA, LTD., TORONTO, ONTARIO
Printed in the United States of America

# Contents

# The Medieval World

The passing of the Roman Empire in the west in the fifth century A.D., often called "the fall of Rome," is generally accepted as marking the end of ancient times and the beginning of what in Europe is known as the "medieval" period or the "Middle Ages." Much of Europe was overrun again by forests and wild animals. Trade, travel by land, and shipping almost ended. Many cities vanished, and those that remained dwindled in size. Ignorance prevailed, even in government and the church. Governments were weak. Who would care for the sick, the orphan, the aged, the stranger, the destitute?

In the three centuries leading to the time of Charlemagne (A.D. 768–814), conditions slowly improved. A new world seemed in the making through the co-operation of the church and the nation of Franks. But many of the gains were lost again in the ninth and tenth centuries. Invasions of Vikings from the north, Muslims from the south, and Huns again from the east coincided with civil wars at home. The little learning of these "Dark Ages" was threatened with complete extinction. Some new substitute for government had to be found, some economic system established. The answers to these problems were the systems of feudalism and manorialism.

Then, in the eleventh century, one of the most tremendous periods of rapid human development began. The following three centuries, Europe's "high" Middle Ages, were crowded with exciting personalities and events. Cities multiplied in number and size; within their walls, cathedrals soared skyward, and universities were born. The first national states began to emerge. Great wars of religion, called "crusades," were waged against the Muslims, and finally a great war took place between England and France (the Hundred Years War). The long struggle for liberty began. Modern languages were born and became the parents of great new literature. Art, architecture, law, philosophy, and commerce flourished.

Throughout the Middle Ages, men wrote of good things and bad, of life as it is and life as it ought to be, and of the world of fact and the world of fancy.


## The Huns *

AMMIANUS MARCELLINUS

*Sweeping out of western Asia against the Chinese to the east and the German tribal neighbors of the Roman Empire to the west, the Huns and their chieftan Attila typified the most destructive elements of the fourth century. The Roman historian Marcellinus (c. A.D. 400) describes them according to stories then circulating in Europe.*

. . . The people called Huns . . . are a race savage beyond all parallel.

At the very moment of their birth the cheeks of their infant children are deeply marked by an iron, in order that the usual vigour of their hair, instead of growing at the proper season, may be withered by the wrinkled scars; and accordingly they grow up without beards, and consequently without any beauty . . . ; they are of great size, and low legged, so that you might fancy them two-legged beasts, or the stout figures which are hewn out in a rude manner with an axe on the posts at the end of bridges.

* Ammianus Marcellinus, *The Roman History*, London, Henry G. Bohn, 1862 (translated by C. D. Yonge).

They are certainly in the shape of men, however uncouth, but are so hardy that they neither require fire nor well-flavoured food, but live on the roots of such herbs as they get in the fields, or on the half-raw flesh of any animal, which they merely warm rapidly by placing it between their own thighs and the backs of their horses.

They never shelter themselves under roofed houses, but avoid them as people ordinarily avoid sepulchres as things not fitted for common use. Nor is there even to be found among them a cabin thatched with reed; but they wander about, roaming over the mountains and the woods, and accustom themselves to bear frost and hunger and thirst from their very cradles. And even when abroad they never enter a house unless under the compulsion of some extreme necessity; nor, indeed, do they think people under roofs as safe as others.

They wear linen clothes, or else garments made of the skins of field-mice: nor do they wear a different dress out of doors from that which they wear at home; but after a tunic is once put round their necks, however it becomes worn, it is never taken off or changed till, from long decay, it becomes actually so ragged as to fall to pieces.

They cover their heads with round caps, and their shaggy legs with the skins of kids; their shoes are not made on any lasts, but are so unshapely as to hinder them from walking with a free gait. And for this reason they are not well suited to infantry battles, but are nearly always on horseback. . . . There is not a person in the whole nation who cannot remain on his horse day and night. On horseback they buy and sell, they take their meat and drink, and there they lean forward on the narrow neck of their steed, and yield to sleep so deep as to indulge in every variety of dream.

And when any deliberation is to take place on any weighty matter, they all hold their common council on horseback. They are not under the authority of a king, but are contented with the irregular government of their nobles, and under their lead they force their way through all obstacles.

Sometimes when provoked, they fight; and when they go into battle, they form in a solid body, and utter all kinds of terrific yells. They are very quick in their operations, of exceeding speed, and fond of surprising their enemies. With a view to this, they suddenly disperse, then reunite, and again, after having inflicted vast loss upon the enemy, scatter themselves over the whole plain in irregular formations: always avoiding a fort or an entrenchment.

And in one respect you may pronounce them the most formidable of all warriors, for when at a distance they use missiles of various kinds tipped with sharpened bones instead of the usual points of javelins, and these bones are admirably fastened into the shaft of the javelin or arrow; but when they are at close quarters they fight with the sword, without any regard for their own safety; and often while their antagonists are warding off their blows they entangle them with twisted cords, so that, their hands being fettered, they lose all power of either riding or walking.

None of them plough, or even touch a plough-handle: for they have no settled abode, but are homeless and lawless, perpetually wandering with their waggons, which they make their homes; in fact they seem to be people always in flight. . . .

In truces they are treacherous and inconstant, being liable to change their minds at every breeze . . . ; and, like brute beasts, they are utterly ignorant of the distinction between right and wrong. . . .

## *The Regular Clergy and the Benedictine Rule* *

BENEDICT OF NURSIA

> *In a world torn apart and falling into decay, groups of Christian monks created small islands of peace. Eventually such monks and nuns (and their leaders, called abbots, abbesses, priors, or prioresses) came to be known as "regular" clergy (from living under a* regula, *a set of rules). They were distinct from the "secular" clergy, the priests and bishops who lived in the villages, towns, and cities among the people. Although the regular clergy originally came into being through a desire to withdraw from the world, the locations of their houses made them natural places for travelers seeking refuge; their labors in the fields helped to develop agriculture; their labors with the pen made the monasteries centers of learning; and their discipline under rule, combined with their religious devotion, made them effective missionaries. Many of the later groups (such as the Cistercians, Franciscans, and Dominicans of the twelfth and thirteenth*

* Oliver J. Thatcher, Edgar H. McNeal, *A Source Book for Mediæval History*, New York, Charles Scribner's Sons, 1905.

*centuries) followed the example of the great Benedictine order, founded in* A.D. *529 at Monte Cassino, Italy. Saint Benedict of Nursia lays down the basic requirements of poverty, chastity, obedience, and work for the common good.*

(Take counsel) Whenever important matters arise in the monastery, the abbot should call together the whole congregation, and tell them what is under consideration. After receiving the advice of the brothers, he should reflect upon it and then do what seems best. . . . Let everyone in the monastery obey the rule in all things, and let no one depart from it to follow the desires of his own heart. Let no one of the brothers presume to dispute the authority of the abbot within or outside the monastery.

(Be instruments of good works) The brother is bound first, to love the Lord God with all the heart, and with all the soul, and with all the strength, and then his neighbor as himself . . . to feed the poor, to clothe the naked, to visit the sick, to bury the dead, to offer help in trouble, to comfort the sorrowing . . . not to injure others, but to suffer injuries patiently; to love his enemies. . . .

(Be obedient) The first grade of humility is obedience without delay, which is becoming to those who hold nothing dearer than Christ. So, when one of the brothers receives a command from a superior, he should obey it at once. . . .

(Be silent) It is the business of the master to speak and instruct, and that of the disciple to hearken and be silent. And if the disciple must ask anything of his superior, let him ask it reverently and humbly, lest he seem to speak more than is becoming. . . .

(Be humble) Brethren, if we wish to attain to the highest measure of humility and to that exaltation in heaven which is only to be gained by lowliness on earth, we must raise to heaven by our deeds a ladder. . . . Our body and soul are two sides of the ladder, in which by deeds consistent with our holy calling we insert steps whereby we may ascend to heaven. . . . The brother should be contented with any lowly or hard condition in which he may be placed, and should always look upon himself as an unworthy laborer . . . should not be easily provoked to laughter . . . when he speaks, should do so slowly and without laughter, softly and gravely, using few words and reasonable. . . .

(Own no property) No one shall presume to give or receive anything except by the order of the abbot; no one shall possess anything of his own, books, paper, pens, or anything else. . . .

(Labor daily) Idleness is the great enemy of the soul, therefore . . . always be occupied, either in manual labor or in holy reading. . . . From Easter to the first of October the brothers shall go to work at the first hour [6 A.M.] and labor until the fourth hour [10 A.M.], and the time from the fourth to the sixth hour [noon], they shall lie down and rest in silence; but anyone who wishes may read, if he does it so as not to disturb anyone else. Nones shall be observed a little earlier, about the middle of the eighth hour [2:30 P.M.] and the brother shall go back to work, laboring until vespers [5, 6, 7 P.M.]. But if the condition of the locality or the needs of the monastery, such as may occur at harvest time, should make it necessary to labor longer hours, they shall not feel themselves ill-used, for true monks should live by the labor of their own hands, as did the apostles and the holy fathers. . . .

## Clovis and the Franks *

Gregory of Tours

> Of the tribes that invaded the Roman Empire, the future lay with the Franks west of the Rhine. Brought by their chief, Clovis, into communion with the Roman Catholic Church, they felt free of the German ties of blood relationship, and so attacked the other Germans who were pagan or who adhered to the Arian version of Christianity. The Franks would reach their peak under Charlemagne three centuries later, from whose empire modern European civilization would grow. Bishop Gregory of Tours (died A.D. 594) tells of Clovis's conversion and of some of his exploits.

. . . The army of Clovis seemed about to be cut in pieces. Then the king raised his hands fervently toward the heavens and breaking into tears, cried: "Jesus Christ . . . who it is said givest help to the oppressed and victory to those who put their trust in thee, I invoke thy marvellous help. If thou wilt give me victory over my enemies and I prove that power which thy followers say they have proved concerning thee, I will

* Bishop Gregory of Tours, History of the Franks, as quoted in Frederic A. Ogg, A Source Book of Mediæval History, New York, American Book Company, 1907.

believe in thee, and will be baptized in thy name; for I have called upon my own gods and it is clear that they have neglected to give me aid. Therefore I am convinced that they have no power, for they do not help those who serve them. . . ." When he had offered this prayer the Alemanni [a German people occupying a region about the upper waters of the Rhine and Danube] turned their backs and began to flee. And when they learned that their king had been slain, they submitted at once to Clovis. . . .

Then the queen sent secretly to the blessed Remigius, bishop of Rheims, and asked him to bring the king the gospel of salvation. . . .

Clovis at length engaged in battle with Alaric, king of the Goths. . . . The Goths fought with javelins, but the Franks charged upon them with lances. Then the Goths took to flight, as is their custom, and the victory, with the aid of God, fell to Clovis. . . . Thus, crowned with victory, he returned to Tours and bestowed a great number of presents upon the holy church. . . .

Now while Clovis was living at Paris he sent secretly to the son of Sigibert [king of a tribe of Franks living along the middle Rhine], saying: "Behold now your father is old and lame. If he should die his kingdom would come to you and my friendship with it." So the son of Sigibert, impelled by his ambition, planned to slay his father. And when Sigibert set out for Cologne and crossed the Rhine to go through the Buchonian forest, his son had him slain by assassins while he was sleeping in his tent, in order that he might gain the kingdom for himself. . . . He sent messengers to Clovis to announce the death of his father and to say: "My father is dead and I have his treasures, and likewise his kingdom. Now send trusted men to me, that I may give them for you whatever you would like. . . ." Clovis replied: "I thank you for your kindness and will ask you merely to show my messengers all your treasures, after which you may keep them yourself." And when the messengers of Clovis came, the son of Sigibert showed them the treasures which his father had collected. And while they were looking at various things, he said: "My father used to keep his gold coins in this little chest." And they said, "Put your hand to the bottom that you may show us everything." But when he stooped to do this, one of the messangers struck him on the head with his battle-ax, and thus he met the fate he had visited upon his father.

Now when Clovis heard that both Sigibert and his son were dead, he came to that place and called the people together and said to them: "Hear what has happened. While I was sailing on the Scheldt River, Cloderic, son of Sigibert, my relative, attacked his father, pretending that I had wished him to slay him. . . . But while Cloderic was opening his father's treasure chest, some man unknown to me struck him down. I am in no way guilty of these things, for I could not shed the blood of my relatives, which is very wicked. But since these things have happened, if it seems best to you, I advise you to unite with me and come under my protection." And those who heard him applauded his speech, and, raising him on a shield, acknowledged him as their king. Thus Clovis gained the kingdom of Sigibert and his treasures, and won over his subjects to his own rule. . . .

Then Clovis made war on his relative Ragnachar. And when the latter saw that his army was defeated, he attempted to flee; but his own men seized him and his brother Richar and brought them bound before Clovis. Then Clovis said: "Why have you disgraced our family by allowing yourself to be taken prisoner? It would have been better if you had been slain." And raising his battle-ax, he slew him. Then turning to Richar, he said, "If you had aided your brother he would not have been taken"; and he slew him with the ax also. Thus by their death Clovis took their kingdom and treasures. And many other kings and relatives of his, who he feared might take his kingdom from him, were slain, and his dominion was extended over all Gaul. . . .

## *A New Religion Rises in Arabia* *

MUHAMMAD

> *While Gregory was recording the* History of the Franks, *a young man was growing up in Arabia whose followers would one day challenge the Franks for control of Europe. The teachings of Muhammad (570–632) were later collected in* The Koran. *They reflected Judaism, Christianity, and Arab paganism, although in later life Muhammad turned against Jews for rejecting him as God's messenger*

* *The Koran* (an original translation by James H. Hanscom).

*and against Christians for believing Jesus to be more than a prophet. His religion, Islam (Submission to God), not only emphasized the unity of God but also served to unite the many tribes of Arabs into a single fighting community. Within a century after Muhammad's death in 632, Islam had spread eastward into Persia and westward into Spain, from which it threatened to overrun Christian Europe. In the following excerpts from The Koran, Muhammad speaks in words which he claimed to have received from Heaven.*

In the Name of Allah, the God of Mercy, the Merciful!

Praise Allah, universal Lord, compassionate and merciful,
King on the Judgment Day!
Thee only do we worship. To Thee do we pray
That Thou shalt guide us on the road that leads straight to Thee,
The road of those who have known Thy grace,
With whom Thou art not angered,
Who have not gone astray.

Every man's fate have We fastened about his neck.
On the day when the dead arise We will bring to each
A book which shall be opened wide, and We shall say
"Read your book, you alone are accountable
For the record against you this day."
. . . To each man's loss alone shall his sins be charged;
None shall carry the weight of another's burden.

Set no other god beside Allah . . .
Who hath ordered that you worship none but Him.
Show kindness to your parents, and to your kindred,
And to the poor, and to the wayfaring stranger.
Commit no adultery, for this is taboo and sinful.
Slay none whom Allah hath forbidden you to slay.
Rob not the orphan.
Keep your promises.
Cheat not when you sell.
Walk humbly on the earth.
Other than this is evil, a stench before the Lord.

He who fears Allah will heed the warning,
Only the evil one will ignore it
And he will be exposed to the fires of Hell
In which is living death.

As to those who have believed and lived righteously
. . . For them the gardens of Paradise
Where rivers flow in the cool shade,
Where they shall wear bracelets of gold
And green robes of silk and rich brocade,
Resting themselves on thrones or lying in bliss
On couches of ease.

Infidels are they who say, "God is the Messiah, son of Mary,"
For the Messiah said only, "Children of Israel, worship God, my
Lord and your Lord."
Whoever shall join other gods to God, God shall ban him from Paradise
And he shall dwell in Hellfire where no help comes to the wicked.

You followers of the Bible!
Be moderate in your beliefs,
And of Allah, speak only the truth.
The Messiah, Jesus, son of Mary, is only an apostle of God . . .
Believe therefore in God and His apostles and say not
"O Trinity!"
God is only one God;
In His glory He would have no son!

## The Muslims Are Turned Back at Tours *

E. S. CREASY

> After a rapid conquest of most of Spain (A.D. 711–713), the
> Muslims began raiding France in preparation for a full-scale

* E. S. Creasy, *The Fifteen Decisive Battles of the World from Marathon to
Waterloo*, New York, American Book Exchange, 1881.

*invasion. For some time leadership in the Frankish nation
had been slipping from the hands of the kings into those of
their household supervisors, called "mayors of the palace."
One of the mayors of the palace, Charles, saw that the
destiny of Europe rested with the Franks, and he determined
to assemble a force of cavalry of the kind that had won many
Muslim victories. Church and state co-operated willingly,
selling possessions to equip horsemen. The Muslims were
met in 733 by Charles, who won for himself in this battle the
name* Martel *("the Hammer"). This Christian victory was
judged by the nineteenth-century author E. S. Creasy to
have been one of the great turning points of history.
Through him we hear the voices of Christians and Muslims
telling of the great battle near Tours.*

The monkish chroniclers, from whom we are obliged to glean a nar-
rative of this memorable campaign, bear full evidence to the terror which
the Saracen invasion inspired. . . . The Saracens, say they, and their
king . . . came out of Spain, with all their wives, and their children,
and their substance, in such great multitudes that no man could reckon
or estimate them. They brought with them all their armor, and whatever
they had, as if they were thenceforth always to dwell in France. . . .

. . . The Arabian writers who recorded the conquests and wars of their
countrymen in Spain have narrated also the expedition into Gaul of their
great emir, and his defeat. . . .

. . . Say the Arabian Chroniclers ". . . . All the nations of the Franks
trembled at that terrible army, and they betook themselves to their king
Caldus [Charles], and told him of the havoc made by the Moslem horsemen, and how they rode at their will through all the land. . . . The king
bade them be of good cheer, and offered to aid them. And in the 114th
year [of the Hegira] he mounted his horse, and he took with him a host
that could not be numbered, and went against the Moslems. And he
came upon them at the great city of Tours. And Abderraham and other
prudent cavaliers saw the disorder of the Moslem troops, who were loaded
with spoil; but they did not venture to displease the soldiers by ordering
them to abandon every thing except their arms and war-horses. And
Abderraham trusted in the valor of his soldiers, and in the good fortune
which had ever attended him. But (the Arab writer remarks) such defect
of discipline always is fatal to armies. . . ."

[The Arab writers continue], "Near the River Owar [probably the Loire] the two great hosts of the two languages and the two creeds were set against each other. The hearts of Abderraham, his captains, and his men, were filled with wrath and pride, and they were the first to begin the fight. The Moslem horsemen dashed fierce and frequent forward against the battalions of the Franks, who resisted manfully, and many fell dead on either side until the going down of the sun. Night parted the two armies; but in the gray of the morning the Moslems returned to the battle. Their cavaliers had soon hewn their way into the center of the Christian host. But many of the Moslems were fearful for the safety of the spoil which they had stored in their tents, and a false cry arose in their ranks that some of the enemy were plundering the camp; whereupon several squadrons of the Moslem horsemen rode off to protect their tents. But it seemed as if they fled; and all the host was troubled. And while Abderraham strove to check their tumult, and to lead them back to battle, the warriors of the Franks came around him, and he was pierced through with many spears, so that he died. Then all the host fled before the enemy, and many died in flight. . . ."

. . . Christendom, though disunited was safe. . . .

## Charlemagne *

EINHARD

> *The family of Charles Martel rose steadily in power, his son Pepin the Short and his grandson Charlemagne (Charles the Great) being kings of the Franks. This rise was climaxed on Christmas Day, 800, when Pope Leo III hailed Charlemagne as "Roman emperor." The empire of Charlemagne, called "Carolingian" (from "Carolus," Charles), consisted of the vast Frankish domains plus the states of the church in Italy. The Carolingian period was one of considerable progress, in which the roots of modern western civilization were developed. Some of the gains were temporarily lost, however, in the dark ninth and tenth centuries. We first see*

* Einhard, *Life of Charlemagne*, as quoted in Frederic A. Ogg, *A Source Book of Mediæval History*, New York, American Book Company, 1907.

*Charlemagne through the eyes of his friend and servant Einhard, as recorded in his* Life of Charlemagne.

Charles was large and strong, and of lofty stature, though not excessively tall. The upper part of his head was round, his eyes very large and animated, nose a little strong, hair auburn, and face laughing and merry. . . . His health was excellent, except during the four years preceding his death, when he was subject to frequent fevers; toward the end of his life he limped a little with one foot. . . . In accordance with the national custom, he took frequent exercise on horseback and in the chase. . . .

His custom was to wear the national, that is to say, the Frankish, dress—next his skin a linen shirt and linen breeches, and above these a tunic fringed with silk; while hose fastened by bands covered his lower limbs, and shoes his feet. In winter he protected his shoulders and chest by a close-fitting coat of otter or marten skins. Over all he flung a blue cloak, and he always had a sword girt about him, usually one with a gold or silver hilt and belt. . . . On great feast-days he made use of embroidered clothes, and shoes adorned with precious stones; his cloak was fastened with a golden buckle, and he appeared crowned with a diadem of gold and gems; but on other days his dress differed little from that of ordinary people. . . .

Charles had the gift of ready and fluent speech, and could express whatever he had to say with the utmost clearness. He was not satisfied with ability to use his native language merely, but gave attention to the study of foreign ones, and in particular was such a master of Latin that he could speak it as well as his native tongue; but he could understand Greek better than he could speak it. . . . He most zealously cherished the liberal arts, held those who taught them in great esteem, and conferred great honors upon them. . . . He learned to make calculations, and used to investigate with much curiosity and intelligence the motions of the heavenly bodies. He also tried to write, and used to keep tablets and blanks in bed under his pillow, that at leisure hours he might accustom his hand to form the letters; however, as he began his efforts late in life, and not at the proper time, they met with little success.

He cherished with the greatest fervor and devotion the principles of the Christian religion, which had been instilled into him from infancy. Hence it was that he built the beautiful basilica at Aix-la-Chapelle, which he adorned with gold and silver . . . and with rails and doors of solid brass. . . .

# General Capitulary for the Missi *

CHARLEMAGNE

> To bring unity to his sprawling empire, Charlemagne appointed traveling agents, called missi dominici, who acted as his personal representatives and had wide power over local administrators in assigned districts. Their instructions appear in Charlemagne's General Capitulary for the Missi of 802.

. . . The most serene and most Christian lord emperor Charles has chosen from his nobles the wisest and most prudent men . . . and has sent them throughout his whole kingdom. . . . Moreover, where anything which is not right and just has been enacted in the law, he has ordered them to inquire into this most diligently and to inform him of it; he desires, God granting, to reform it. And let no one, through his cleverness or astuteness, dare to oppose or thwart the written law, as many are wont to do, or the judicial sentence passed upon him, or to do injury to the churches of God or the poor or the widows or the wards of any Christian. But all shall live entirely in accordance with God's precept, justly and under a just rule. . . . And let the missi themselves make a diligent investigation whenever any man claims that an injustice has been done to him by any one. . . . And if there shall be anything of such a nature that they, together with the provincial counts, are not able of themselves to correct it and do justice concerning it, they shall . . . refer this, together with their reports, to the judgment of the emperor; and the straight path of justice shall not be impeded by any one on account of flattery or gifts from any one, or on account of any relationship, or from fear of the powerful.

Concerning the fidelity to be promised to the lord emperor. And he commanded that every man in his whole kingdom, whether ecclesiastic or layman . . . should now promise to him as emperor the fidelity which he had previously promised to him as king; and all of those who had not yet made that promise should do likewise, down to those who were twelve years old. . . .

Concerning embassies coming from the lord emperor. That the counts . . . shall provide most carefully, as they desire the grace of the lord

* University of Pennsylvania, Translations and Reprints from the Original Sources of European History, vol. 6, no. 5, Philadelphia, 1900.

emperor, for the *missi* who are sent out, so that they may go through their departments without any delay; and he commands to all everywhere that they ought to see to it that no delay is encountered anywhere, but they shall cause them to go on their way in all haste and shall provide for them in such a manner as our *missi* may direct. . . .

[He has said] . . . We desire all our decrees to be known in our whole kingdom through our *missi* now sent out . . . so that each one in his ministry or profession may keep our ban or decree, or where it may be fitting to thank the citizens for their good will, or to furnish aid, or where there may be need still of correcting anything. . . .

## The Northmen Terrorize Europe *

> For three centuries (800–1100) the warriors of Scandinavia in their longboats raided, invaded, and colonized neighboring Europe. Europe knew them under a variety of names: "Danes" in Ireland and England, "Norse" in Iceland, Greenland, and Vinland in North America, "Northmen" or "Normans" in France, "Rus" in the eastern lands which would one day be called Russia, "Varangians" in far-off Constantinople. Some monkish chronicles recording in horror their deeds of fire and sword spoke of them simply as "the host." All Europe prayed, "From the fury of the Northmen, Good Lord, deliver us!" But while they slew in the name of Thor and Wotan, especially the missionaries who met them as agents of the "White Christ," the work of conversion went on. By the time they were permanently settled overseas, they had adopted Christianity and the culture of the Carolingian empire and Saxon England. A scribe in the monastery of St. Vaast records their ninth-century raids.

(882) . . . The Northmen in the month of October intrenched themselves at Condé, and horribly devastated the kingdom of Carloman. . . .

[King Carloman gave them battle] and the Franks were victorious and killed nigh a thousand of the Northmen. Yet they were in no wise dis-

* *Annals of St. Vaast* as quoted in James H. Robinson, *Readings in European History*, vol. 1, New York, Ginn and Company, 1904.

comfited by this battle. . . . They went from Condé back to their ships, and thence laid waste the whole kingdom with fire and sword as far as the Oise. They destroyed houses, and razed monasteries and churches to the ground. . . .

(883) . . . In the spring the Northmen left Condé and sought the country along the sea. Here they dwelt through the summer; they forced the Flemings to flee from their lands, and raged everywhere, laying waste the country with fire and sword. As autumn approached, Carloman, the king, took his station with his army in the canton of Vithman at Mianai, opposite Lavier, in order to protect the kingdom. The Northmen at the end of October came to Lavier with cavalry, foot soldiers, and all their baggage. Ships, too, came from the sea up the Somme and forced the king and his whole army to flee and drove them across the river Oise. The invaders went into winter quarters in the city of Amiens and devastated all the land to the Seine and on both sides of the Oise, and no man opposed them; and they burned with fire the monasteries and churches of Christ. . . .

(885) . . . On the twenty-fifth of July the whole host of the Northmen forced their way to Rheims. Their ships had not yet come, so they crossed the Seine in boats they found there, and quickly fortified themselves. The Franks followed them. All those who dwelt in Neustria and Burgundy gathered to make war upon the Northmen. But when they gave battle it befell that Ragnold, duke of Maine, was killed, with a few others. Therefore all the Franks retreated in great sorrow and accomplished nothing.

Thereupon the rage of the Northmen was let loose upon the land. They thirsted for fire and slaughter; they killed Christian people and took them captive and destroyed churches; and no man could resist them.

Again the Franks made ready to oppose them, not in battle, but by building fortifications to prevent the passage of their ships. They built a castle on the river Oise at the place which is now called Pontoise, and appointed Aletramnus to guard it. Bishop Gauzelin fortified the city of Paris.

In the month of November the Northmen entered the Oise, and besieged the castle the Franks had built. They cut off the water supply from the castle's garrison, for it depended on the river for water and had no other. Soon they who were shut up in the castle began to suffer for lack of water. What more need be said? They surrendered on condition that they be allowed to go forth unharmed. After hostages had been exchanged, Aletramnus and his men went to Beauvais. The Northmen burned the castle and carried off all that had been left by the garrison, who had been permitted to depart only on condition that they would leave everything behind except their horses and arms.

Elated with victory, the Northmen appeared before Paris, and at once attacked a tower, confident that they could take it quickly because it was not yet fully fortified. But the Christians defended it manfully and the battle raged from morning till evening. The night gave a truce to fighting and the Northmen returned to their ships. Bishop Gauzelin and Count Odo worked with their men all night long to strengthen the tower against assaults. The next day the Northmen returned and tried to storm the tower, and they fought fiercely till sunset. The Northmen had lost many of their men and they returned to their ships. They pitched a camp before the city and laid siege to it and bent all their energies to capture it. But the Christians fought bravely and stood their ground.

(886) . . . The Northmen ceased not to attack the city daily; many were killed and still more were disabled by wounds, and food began to give out in the city. At this time Hugo, the venerable abbot, departed this life and was buried in the monastery of St. German Antisdoro. Odo saw how the people were falling into despair, and he went forth secretly to seek aid from the nobles of the kingdom, and to send word to the emperor that the city would soon be lost unless help came. . . .

[The siege had lasted eight months when the emperor came to relieve the city.] It was in the autumn that he appeared before Paris with a very strong army. . . . But he did not force them to raise the siege. He made terms with them and signed a shameful treaty. He promised to pay a ransom for the city, and gave them leave to march unopposed into Burgundy, to plunder it during the winter.


## *The Establishment of the Normans in France* *

> *The Scandinavian warriors who adopted Christianity and settled in France came to be called "Normans." One group of*

* *Chronicles of St. Denis*, as quoted in Frederic A. Ogg, *A Source Book of Mediæval History*, New York, American Book Company, 1907.

*Normans, led by a duke named Rollo, took possession of a part of northern France on the English Channel, an area ever since called "Normandy." In time they adopted the language and customs of France, but it was many years before they ended their raids on other areas. A scribe in the monastery of Saint Denis, near Paris, tells of Rollo's relations with the king of France and his rule of Normandy.*

The king had at first wished to give Rollo the province of Flanders, but the Norman rejected it as being too marshy. Rollo refused to kiss the foot of Charles when he received from him the duchy of Normandy. "He who receives such a gift," said the bishops to him, "ought to kiss the foot of the king." "Never," replied he, "will I bend the knee to any one, or kiss anybody's foot." Nevertheless, impelled by the entreaties of the Franks, he ordered one of his warriors to perform the act in his stead. This man seized the foot of the king and lifted it to his lips, kissing it without bending and so causing the king to tumble over backwards. At that there was a loud burst of laughter and a great commotion in the crowd of onlookers. King Charles, Robert, Duke of the Franks, the counts and magnates, and the bishops and abbots, bound themselves by the oath of the Catholic faith to Rollo, swearing by their lives and their bodies and by the honor of all the kingdom, that he might hold the land and transmit it to his heirs from generation to generation throughout all time to come. . . .

In the year of our Lord 912 Rollo was baptized in holy water in the name of the sacred Trinity by Franco, archbishop of Rouen. . . . Rollo devotedly honored God and the Holy Church with his gifts. . . . The pagans, seeing that their chieftain had become a Christian, abandoned their idols, received the name of Christ, and with one accord desired to be baptized. Meanwhile the Norman duke made ready for a splendid wedding and married the daughter of the king according to Christian rites.

Rollo gave assurance of security to all those who wished to dwell in his country. The land he divided among his followers, and, as it had been a long time unused, he improved it by the construction of new buildings. It was peopled by the Norman warriors and by immigrants from outside regions. . . . He rebuilt the churches, which had been entirely ruined; he restored the temples, which had been destroyed by the ravages of the pagans; he repaired and added to the walls and fortifications of the cities. . . .

# Feudalism

*After the collapse of the Carolingian Empire in the tenth century, central government ceased to be effective. In a lawless age, men turned for security to personal relationships. One man would promise his loyalty ("homage") and service to one stronger than he in return for favors, such as protection or land grants. Such relationships, called "feudal," ran all the way from kings and emperors down to peasants. Feudalism was rarely a clearly organized system. Feudal ties became complicated when one man received several grants, thereby owing loyalty to more than one person at the same time. The homage oath of Bernard of Carcassonne shows a simple relationship of one man to one lord even though several fiefs (land grants) are involved. That of John of Toul shows an attempt to solve possible conflicting loyalty claims.*

## HOMAGE OATH OF BERNARD OF CARCASSONNE *

In the name of the Lord, I, Bernard Atton, Viscount of Carcassonne, in the presence of my sons, Roger and Trencavel, and of Peter Roger of Barbazan, and William Hugo, and Raymond Mantelli, and Peter de Vietry, nobles, and of many other honorable men, who had come to the monastery of St. Mary of Grasse . . . ; since lord Leo, abbot of the said monastery, has asked me, in the presence of all those above mentioned, to acknowledge to him fealty and homage for the castles, manors, and places which . . . my ancestors held from him and his predecessors and from the said monastery as a fief, and which I ought to hold as they held, I have made to the lord abbot Leo acknowledgment and homage as I ought to do.

Therefore, let all present and to come know that I the said Bernard Atton, lord and viscount of Carcassonne, acknowledge verily to thee my lord Leo, by the grace of God, abbot of St. Mary of Grasse, and to thy successors that I hold and ought to hold as a fief, in Carcassonne, the following: that is to say, the castles of Confoles, of Leocque, of Capendes . . . ; and the manors of Mairac, of Albars, and of Musso. . . . Moreover, I acknowledge that I hold from thee and from the said monastery as a fief

* University of Pennsylvania, *Translations and Reprints from the Original Sources of European History*, vol. 4, no. 4, Philadelphia, 1898.

the castle of Termes in Narbonne; and in Minerve the castle of Ventaion, and the manors of Cassanolles, and of Ferral and Aiohars; and in Le Rogès, the little village of Longville; and for each and all of which I make homage and fealty to thee my said lord abbot Leo and to thy successors, and I swear upon these four gospels of God that I will always be a faithful vassal to thee and to thy successors and to St. Mary of Grasse in all things in which a vassal is required to be faithful to his lord, and I will defend thee, my lord, and all thy successors, and the said monastery . . . and their possessions at my own cost; and I will give to thee power over all the castles and manors described, in peace and war, whenever they shall be claimed by thee or by thy successors.

Moreover I acknowledge that, as a recognition of the above fiefs, I and my successors ought to come to the said monastery, at our own expense, as often as a new abbot shall have been made, and there do homage. . . . And when the abbot shall mount his horse I and my heirs, viscounts of Carcassonne, and our successors ought to hold the stirrup for the honor . . . ; and to him and all who come with him, to as many as two hundred beasts, we should make the abbot's purveyance in the borough of St. Michael of Carcassone, the first time he enters Carcassonne, with the best fish and meat and with eggs and cheese, honorably according to his will, and pay the expense of shoeing of his horses, and for straw and fodder as the season shall require.

And if I or my sons or their successors do not observe to thee or to thy successors each and all the things declared above, and should come against these things, we wish that all the aforesaid fiefs should by that very fact be handed over to thee and to the said monastery. . . .

Made in the year of the Lord 1110, in the reign of Louis. . . .

### Homage Oath of John of Toul *

I, John of Toul, make known that I am the liege man of the lady Beatrice, countess of Troyes, and of her son, Theobald, count of Champagne, against every creature, living or dead, saving my allegiance to lord Enjorand of Coucy, lord John of Arcis, and the count of Grandpré. If it should happen that the count of Grandpré should be at war with the countess and count of Champagne on his own quarrel, I will aid the count of Grandpré in my own person, and will send to the count and the countess

* Oliver J. Thatcher, Edgar H. McNeal, *A Source Book for Mediæval History*, New York, Charles Scribner's Sons, 1905.

of Champagne the knights whose service I owe to them for the fief which I hold of them. But if the count of Grandpré shall make war on the countess and the count of Champagne on behalf of his friends and not in his own quarrel, I will aid in my own person the countess and count of Champagne, and will send one knight to the count of Grandpré for the service I owe him for the fief which I hold of him, but I will not go myself into the territory of the count of Grandpré to make war on him.

## The Ordeal of the Red-hot Iron *

> In the absence of national law, the people of the feudal age fell back on some of the customs of their barbarian German ancestors. Trial by ordeal was based on the idea that an innocent person would come through a test alive and well, while a guilty one would perish. The only change from old Germanic custom lay in the fact that now the decision was supposed to be made by the Christian God instead of, as formerly, by the pagan gods of the north. This is a description of one kind of ordeal, the red-hot iron, in 928.

If anyone shall have given pledge to undergo the ordeal of iron . . . , let him go three days beforehand to the priest whose duty it is to bless him with the sign of the cross; and let him live upon bread, water, salt and herbs, and hear mass each one of the three days; and let him make his offering and go to the holy communion on the day when he is to be examined by the ordeal; and before he is examined let him swear that by the law of the realm he is innocent of the charge. . . . Concerning the ordeal we enjoin in the name of God and by the command of the archbishop and of all our bishops that no one enter the church after the fire has been brought in with which the ordeal is to be heated except the priest and him who is to undergo judgment. And let nine feet be measured off from the stake to the mark, by the feet of him who is to be tried. . . . And when the ordeal is ready let two men from each side go in and certify that it is as hot as we have directed it to be. Then let an equal number from both sides enter and stand on either side of the judgment

* University of Pennsylvania, *Translations and Reprints from the Original Sources of European History*, vol. 4, no. 4, Philadelphia, 1898.

place along the church. . . . And let the priest sprinkle them all with water and let them bow themselves everyone to the holy water and let the holy Gospel and the cross be given them all to kiss. . . . And let the accused drink of the holy water and then let the hand with which he is about to carry the iron be sprinkled, and so let him go [to the ordeal]. Let the nine feet that were measured off be divided into three sections. In the first division let him hold his right foot, close to the stake. Then let him move his right foot across the second into the third division, where he shall cast the iron in front of him and hasten to the holy altar. Then let his hand be sealed up, and on the third day let examination be made whether it is clean or foul within the wrapper. And whoever shall transgress these laws, be the ordeal of no worth in his case, but let him pay the king a fine of twenty shillings.

## A Law Against the Ordeal *

### EMPEROR FREDERICK II

> With the development of national states in the high Middle Ages, the courts and the justice of kings and emperors came to oppose trial by ordeal. We read here a law against the ordeal by the Holy Roman Emperor Frederick II (1220–1250). Notwithstanding such laws, in some countries the practice—as applied to witches—lasted into the seventeenth century.

The laws which are called by certain ingenuous persons *paribiles,* which neither regard nature nor give heed to the truth, We, who investigate the true science of laws and reject their errors, abolish from our tribunals; forbidding by the edict published under sanction of our name all the judges of our kingdom ever to impose on any of our faithful subjects these *paribiles* laws, which ought rather to be called laws that conceal the truth; but let them be content with ordinary proofs such as are prescribed in the ancient laws and in our constitutions. Indeed, we consider that they deserve ridicule rather than instruction who have so little understand-

* University of Pennsylvania, *Translations and Reprints from the Original Sources of European History,* vol. 4, no. 4, Philadelphia, 1898.

ing as to believe that the natural heat of red-hot iron grows mild, nay, (what is more foolish) even turns to coldness without the working of an adequate cause; or who assert that on account of a troubled conscience alone a criminal does not sink into the cold water, when rather it is the holding in of sufficient air that does not allow of his being submerged.

## Feudal Warfare *

WILLIAM STEARNS DAVIS

> *The feudal age was one of constant turmoil. If one was not being attacked by Vikings, Muslims, or Huns, he was sure to be beset by an aggressive neighbor or to be summoned to help his feudal overlord with military aid. Most fighting was in hit-and-run raids to seize prisoners for ransom. Since most of the feudal nobles were illiterate, we have few accounts from the period, and view it instead through the eyes of a modern scholar.*

In spite of the efforts of clergy and of kings it will be truthfully written of feudal France that "war was practically a permanent scourge almost everywhere. *In the society of that day war was the normal state.*" When these wars are waged by mighty kings one can at least take the comfort that perhaps they are settling long-standing questions concerning many people, and, however dreadful, may pave the way for lasting peace. . . . But most of the wars are for miserably petty stakes. Time was when every insignificant sire holding a feeble tower considered that he had the right to declare war on any neighbor with whom he argued the rights to a trout stream. Yet the case is changing. Suzerains are insisting that the lower class of vassals arbitrate their quarrels and not embroil the neighborhood. Nevertheless, the superior type of barons still claim war as their "noble right." The amount of local fighting can hardly be computed.

There is something abnormal about a powerful seigneur who (if blessed with a long lifetime) does not have at least *one* war with each

* From *Life on a Mediæval Barony* by William Stearns Davis, copyright 1923 by Harper & Brothers, renewed 1950 by Alice Redfield Davis. Reprinted by permission of Harper & Row, Publishers, Incorporated.

of his several suzerains, a war with the bishops and abbots with whom he has contact, a war with each neighboring noble of equal rank . . . and a war with at least some of his own vassals. A war can start out of a dispute about a bit of land, an ill-defined boundary, or the exact obligations of a feudal tenure. Theoretically, the suzerain can interfere between wrangling vassals. Practically, he had better let them fight it out, at least till there seems real danger that their fiefs will be permanently injured. Then he can sometimes compel a truce.

. . . Younger brothers battle with elder brothers over the inheritance. Nephews attack uncles who seem prolonging their guardianship. Sons even attack a widowed mother to seize her dower lands. . . .

Nevertheless, certain limitations are intruding, customs that have nearly the force of law. For example, if a vassal attacks his suzerain, none but his own family (among his noble followers) can aid him. Also, in any case, at least a week's notice must be given ere the war is commenced. After the war does begin, forty days' respite must also be granted your foe's relatives ere attacking them. In the interval they are entitled to proclaim their neutrality and so to become safe. Again, one is supposed to respect priests and women and minors. . . .

As for that motive which prevails in other ages for waging wars—*patriotism*—often it does not seem to exist so vitally. . . . The great significant tie is that of *personal loyalty*. It is horrible to betray the prince to whom you have sworn fealty. A suzerain will call out his host by a summons to "my vassals," he will seldom think of appealing to "my fellow countrymen."

We have said that wars are incessant; yet there is one strange thing about them—*pitched battles are very rare*. The campaigns abound in petty skirmishes—valorous duels, surprises of small castles, occasional clashes of cavalry, and, above all, in the pitiless ravaging of the lands, farms, and villages of the helpless peasantry. What better way to put pressure on your foe than to reduce his villeins to such misery that they can render him nothing in money or kind and that he thus be brought to poverty? If you have the weaker force you will not think of meeting an invader in battle. You will shut yourself up in your castles when you see the burning villages, stifle your pride, remain passive, and trust that after the "forty days' service" of your enemy's vassals is expired they will weary of the operations and not venture to besiege your strongholds. Then when the foe's army is beginning to disperse you can employ some neutral baron or abbot to negotiate peace.

Even when kings are in the field, with really large armies, somehow the opposing forces seldom risk a decisive encounter. They maneuver, skirmish, and negotiate underhandedly with the uncertain elements in the hostile camp. The upshot often is that the invading army, having devoured all the provisions in the open country and not daring to besiege strong cities with a powerful enemy close at hand, retreats homeward.

Of course, sometimes there are great battles with great results. Such in the eleventh century was Senlac [Hastings], when Duke William the Norman won all England. . . . Such marked several of the Crusades against the Infidels, particularly the great and successful First Crusade, and the Third Crusade, when Richard the Lion Hearted seemed to come nearer than any other feudal general to being a really able tactician, if not a great strategist. . . .

Enormous pains have been taken in training the individual warrior. For personal prowess the French cavalier is as formidable an individual as ever shared the sins of mankind. But he is trained only in simple evolutions when maneuvering in companies. He dislikes taking orders. He wearies of long campaigns. His camps are very unhygienic and subject to pestilence. Wars, in short, are to him superb games, exciting, spiced with danger. . . . .

## *Knighthood* *

PETER OF BLOIS

> *Slowly ideas of "chivalry" developed, which added other values to the early concept of mere physical prowess. As late as 1200, however, we hear Peter of Blois bewail the behavior of the knighthood of his day.*

. . . The knighthood of today! Why, it consists of disorderly living! In these military circles, who is it that is reputed the strongest and most worthy of esteem? It is he who says the most abominable things, who swears the most violently, who treats the ministers of God the worst,

* Achille Luchaire, *Social France at the Time of Philip Augustus,* New York, Henry Holt & Co., 1912 (translated by Edward B. Krehbiel). Reprinted by permission of Holt, Rinehart & Winston, Inc.

and who respects the church least. . . . What has become of military art . . . ? It no longer exists: it is the art of giving oneself up to all sorts of excesses. . . . Formerly the soldiers swore to defend the state, to stand firm in the field of battle, and to sacrifice their lives for the public interest; today our knights receive their swords from the hand of the priest, and thus declare that they are the sons of the church, that their arms serve to defend the priesthood, to protect the poor, to pursue malefactors, and to save their country. But in reality they do just the opposite: they have hardly donned the baldric [belt worn to support a sword] before they rise against the anointed of the Lord. . . . They despoil and ransom the subjects of the church; they crush the miserable with unequaled cruelty; they seek the satisfaction of . . . their extraordinary desires in the pain of others. . . . Our soldiers, who ought to employ their strength against the enemies of the cross and of Christ, use it to vie with each other in debauchery and drunkenness; they waste their time in sloth; . . . by their degenerate and impure lives they dishonor their name and their profession.

## Knightly Diversion in Time of Peace

> Knights kept themselves in training for war by combats which, although supposedly peaceful, often became violent and fatal. "Jousts," or "tourneys," were contests between armed horsemen, held to celebrate holidays and important events in the life of a noble family. Sometimes a legal dispute would be settled in this way, the contestants having asked God to give the victory to the righteous. We hear first a challenge, then a description of a tournament involving two knights, and finally of a "Mêlée," a general free-for-all.

### A Challenge *

From the great desire we entertain to become acquainted with the nobles, gentlemen, and knights and esquires bordering on the kingdom of France, as well as with those in the more distant countries, we propose being at St. Inglevere, in Picardy, the 20th day of May next ensuing, and to remain there for thirty days complete; and on each of these thirty days,

* John Burke, ed., *The Patrician*, vol. 1, London, 1846.

excepting the Fridays, we will deliver from their vows all knights, esquires, and gentlemen, from whatever countries they may come, with five courses with a sharp or blunt lance, according to their pleasure, or with both lances if more agreeable. On the outside of our tents will be hung our shields, blazoned with our arms; that is to say, with our targets of war and our shields of peace. Whoever may choose to tilt with any of us, has only to come himself, or to send a proxy the preceding day to touch with a rod either of these shields according to his courage. If he touch the target, he shall find an opponent ready on the morrow to engage him in a mortal combat with three courses with a lance; if the shield, he shall be tilted with a blunted lance; and if both shields are touched, he shall be accommodated with both sorts of combat. Every one who may come, or send to touch our shields, must give in his name to the persons who shall be appointed to the care of them. And all such foreign knights, and squires as shall be desirous of tilting with us shall bring with them some noble friend, and we will do the same on our parts, who will order what may be proper to be done on either side. We especially intreat such noble knights and esquires as may accept our challenge, to believe that we do not make it through presumption, pride, or any ill-will, but solely with a view of having their honourable company, and making acquaintance with them, which we desire from the bottom of our hearts. None of our targets shall be covered with steel or iron, any more than those who may tilt with us; nor shall there be any fraud, deceit or trick made use of, but what shall be deemed honourable by the judges of the tournament. And that all gentlemen, knights, and esquires, to whom these presents shall come, may depend on their authenticity, we have set to them our seals, with our arms this twentieth day of November at Montpellier in the year of Grace, 1389.

Signed,

REGINALD DE ROYE.
BOUCICAUT.
SAIMPI.

## A JOUST *

. . . Sir John Holland and Sir Reginald de Roye armed themselves, and rode into a spacious close in Entença, well sanded, where the tilts were

* Sir Jean Froissart, *Chronicles,* vol. 1, New York, The Colonial Press, 1901 (translated by Thomas Johnes).

to be performed. Scaffolds were to be erected for the ladies, the kings, the duke, and the many English lords who came to witness this combat. The two knights entered the lists so well armed and equipped that nothing was wanting. Their spears, battle-axes, and swords were brought them; and each, being mounted on the best of horses, placed himself about a bow-shot distant from the other, and at times pranced about on his horses; for they knew that every eye was upon him.

All things were now arranged for the combat, which was to include everything except pushing it to extremity, though no one could foresee what mischief might happen, nor how it would end: for they were to tilt with pointed lances, then with swords, which were so sharp that a helmet could scarcely resist their strokes; and these were to be succeeded by battle-axes and daggers, each so well tempered that nothing could withstand them. It was indeed a perilous combat. Having braced their targets, and viewed each other through the visors of their helmets, they spurred their horses, spear in hand. Though they allowed their horses to gallop as they pleased, they advanced on as straight as a line, as if it had been drawn with a cord; and hit each other on their visors with such force that Sir Reginald's lance was shivered into four pieces, which flew to a greater height than they could have been thrown. All present allowed this to have been gallantly done. Sir John Holland's blow was not equally successful, and I will tell you why. Sir Reginald had but slightly laced on his helmet, so that it was held by one thong only, which broke at the blow, and the helmet flew over his head, leaving Sir Reginald bare-headed. Each passed the other, and Sir John bore his lance without halting. The spectators cried out, that it was a handsome course. The knights returned to their stations, where Sir Reginald's helmet was fitted on again, and another lance given to him. Sir John grasped his own, which was not injured. When ready, they set off at full gallop; for they held excellent horses under them, which they well knew how to manage; again they struck each other on the helmets, so that sparks of fire came from them, but chiefly from Sir John Holland's, who received a very severe blow, for this time the lance did not break; neither did Sir John's, but it hit the visor of his adversary, though without much effect, passing through and leaving it on the crupper of the horse, and Sir Reginald was once more bare-headed. "Ah," cried the English, "he does not fight fair; why is his helmet not as well buckled on as Sir John Holland's? tell him to put himself on an equal footing with his adversary." "Hold your tongues," said the duke, "let them alone: in arms, everyone takes what advantage he can. If there is any advantage in the fastening on the helmet, Sir John may do the same; but, for my part, were I in their situation, I would lace my helmet as tight as possible." The English, on this, did not interfere further. The ladies declared that the combatants had nobly jousted; they were also very much praised by the King of Portugal. The third course now began: Sir John and Sir Reginald eyed each other to see if any advantage were to be gained, for their horses were so well trained that they could manage them as they pleased; and sticking spurs into them, they hit their helmets so sharply that their eyes struck fire, and the shafts of their lances were broken. Sir Reginald was again unhelmed, for he could never avoid this, and they passed each other without falling. All again declared that they had well tilted, though the English, with the exception of the Duke of Lancaster, greatly blamed Sir Reginald.

After the courses of the lance, the combatants fought three rounds with swords, battle-axes, and daggers, without either of them being wounded. The French then carried off Sir Reginald to his lodgings, and the English did the same to Sir John Holland.

## THE MÊLÉE *

The next day there is the climax to the festival, the mêlée. Really, it is nothing less than a pitched battle on a small scale. The details have been arranged at a council of the more prominent seigneurs at the castle. About forty knights on a side are to fight under the leadership of the Viscount of Gemours and the Baron of Dompierre. The space in the lists is insufficient. They go to a broad, convenient meadow across the Claire, where the noncombatants can watch from a safe distance. The marshals array the two companies "at least a bowshot apart." Groups of friendly knights are set together and are placed opposite to groups of rivals with whom they are anxious to collide. The great banners of the houses of Gemours and Dompierre flutter in the center of each respective array, and all the little banderoles of the various knights wave with them. . . .

Each baron is expected to charge a particular foe, but all are liable to be swerved in the great rush of men and horses. The two flashing squadrons of cavalry come together like thunderbolts. All the danger of the jousts is present, and another more terrible—that of being trampled to

---

* From *Life on A Mediæval Barony* by William Stearns Davis, copyright 1923 by Harper & Brothers, renewed 1950 by Alice Redfield Davis. Reprinted by permission of Harper & Row, Publishers, Incorporated.

death, if once down, by the raging horses. There is no real leadership. Gemours and Dompierre merely try to set examples of valor and to push their banners forward as rallying points. At first the fighting is good-humored, but when the lances are broken and everyone is smiting one another with sword or mace, the contest becomes desperate. A fearful cloud of dust rises, almost blinding to the combatants, and rendering their blows more reckless.

After the fight has progressed some time, certain of the less adventurous knights begin to drop out. The squires dive into the murk of warriors and horses and drag to safety now this, now another fallen cavalier. At last, just as Conon is considering whether he should not proclaim a "draw," the Gemours banner is observed to topple. A desperate attempt is made to right it, but it sinks again amid a rending shout from the victors. The uplifted hands fall. The frantic horses are brought under control. "A Dompierre! A Dompierre!" bawl all the heralds. And so the mêlée ends.

No one, thanks to excellent armor, is dead, although one heir to a barony is in a desperate condition and several shoulders and thighs are broken. It is futile to count the shattered collar bones and ribs. . . .

## Knighthood Becomes Ornamental *

SIR JEAN FROISSART

> By the fourteenth century, knights in armor no longer pro-
> vided the most efficient fighting force. But the prestige of
> knighthood was not lightly to be abandoned. It began to
> be surrounded by glamour, and knights were now thought to
> be virtuous men. In 1370 Giovanni Boccaccio told of a
> twelve-point oath, which he says was taken by the Knights
> of the Round Table of the mythical King Arthur a thousand
> years before. This fictional picture has colored our view of
> knighthood ever since. According to Boccaccio, a knight
> would swear never to surrender, or to behave dishonorably,
> or to break a promise, or to do violence, or to injure another,
> or to lie about his actions. He would further swear to track

* Sir Jean Froissart, *Chronicles*, as quoted in George F. Beltz's *Memorials of the Order of the Garter*, London, William Pickering, 1841.

*down monsters, to protect the weak, to fight for his friends,*
*to risk his life for his place of birth, to practice religion, and*
*to be as hospitable as his means would allow. Six hundred*
*years later the English poet Tennyson boiled it all down*
*to "Live pure, speak truth, right the wrong, follow the king,"*
*a code much more reminiscent of a modern Boy Scout than a*
*medieval knight. One of the signs that knighthood was*
*becoming ornamental was the establishment of "orders" of*
*knighthood. The first was the Order of the Garter, founded*
*by King Edward III of England about 1344. Froissart*
*describes the event in his* Chronicles.

At this time Edward king of England resolved to rebuild the great castle of Windsor, formerly built and founded by king Arthur, and where was first set up and established the noble Round Table, from whence so many valiant men and knights had issued forth to perform feats of arms and prowess throughout the world. And the said king created an Order of knights, to consist of himself, his children, and the bravest of his land. They were to be in number *forty,* and to be called knights of the blue Garter; their feast to be kept and solemnised at Windsor annually on St. George's day. And, in order to institute this festival, the king of England assembled earls, barons, and knights from his whole realm and signified to them his purpose and great desire to found the same. In this they joyfully concurred; for it appeared to them to be an honourable undertaking, and calculated to nourish affection amongst them. Then were elected *forty* knights known and celebrated as the bravest of all the rest; and they bound themselves to the king, under their seals, by oath and fealty, to keep the feast, and obey the ordinances which should be agreed upon and devised. And the king caused a chapel of St. George to be built and founded within the castle of Windsor; established canons therein for the service of God; and provided and endowed them with a good and liberal revenue. And, in order that the said feast might be promulgated in all countries, the king of England sent his heralds to publish and proclaim the same in France, Scotland, Burgundy, Hainault, Flanders, Brabant, and the German empire; granting to all knights and esquires, who should be willing to come, safe-conduct until fifteen days after the feast. And there was to be held at this feast a jousting by *forty* knights, within the lists, against all comers, and also by *forty* esquires. And this feast was to be celebrated on St. George's Day next coming, which would be in the year of grace ONE THOUSAND THREE HUNDRED AND FORTY-FOUR, at Windsor castle. And the queen of England, accompanied by three hundred ladies and damsels, all noble and gentlewomen, and uniformly apparelled, were to be present.

## Another Version of the Garter Founding *

Elias Ashmole

> A different tradition tells how at a court ball a blue garter fell from the leg of Joan of Kent, wife of Edward the "Black Prince" and daughter-in-law of King Edward. Such blue garters were being worn by persons dabbling in witchcraft as a sign by which they could recognize each other. To save the girl from possible arrest and death, the king turned the whole thing off as a joke with his famous remark "Honi soit qui mal y pense," which remains the motto of the order to this day. This account was still believed in the eighteenth century, as we now see.

. . . The most Noble and Illustrious *Order of the Garter;* which, if we consider either its Antiquity, or the Nobleness of the Personages, that have been enroll'd, it excels and outvies all other Institutions of Honour in the whole World. It owes its Original, as is confessed on all Hands, to *Edward* III, King of *England* and *France;* yet as to the Occasion, there are several Opinions. . . . The vulgar and more general is, that the Garter of *Joan,* Countess of *Salisbury,* dropping casually off as she danced in a solemn Ball, King *Edward* stooping took it up from the Ground, whereupon some of his Nobles smiling, as at an amorous Action, and he observing their sportive Humour, turned it off with a Reply in *French, Honi soit qui mal y pense* [Evil to him who evil thinks]; but withal added, in disdain of their Laughter, *That shortly they should see that Garter advanced to so high an Honour and Renown as to account themselves happy to wear it.*

* Elias Ashmole, *The History of the most Noble Order of the Garter,* London, A. Bell, W. Taylor, & J. Baker, & A. Collins, 1715.

# Tale Tellers and Songsters *

JOHN RUTHERFORD

*In the feudal centuries the most honored guest in the village,
the manor house, or the castle was the wandering minstrel.
His stock in trade included news of far-off places, tales of
heroic events present and past, histories, comedies, tragedies.
Great collections of song-stories grew up, clustered around
Arthur of Britain, Siegfried of the Rhineland, Vainamoinan
of Finland, Charlemagne and his paladins Roland and
Olivier, The Cid in Spain, and Alexander the Great. Or the
latest news from the crusades might be interspersed with
simple songs such as the following, addressed to the night-
ingale.*

| | |
|---|---|
| Sile, philomena | *Hush, sweet bird* |
| Pro tempore | *While ere long* |
| Surge cantilena | *My heart is heard* |
| De pectore. | *In song.* |

. . . The profession of the troubadours was probably the best remuner-
ated of the age. . . . Money, clothes, jewels, arms, horses, and unlimited
hospitality were the most usual rewards of the skilled. . . .

Old Provençal poetry abounds in allusions to the munificence of
patrons and the good fortune of the poets. Perhaps, the care with which
it is evident that the latter laboured to inculcate generosity towards themselves did something to produce the desired result. And even more effective
in this way, must have been the denunciations which the disappointed
troubadour never failed to aim at the stinginess of the patron. . . .

It must be admitted that the life of the wandering troubadour possessed
peculiar attractions. . . . They were allowed all the privileges, and more
than all the licence of the pilgrim and the strolling friar; they were free
to come and go where ever they liked . . . and they were always more
welcome than any other class of itinerant. . . . The poorer members of
the profession travelled alone and afoot. . . . They sang chiefly for the
amusement of the lower classes in town and country. . . . And sometimes
the baronial family was compelled to resort to the poor-devil minstrel, in
dearth of all other sources of amusement. . . . If he possessed any original

* John Rutherford, *The Troubadours*, London, Smith, Elder, & Co., 1873.

talent it was certain to be recognized and rewarded. . . . Thereafter his journeys would be made on horseback. . . .

The life of the wandering troubadour had its shadows as well as its lights. One of the chief attractions of his lyrics was their personality. . . . When he could throw a current scandal into a song, or when he could describe a disagreeable character therein to the life, the poem was assured of unusual success. But the poet was also assured of more than ordinary peril. Those were rough and ready times, and the persons censured generally avenged themselves. . . . They would waylay him to administer chastisement, sometimes by a savage whipping, sometimes by slitting or cutting out his tongue, and sometimes by slaying him outright. . . . Sometimes a baron would suspect—or pretend to suspect—that the troubadour was not what he asserted to be, but a spy . . . and then the object of suspicion had to prove his right to the title under which he had announced himself by composing, on the spot and generally in unpleasant circumstances, a song concerning whose originality there could be no doubt. . . .

It must not be supposed that the trobar's craft was to be assumed off-hand. Facility in rhyming, an ear for music, a vein of low humour, a good stock of impudence, and even a capacity for jumping through four hoops, were not the only essentials. . . . Rhyme and cadence, too, had their laws, which could only be infringed by a genius of the highest order. There were also what may be called stage laws. A good song had to be given in an attractive form, in order to render it popular; and, as all the great poets are not blessed with sweet voices, the troubadour who was merely a poet, found it necessary . . . to consort with pleasing singers. . . .

The influence exercised by the troubadours can hardly be exaggerated. By means of their lyrics they swayed the minds of their countrymen. . . . Their opposition was death, their favour the breath of life, to the institutions of their country. . . .

The troubadours were authorities in all matters of taste and etiquette. They prepared the youth of both sexes for society, and they drew up rules for their guidance. It was thus that Amanieu des Escas instructed the young men of rank. . . . "Shun the companionship of fools, impertinents, or meddlers, lest you pass for the same. Never indulge in buffoonery, scandal, deceit, or falsehood. Be frank, generous, and brave; be obliging and kind; study neatness in your dress. . . . There is no great merit in dressing well if you have the means; but a display of neatness and taste on a small income is a sure token of superiority in spirit. . . . Be first up in the morning, and . . . first also in the saddle. . . ."

# The Song of Roland *

> *In 778 Charlemagne's army was returning from an invasion of Muslim Spain when its rear guard, led by Roland, was cut off and destroyed by enemy forces in the passes of the Pyrenees Mountains. Of little significance in itself, the battle nevertheless became the subject of song and story handed down from singer to singer until recorded in the eleventh century as the "Song of Roland." Roland, together with his friend Olivier, came to represent what was considered to be proper knightly conduct—bravery, steadfastness in battle, loyalty to his lord. Such a song of great deeds was known as a chanson de geste. Excerpts follow.*

Archbishop Turpin, above the rest,
Spurred his steed to a jutting crest.
His sermon thus to the Franks he spake:—
"Lords, we are here for our monarch's sake;
Hold we for him, though our death should come;
Fight for the succour of Christendom.
The battle approaches—ye know it well,
For ye see the ranks of the infidel.
Cry *mea culpa*, and lowly kneel;
I will assoil you, your souls to heal.
In death ye are holy martyrs crowned."
The Franks alighted, and knelt on ground;
In God's high name the host he blessed,
And for penance gave them—to smite their best. . . .

Wild and fierce is the battle still:
Roland and Olivier fight their fill;
The archbishop dealeth a thousand blows
Nor knoweth one of the peers repose;
The Franks are fighting commingled all,
And the foe in hundreds and thousands fall;
Choice have they none but to flee or die,
Leaving their lives despighteously.
Yet the Franks are reft of their chivalry,

* *The Song of Roland*, London, C. Kegan Paul & Co., 1900 (translated by John O'Hagan). Reprinted by permission of Routledge & Kegan Paul Ltd.

Who will see nor parent nor kindred fond,
Nor Karl who waits them the pass beyond. . . .

"I will sound," said Roland, "upon my horn,
Karl, as he passeth the gorge, to warn.
The Franks, I know, will return apace."
Said Olivier, "Nay, it were foul disgrace
On your noble kindred to wreak such wrong;
They would bear the stain their lifetime long.
Erewhile I sought it, and sued in vain;
But to sound thy horn thou wouldst not deign.
Not now shall mine assent be won,
Nor shall I say it is knightly done. . . ."

Archbishop Turpin their strife hath heard,
His steed with the spurs of gold he spurred,
And thus rebuked them, riding near:
"Sir Roland, and thou, Sir Olivier,
Contend not, in God's great name, I crave.
Not now availeth the horn to save;
And yet behoves you to wind its call,—
Karl will come to avenge our fall,
Nor hence the foemen in joyance wend.
The Franks will all from their steeds descend;
When they find us slain and martyred here,
They will raise our bodies on mule and bier,
And, while in pity aloud they weep,
Lay us in hallowed earth to sleep;
Nor wolf nor boar on our limbs shall feed."
Said Roland, "Yea, 'tis a goodly rede.". . .

Roland feeleth his hour at hand;
On a knoll he lies towards the Spanish land.
With one hand beats he upon his breast:
"In thy sight, O God, be my sins confessed.
From my hour of birth, both the great and small.
Down to this day, I repent of all."
As his glove he raises to God on high,
Angels of heaven descend him nigh.

# The Song of the Cid *

*Spain's national hero of the feudal period was Ruy Diaz de Bivar, known as "the Cid," who played an active part in the beginning of the reconquest of Spain from the Muslims by the Christians. His exploits are recounted in Spain's great medieval epic.*

. . . "From water they have cut us off, our bread is running low;
If we would steal away by night, they will not let us go;
Against us there are fearful odds if we make choice to fight;
What would ye do now, gentlemen, in this our present plight?"
Minaya was the first to speak: said the stout cavalier,
"Forth from Castile the Gentle thrust, we are but exiles here;
Unless we grapple with the Moor bread he will never yield;
A good six hundred men or more we have to take the field;
In God's name let us falter not, nor countenance delay,
But sally forth and strike a blow upon to-morrow's day."
"Like thee the counsel," said my Cid; "thou speakest to my mind;
And ready to support thy word thy hand we ever find."
Then all the Moors that bide within the walls he bids to go
Forth from the gates, lest they, perchance, his purpose come to know.
In making their defences good they spend the day and night,
And at the rising of the sun they arm them for the fight.
Then said my Cid: "Let all go forth, all that are in our band;
Save only two of those on foot, beside the gate to stand.
Here they will bury us if death we meet on yonder plain,
But if we win our battle there, rich booty shall we gain.
And thou Pero Bermuez, this my standard thou shalt hold;
It is a trust that fits thee well, for thou art stout and bold;
But see that thou advance it not unless I give command."
Bermuez took the standard and he kissed the Champion's hand.
Then bursting through the Castle gates upon the plain they show;
Back on their lines in panic fall the watchmen of the foe.
And hurrying to and fro the Moors are arming all around,
While Moorish drums go rolling like to split the very ground;
And in hot haste they mass their troops behind their standards twain,
Two mighty bands of men-at-arms—to count them it were vain.
And now their line comes sweeping on, advancing to the fray,

* John Ormsby, ed., *The Poem of the Cid*, London, Longmans, Green & Co., 1879.

Sure of my Cid and all his band to make an easy prey.
"Now steady, comrades," said my Cid; "our ground we have to stand;
Let no man stir beyond the ranks until I give command."
Bermuez fretted at the word, delay he could not brook;
He spurred his charger to the front, aloft the banner shook:
"O loyal Cid Campeador, God give thee aid! I go
To plant thy ensign in among the thickets of the foe;
And ye who serve it, be it yours our standard to restore.". . .
Then cried my Cid—"In charity, on to the rescue—ho!"
With bucklers braced before their breasts, with lances pointing low,
With stooping crests and heads bent down above the saddlebow,
All firm of hand and high of heart they roll upon the foe. . . .
Down go three hundred Moors to earth, a man to every blow;
And when they wheel, three hundred more, as charging back they go.
It was a sight to see the lances rise and fall that day;
The shivered shields and riven mail, to see how thick they lay;
The pennons that went in snow-white come out a gory red;
The horses running riderless, the riders lying dead;
While Moors call on Mohammed, and "St. James!" the Christians cry,
And sixty score of Moors and more in narrow compass lie.

Above his gilded saddlebow there played the Champion's sword; . . .
And now are both king Galve and Fariz [the Moslem leaders] in retreat;
Great is the day for Christendom, Great is the Moors' defeat! . . .


## Arthur's Last Battle *

> Most popular of all heroic subjects was the legendary King
> Arthur of Britain and his Round Table. Supposed to have
> lived sometime between the first and fifth centuries, his
> return was still awaited a thousand years later.

I neither know who lost, nor who gained that day. No man wists
[knows] the name of overthrower or of overthrown. All are alike forgotten,
the victor with him who died. . . . There perished the brave and comely

* Wace, *Roman de Brut, Arthurian Chronicles*, Everyman's Library, London, J. M.
Dent & Sons Ltd., and New York, E. P. Dutton & Co. Inc., 1928 (translated by
Mason).

youth Arthur had nourished and gathered from so many and far lands, there also the knights of his Table Round, whose praise was bruited about the whole world. . . . Arthur himself was wounded in his body to his death. He caused him(self) to be borne to Avalon for the searching of his hurts. He is yet in Avalon, awaited of the Britons; for as they say and deem he will return from whence he went and live again. I, Master Wace, the writer of this book, cannot add more to this matter of his end than was spoken by Merlin the prophet. Merlin said of Arthur—if I read aright—that his end should be hidden in doubtfulness. . . . To . . . (the) Earl of Cornwall, and his near kin, Arthur committed the realm, commanding him to hold it as king until he returned to his own. The earl took the land to his keeping. He held it as bidden, but nevertheless Arthur came never again.

## Manorial Farms

EILEEN POWER, ROWLAND E. P. ERNLE

> *In the same centuries when feudalism provided the political structure of society, the principal economic unit was the manor. Each manor tried to produce everything needed for food, clothing, and shelter, and among the peasants were not only farmers but also such craftsmen as millers, carpenters, wheelwrights, and smiths. The villagers' huts had no furniture other than a pallet for sleeping and possibly a crude table and stools. The manor house, although larger, was also furnished simply, with primitive sanitation and no elegance. Again we must rely on modern descriptions.*

### MANORS IN CAROLINGIAN TIMES *

. . . The lands of the Abbey of St. Germain were divided into a number of estates, called *fiscs*, each of a convenient size to be administered by a steward. On each of these *fiscs* the land was divided into seigniorial and tributary lands; the first administered by the monks through a steward or

* Eileen Power, *Medieval People*, London, Methuen & Co. Ltd., 1924. Published in the U.S.A. by Barnes & Noble, Inc.

some other officer, and the second possessed by various tenants, who received and held them from the abbey. These tributary lands were divided into numbers of little farms, called manses. . . .

Beside the seigniorial manse, there were a number of little dependent manses. These belonged to men and women who were in various stages of freedom, except for the fact that all had to do work on the land of the chief manse. There is no need to trouble with the different classes, for in practice there was very little difference between them. . . . The most important people were those called *coloni,* who were personally free (that is to say, counted as free men by the law), but bound to the soil, so that they could never leave their farms and were sold with the estate, if it were sold. . . . In return for these holdings the owner or joint owners of every manse had to do work on the land of the chief manse for about three days in the week. The steward's chief business was to see that they did their work properly, and from every one he had the right to demand two kinds of labour. The first was *field work:* every year each man was bound to do a fixed amount of ploughing on the domain land (as it was called later on), and also to give . . . an unfixed amount of ploughing, which the steward could demand every week when it was needed; . . . The second kind of labour which every owner of a farm had to do on the monks' land was called handwork, that is to say, he had to help repair buildings, or cut down trees, or gather fruit, or make ale, or carry loads—anything, in fact, which wanted doing and which the steward told him to do. It was by these services that the monks got their own seigniorial farm cultivated. On all the other days of the week these hard-worked tenants were free to cultivate their own little farms, and we may be sure that they put twice as much elbow grease into the business.

But their obligation did not end here, for not only had they to pay services, they also had to pay certain rents to the big house. There were no State taxes in those days, but every man had to pay an army due . . . ; this took the form of an ox and a certain number of sheep, or the equivalent in money: "He pays to the host two shillings of silver" comes first on every freeman's list of obligations. The farmers also had to pay in return for any special privileges granted to them by the monks; they had to carry a load of wood to the big house, in return for being allowed to gather firewood in the woods . . . ; they had to pay some hogsheads of wine for the right to pasture their pigs in the same precious woods; every third year they had to give up one of their sheep for the right to graze upon the fields of the chief manse; they had to pay a sort of poll-tax of 4d. a head. In addition to these special rents every farmer had also to pay other rents in produce; every year he owed the big house three chickens and fifteen eggs and a large number of planks, to repair its buildings; often he had to give it a couple of pigs; sometimes corn, wine, honey, wax, soap, or oil. If the farmer were also an artisan and made things, he had to pay the produce of his craft; a smith would have to make lances for the abbey's contingent to the army, a carpenter had to make barrels and hoops and vine props, a wheelwright had to make a cart. Even the wives of the farmers were kept busy, if they happened to be serfs; for the servile women were obliged to spin cloth or to make a garment for the big house every year. . . .

That, in a few words, is the way in which the monks of St. Germain and the other Frankish landowners of the time of Charlemagne managed their estates. Let us try, now, to look at those estates from a more human point of view and see what life was like to a farmer who lived upon them. The abbey possessed a little estate called Villaris, near Paris, in the place now occupied by the park of Saint Cloud. When we turn up the pages in the estate book dealing with Villaris, we find that there was a man called Bodo living there. He had a wife called Ermentrude and three children called Wido and Gerbert and Hildegard; and he owned a little farm of arable and meadow land, with a few vines. And we know very nearly as much about Bodo's work as we know about that of a small-holder in France to-day. Let us try and imagine a day in his life. On a fine spring morning towards the end of Charlemagne's reign Bodo gets up early, because it is his day to go and work on the monks' farm, and he does not dare to be late, for fear of the steward. To be sure, he has probably given the steward a present of eggs and vegetables the week before, to keep him in a good temper; but the monks will not allow their stewards to take big bribes (as is sometimes done on other estates), and Bodo knows that he will not be allowed to go late to work. It is his day to plough, so he takes his big ox with him and little Wido to run by its side with a goad, and he joins his friends from some of the farms near by, who are going to work at the big house too. They all assemble, some with horses and oxen, some with mattocks and hoes and spades and axes and scythes, and go off in gangs to work upon the fields and meadows and woods of the seigniorial manse, according as the steward orders them. . . . Frambert is going to make a fence round the wood, to prevent the rabbits from coming out and eating the young crops; Ermoin has been told off to cart a great load of firewood up to the house; and Ragenold is mending a hole in the roof of a barn. Bodo goes whistling off in the cold with his oxen and his little boy; and it is no use to follow him farther, because he ploughs all day and eats his meal under a tree with the other ploughmen, and it is very monotonous.

Let us go back and see what Bodo's wife, Ermentrude, is doing. She is busy too; it is the day on which the chicken-rent is due—a fat pullet and five eggs in all. She leaves her second son, aged nine, to look after the baby Hildegard and calls on one of her neighbours, who has to go up to the big house too. . . .

She finds the steward, bobs her curtsy to him, and gives up her fowl and eggs. . . . She goes back to her own farm and sets to work in the little vineyard; then after an hour or two goes back to get the children's meal and to spend the rest of the day in weaving warm woollen clothes for them. All her friends are either working in the fields on their husband's farms or else looking after the poultry, or the vegetables, or sewing at home; for the women have to work just as hard as the men on a country farm. . . .

### Manors in High Medieval Times *

. . . In the thirteenth century, muscles were more essential to the prosperity of the landlord than money rents. The cultivators of the soil grew their produce, not for sale, but for their own consumption. Each manor or village was isolated and self-sufficing. Only in the neighbourhood of towns was there any market for the produce of the farm. Few manufactured articles were bought. Salt, tar, iron (bought in four-pound bars), mill-stones, steel for tipping the edges of implements, canvas for the sails of the wind-mill, cloths for use in the dairy, in the malthouse, or in the grange, together with the dresses of the inhabitants of the hall, and a few vessels of brass, copper, or earthenware, satisfied the simple needs of the rural population. Hands were therefore more required than money on manorial estates. If the manor was well stocked with labour, the land paid; when the stock of labour shrank, the profits dwindled. It was in order to retain a sufficient supply of labour on the land that bondmen were restrained from leaving the manor to assume . . . the flat cap of the apprentice, to become soldiers or to work outside the manor. Even their marriages were carefully controlled by licenses. It was, again, in order to

* Lord Rowland E. P. Ernle, *English Farming Past and Present*, London, Longmans, Green & Co. Ltd., 1927.

exact and supervise the due performance of labour services that the lord of the manor maintained his large official staff—his seneschal, if he owned several manors, his steward, his bailiff, and the various foremen of the labourers. . . .

## Child Marriages *

EILEEN POWER

> Since land was the basis of all wealth and power, the Middle Ages saw many famous instances of child "marriage," whose object was the transfer of property from one family to another. We must understand, however, that the "marriages" were in many cases only betrothal or engagement ceremonies.

Modern opinion, which is happily in favour of falling in love, and of adult marriages, is often shocked by the air of business which pervades matchmaking in the days of chivalry, and by the many cases of grown men married to little girls not yet out of their teens. In those days it was held that a boy came of age at fourteen and a girl at twelve. . . . For reasons of property, or to settle family feuds, or simply to assure their own future, babies in cradles were sometimes betrothed and even married; all that the Church required was that children should be free when they came of age (at the ages of fourteen and twelve!) to repudiate the contract if they so desired. Nothing seems to separate modern England from the good old days so plainly as the case of little Grace de Saleby, aged four, who for the sake of her broad acres was married to a great noble, and on his death two years later to another, and yet again, when she was eleven, to a third, who paid three hundred marks down for her. There is an odd mixture of humour and pathos in the story of some of these marriages. John Rigmarden, aged three, was carried to church in the arms of a priest, who coaxed him to repeat the words of matrimony, but half-way through the service the child declared that he would learn no more that day, and the priest answered, "You must speak a little more, and then go play you."

* Eileen Power, *Medieval People*, London, Methuen & Co. Ltd., 1924. Published in the U.S.A. by Barnes & Noble, Inc.

# Runaway Serfs *

EMPEROR HENRY VII

> *Stories of the good life for the rapidly growing cities of the high Middle Ages often contributed to the dissatisfaction of serfs, who were legally bound to the land on which they were born. When some of the cities established the custom of granting free citizenship to those who dwelt within the city walls for at least one year and a day, runaways from the farms multiplied. In the early fourteenth century the Holy Roman Emperor Henry VII tried to regulate the problem.*

. . . When a quarrel arose between our cities of Elsass and the nobles and ministerials of the same province in regard to the serfs who had run away and gone to the cities, or might hereafter do so, . . . it was settled by the following decision: If a serf belonging to a noble or ministerial runs away and goes to one of our cities and stays there, his lord may recover him if he can bring seven persons who are of the family of the serf's mother, who will swear that he is a serf, and belongs to the said lord. If the lord cannot secure seven such witnesses, he may bring two suitable witnesses from among his neighbors, who will swear that before the serf ran away the said lord had been in peaceable possession of him, . . . and he may then recover his serf. We also decree and command that all nobles and ministerials who wish to recover their serfs may enter a city for this purpose with our permission and protection, and no one shall dare injure them. . . .

# Falconry—Hunting with Hawks **

WILLIAM STEARNS DAVIS

> *The damp, comfortless houses of the upper medieval classes on the manors made outdoor sports especially attractive.*

* Oliver J. Thatcher, Edgar H. McNeal, *A Source Book for Mediæval History*, New York, Charles Scribner's Sons, 1905.
** From *Life on a Mediæval Barony* by William Stearns Davis, copyright 1923 by Harper & Brothers, renewed 1950 by Alice Redfield Davis. Reprinted by permission of Harper & Row, Publishers, Incorporated.

*Falconry and hunting with hounds provided thrills, satis-
fied the desire to kill, and kept one in physical condition for
the next feudal war. Since those who engaged in these
pursuits were the illiterate nobles, we hear their story in the
words of a modern scholar.*

But chess, dice and every other game indoors or outdoors pales before
the pleasure of hawking or hunting. . . . It is even a kind of substitute
for the delights of war. If a visiting knight shows the least willingness,
the baron will certainly urge him to tarry for a hunting party. It will then
depend on the season, the desire of the guests, and reports from the ken-
nels and mews and the forest whether the chase will be with hawks or
with hounds.

. . . Both sports are carried on simultaneously at every castle. If fresh
meat is needed, if most of the riders are men, if time is abundant, probably
the order is "bring out the dogs." If only the sport is wanted, and the
ladies can ride out merely for an afternoon, the call is for the hawks. . . .

Falcons are counted "noble birds"; they rank higher in the social hier-
archy of beasts than even eagles. If one cannot afford large hawks and
falcons one can at least keep sparrow hawks; and "sparrow hawk" is the
nickname for poor sires who only maintain birds large enough to kill
partridges and quails. In short, the possession of a hawk of *some* kind is
almost as necessary for a nobleman as wearing a sword, even with knights
who can seldom go out hunting. However, it takes a rich noble like Conon
to possess a regular falconry with special birds, each trained for attacking
a certain kind of game—hares, kites, herons—with the expert attendants to
care for them.

Falconry has become a complicated art. Very possibly the good folk
in St. Aliquis will have their bodies physicked or bled by physicians much
less skillful in treating human ills than Conon's falconers are in treating
birds. To climb high trees or crags and steal the young hawk out of the
nest is itself no trifling undertaking. Then the prizes must be raised to
maturity, taught to obey whistles and calls, and to learn instantly to do
the bidding of the master. . . . Some birds will return of their own accord to the hand of the master after taking game, but many, including all
sparrow hawks, have to be enticed back by means of a lure of red cloth
shaped like a bird. The falconer swings his lure by a string, and whistles,
and, since the falcon is accustomed to find a bit of meat attached to the
lure, he will fly down promptly and thus be secured. . . .

There are few more acceptable presents to a nobleman or, better still, to a lady, than a really fine bird. Abbots send five or six superior hawks to the king when craving protection for their monasteries. Foreign ambassadors present His Royal Grace with a pair of birds as the opening wedge to negotiations. . . .

Everything about falcons must be compatible with their nobility. The glove on which they are carried is embroidered with gold. The hood which keeps them blindfolded is likewise adorned with gold thread, pearls, and bright feathers. Every bird has attached to his legs two little bells engraved with his owner's name. High in the air they can be heard tinkling. If the bird is lost the peasants discovering it can return it to the owner—and woe to the villein who retains a falcon found in the forest! The local law provides that either he must pay a ruinous fine or let the falcon eat six ounces of flesh from his breast. As for stealing a hunting bird outright, there is hardly a speedier road to the gallows; it is what horse stealing some day will become in communities very far from France.

Assuredly it is an exhilarating sight to see the castle folk go hawking on a fine morning. The baron, baroness, and all their older relatives and guests, each with bird on gauntlet, are on tall horses; the squires and younger people have sparrow hawks to send against the smaller prey, but the leaders of the sport will wait until they can strike a swift duck or heron. Dogs will race along to flush the game. Horns are blowing, young voices laughing, all the horses prancing. Conon gives the word. Away they go—racing over fences, field and fallow, thicket and brook, until fate sends to view a heron. Then all the hawks are unhooded together; there are shouts, encouragement, merry wagers, and helloing as the birds soar in the chase. The heron may meet his fate far in the blue above. Then follow more racing and scurrying to recover the hawks. So onward, covering many miles of country, until, with blood tingling, all canter back to St. Aliquis in a determined mood for supper.

## Order in a Lawless Age

> The ninth and tenth centuries, when the feudal system was taking shape, were especially destructive. The first knights were warlike, quarrelsome and inclined to robbery. Travelers, particularly traders, were molested. Farmers' fields were raided, or crops were wantonly trampled when the endless

little "wars" of the horsebacked ruffians raged across them. In struggling with this problem, the church introduced three ideas: "Sanctuary," the "Truce of God," and the "Peace of God." Sanctuary declared the altar of a church a zone of safety for anyone fleeing from attack. The Truce of God sought to ban violence and theft from Wednesday night to Monday morning, as an extension of the holiness of the Lord's Day. The third forbade violence and theft at all times. Even when feudalism became more civilized, there would be famous violations of these principles; but as knights became less like gangsters, and the time of the church's greatest authority drew near, the three ideas came to have wider acceptance.

## Sanctuary in England under Henry II (1154–1189)*

Whatever accused or guilty person shall flee to a church for the sake of protection, from the time that he shall have reached the porch of such church, he shall on no account be seized by any one pursuing him, except only by the bishop or by his servant. And if, on his flight, he shall enter the house of a priest or his court-yard, he is to have the same security and protection as he would have had in the church, supposing always, that the priest's house and court-yard are standing upon the land of the Church. If the person is a thief or burglar, that which he has wrongfully taken, if he has it in his possession, he is to restore, and if he has entirely made away with it, and has anything of his own by which to make restitution, he is to make restitution in full to him whom he has injured. And if the thief has thus acted according to his usual practice, and shall happen to have frequently made his escape to churches and priests' houses, then, after making restitution of what he has taken away, he is to abjure that country, and not to return thereto; and if he does not make restitution, no one is to presume to harbour him, unless with leave granted by the king.

## The Truce of God, as Proclaimed in Arles, 1035 a.d.**

For the salvation of your souls, we beseech all of you who fear God and believe in him and have been redeemed by His blood, to follow the footsteps of God, and to keep peace one with another, that you may obtain eternal peace and quiet with Him.

* Roger De Hoveden, *Annals*, vol. 1, London, H. G. Bohn, 1853 (translated by Henry T. Riley).
** Oliver J. Thatcher, Edgar H. McNeal, *A Source Book for Mediæval History*, New York, Charles Scribner's Sons, 1905.

This is the peace or truce of God which we have received from heaven through the inspiration of God, and we beseech you to accept it and observe it even as we have done; namely, that all Christians, friends and enemies, neighbors and strangers, should keep true and lasting peace one with another from vespers on Wednesday to sunrise on Monday, so that during these four days and five nights, all persons may have peace, and, trusting in this peace, may go about their business without fear of their enemies.

All who keep the peace and truce of God shall be absolved of their sins by God. . . .

Those who have promised to observe the truce and have wilfully violated it, shall be excommunicated . . . shall be accursed and despised here and in the future world . . . unless they make satisfaction as is described in the following:

If anyone has killed another on the days of the truce of God, he shall be exiled and driven from the land and shall make a pilgrimage to Jerusalem, spending his exile there. If anyone has violated the truce of God in any other way, he shall suffer the penalty prescribed by the secular laws and shall do double penance prescribed by the canons. . . .

We have vowed and dedicated these four days to God: Thursday, because it is the day of the ascension; Friday, because it is the day of his passion; Saturday, because it is the day in which he was in the tomb; and Sunday, because it is the day of the resurrection. . . .

By the power given to us by God through the apostles, we bless and absolve all who keep the peace and truce of God; we excommunicate, curse, anathematize, and exclude from the holy mother church all who violate it. . . .

. . . But if anything has been stolen on other days, and the owner finds it on one of the days of the truce, he shall not be restrained from recovering it, lest thereby an advantage should be given to the thief. . . .

## The Peace of God, as Proclaimed in Puy, 990 a.d. *

Guy of Anjou, by the grace of God bishop, greeting and peace to all who desire the mercy of God. Be it known to all the faithful subjects of God, that because of the wickedness that daily increases among the people, we have called together certain bishops, princes and nobles. And

* Oliver J. Thatcher, Edgar H. McNeal, *A Source Book for Mediæval History*, New York, Charles Scribner's Sons, 1905.

since we know that only the peaceloving shall see the Lord, we urge all men, in the name of the Lord, to be sons of peace.

From this hour forth, no man in the bishoprics over which these bishops rule, and in these counties, shall break into a church. . . .

No man in the counties or bishoprics shall seize a horse, colt, ox, cow, ass, or the burdens which it carries, or a sheep, goat, pig, or kill any of them, unless he requires it for a lawful expedition. On an expedition a man may take what he needs to eat, but shall carry nothing home with him; and no one shall take material for fortifying or besieging a castle except from his own lands or subjects.

Clergymen shall not bear arms; no one shall injure monks or any unarmed persons who accompany them. . . .

No one shall seize or rob merchants.

If anyone breaks the peace and refuses to keep it, he shall be excommunicated and cut off from the church, until he makes satisfaction, and if he refuses to make satisfaction, no priest shall say mass or perform divine services for him, no priest shall bury him or permit him to be buried in consecrated ground; no priest shall knowingly give him communion. . . .

## Medieval Fairs *

EMPEROR FREDERICK I BARBAROSSA

> As conditions improved and it became safer for a merchant to travel with goods, the weekly exchange of local farm produce in the villages expanded into regional fairs. Eventually certain great fairs, held annually, displayed merchandise from many parts of Europe and Asia. Merchants moved from fair to fair selling their goods from stalls rented, with protection, from the local feudal lord. Some of the fairs became permanent banking and trading centers and grew into walled towns. We read the charter for two fairs at Aix-la-Chapelle, granted by the Emperor Frederick Barbarossa in the twelfth century.

* Roy C. Cave, Herbert H. Coulson, *A Sourcebook for Medieval Economic History*, New York, The Bruce Publishing Co., 1936.

In the name of the Holy and Indivisible Trinity, Frederick, by favor of divine clemency, Emperor Augustus of the Romans. Since the royal palace of Aix-la-Chapelle excels all provinces and cities in dignity and honor, both for the praise given there to the body of the most blessed Emperor Charlemagne, which that city alone is known to have, and because it is a royal seat at which the Emperors of the Romans were first crowned, it is fitting and reasonable that we, following the example of the holy lord Charlemagne and of other predecessors of ours, should fortify that same place, which is a pillar of support to the empire, with lavish gifts of liberty and privileges, as if with walls and towers. We have therefore decreed that there should be held twice a year the solemn and universal fairs of Aix-la-Chapelle. And this we have done on the advice of the merchants. Moreover, we have preserved the rights of neighboring cities, so that these fairs may not only not be a hindrance to their fairs but may rather increase their profits. And so, on the advice of our nobles, we have given, out of respect for the most holy lord, the Emperor Charlemagne, this liberty to all merchants. . . . No merchant, nor any other person, may take a merchant to court for the payment of any debt during these fairs, nor take him there for any business that was conducted before the fairs began; but if anything be done amiss during the fairs, let it be made good according to justice during the fairs. Moreover, the first fair shall begin on Quadragesima Sunday, which is six weeks before Easter, and it shall last for fifteen days. The second fair shall begin eight days before the feast of St. Michael and shall continue for eight days after that feast. And all people coming to, staying at, or going from the fairs shall have peace for their persons and goods. And lest the frequent changing of coins, which are sometimes light and sometimes heavy, should redound to the hurt of so glorious a place at any time in the future, on the advice of our court, we have ordered money to be struck there of the same purity, weight, and form, and in the same quantity, and to be kept to the same standard. . . . And a certain abuse has prevailed for a long time in the courts of Aix-la-Chapelle so that if he, who was impleaded for calumny or for any other thing, could not offer satisfaction by compensation for his offense, except he flee from the country at once, he incurred the full penalty . . . ; therefore, we, condemning this bad law forever, have decreed that any one may offer in this our royal town of Aix-la-Chapelle, for any cause for which he has been impleaded, compensation by whatever small thing he is able to take off with his hands while standing upright, without bending his body, such thing as a cloak, tunic, hat, shirt, or other garment. . . . Moreover, we grant and confirm to the merchants of that city that they may have a mint and a house for exchanging their silver and money whenever they decide to go away on business. Whoever out of boldness decides to oppose our decree, or by temerity to break it, shall be in our mercy and will pay a hundred pounds of gold to our court. And in order that all the things we have decreed may be accepted as genuine and be faithfully observed we have ordered this charter to be written and to be sealed by the impression of our seal.

## Growth of Cities and Trade *

K. LAMPRECHT

> *Slowly but steadily the rural predominance of the feudal age gave way to cities and trade. Some of the towns dated back to antiquity, some formed around castles and monasteries. All of them struggled to secure their freedom from the control of barons, bishops, and kings. London, for example, purchased its liberties from King Richard I by supplying him with money for the Third Crusade. The burghers, citizens of the cities, with wealth based on industry and trade, formed one more class in medieval society, the "bourgeoisie." Their interests were often opposed to both the landed feudality and the rising national kingdoms. We hear an account of German cities in the fourteenth century.*

In the glorious days of the medieval towns, say in the second half of the fourteenth century, when a traveler approached a large city, its very appearance suggested to him that he had reached his journey's end. Proudly and almost boastingly the silhouette of the city rose from the horizon, with its turrets and towers, its chapels and churches. . . .

First of all, its strong fortifications impressed the traveler. The narrow city limits included normally the old city market and often a much larger territory. All of this was embraced in the fortifications. Its boundaries were surrounded by ramparts and a wall with a ditch in front. This was often strengthened still more by so-called hedges and widely projecting

* K. Lamprecht, "City Life in Germany," quoted in Dana C. Munro, George C. Sellery, eds., *Medieval Civilization*, New York, The Century Co., 1923.

watch-towers at regular intervals. Even when the ramparts were less strongly fortified, there was at least a beacon [watch-tower] with a wide outlook. . . .

When the stranger was admitted through the barricade at the outposts and approached the city more closely, he might well be astonished, even in the smaller cities, by the extent of the fortifications and mass of towers which surrounded the city, especially at the gates. . . . From the old earthen wall rose arch upon arch, and these arches supported the new walls, which often reached the respectable height of twenty-five to thirty feet. And while the walls were raised, the ditches were at the same time deepened and broadened. . . . Paid soldiers, often nobles from the surrounding country, but always men trained to arms whose business was war, were expressly engaged by the city council. They furnished a small garrison for the gate. . . .

In addition to this regular garrison, which was remarkably small, there were usually, in times of peace, only a few guards posted along the city wall. These were chosen from the citizens and relieved every day. It was their duty to make the rounds of the wall regularly, especially during the night; for this service a path was made along the inner side of the wall. . . . The idea of placing the walk on the wall itself readily occurred to them. For this reason they either made the wall broad enough to have a path behind the battlements which crowned it, or else built a wooden walk on supports at the top of the battlements.

While they thus obtained the desired security for the watchmen on duty, careful rules were made for calling all the citizens to arms. For military purposes most cities were divided into quarters, each of which had its own place of assembly in case of alarm; gathering in these places, they hastened to defend the walls. . . .

. . . Most cities were still to a very great extent engaged in agriculture; at Coblenz, in the second half of the thirteenth century, work on the city walls had to be given up during harvest-time, because of the lack of workmen; at Frankfort in the year 1387 the city employed four herdsmen and six field-guards, and even in the fifteenth century a strict law was enacted against allowing pigs to run about in the city streets. Even in the largest cities there are very many indications of the activities of a widely extended population engaged in agriculture. Cattle-breeding and gardening were actively engaged in along with manufacturing and trade; . . .

Manufacturing and trade . . . were located near the center. Here the guilds often dwelt together in narrow lanes with shops opening upon the street; here by the river or some other road the merchants thronged to the warehouses; here little shops of the retail dealers were snuggled in every corner. . . .

. . . Until some time in the thirteenth century most of the cities had been small. In the west they were often surrounded by the walls of an old Roman city which had grown out of a camp; in the east, recently founded on a small spot of ground, they were scarcely more than large castles. . . . When the development of city life began in the twelfth and thirteenth centuries, the old walls were destroyed; generally the area of the cities began to be extended; . . . Thus the rural population was brought into the city; it was a long time before they gave up their occupations and mode of life; . . . In time, to be sure, the space between the walls and the center of the city, which had once been covered with gardens, was filled with streets, and again the suburbs of the city began to extend beyond the gates. . . .

## Medieval London *

William Fitz-Stephen

> *Typical of many European cities was medieval London, which rose on the forgotten ruins of the Roman city of Londinium. In its filthy streets dogs, pigs, and children competed for room with passers-by on foot and horseback. Every inch of space was used, city bridges being especially popular as locations for shops, storehouses, and homes. If one overlooked dirt, crime, and fire and disease that often carried off large parts of the population, city life could seem very exciting. It did to William Fitz-Stephen, a native of London, who tells us about his city in 1173.*

Among the noble cities of the world that Fame celebrates, the City of London of the Kingdom of the English, is the one seat that pours out its fame more widely, sends to farther lands its wealth and trade, lifts its head higher than the rest. It is happy in the healthiness of its air, in the strength of its defences, the nature of its site, the honour of its citizens. . . .

* Elizabeth Kendall, *Source-Book of English History*, New York, The Macmillan Company, 1900.

It has on the east the Palatine Castle, very great and strong. . . . On the west are two towers very strongly fortified, with the high and great wall of the city having seven double gates, and towered to the north at intervals. London was walled and towered in like manner on the south, but the great fish-bearing Thames river which there glides . . . by course of time washed against, loosened, and thrown down these walls. Also upwards to the west the royal palace is conspicuous above the same river, an incomparable building with ramparts and bulwarks, two miles from the city, joined to it by a populous suburb. . . .

Also there are, on the north side, pastures and a pleasant meadow land, through which flow river streams. . . . Very near lies a great forest, with woodland pastures, wild animals, stags, deer, boars, and wild bulls. . . .

That city is . . . populous with many inhabitants, so that in the time of slaughter of war under King Stephen, of those going out to muster twenty thousand horsemen and sixty thousand men on foot were estimated to be fit for war. . . .

Those engaged in the several kinds of business . . . are distributed every morning into their several localities and shops. Besides, there is in London on the river bank . . . a public cook shop; there eatables are to be found every day. . . . If there should come suddenly to any of the citizens friends, weary from a journey and too hungry to like waiting till fresh food is bought and cooked . . . one runs to the river bank, and there is all that can be wanted. . . . Outside one of the gates . . . is a certain field. . . . Every Friday, unless it be a higher day of appointed solemnity, there is in it a famous show of noble horses for sale. Earls, barons, knights, and many citizens who are in town, come to see or buy. . . . In another part of the field stand by themselves the goods proper to rustics, implements of husbandry, swine . . . cows . . . oxen. . . . To this city from every nation under heaven merchants delight to bring their trade by sea. . . .

Let us now come to the sports and pastimes. . . . Every Friday in Lent a fresh company of young men comes into the field on horseback, and the best horseman conducteth the rest. Then march forth the citizens' sons and other young men, with disarmed lances and shields, and there they practise feats of war. . . .

When the great fen, or moor, which watereth the walls of the city on the north side, is frozen many young men play upon the ice . . . ; some tie bones to their feet and under their heels; and shoving themselves by a little picked staff, do slide as swift as a bird flieth in the air. . . .

# A Complaint about Medieval Children *

BARTHOLOMEW ANGLICUS

*"Children will be children!" The complaints of an English Franciscan of the thirteenth century about the young children of his time have a modern ring.*

. . . Some children . . . lead their lives without thought and care. And set their courages only of mirth and liking, and dread no perils more than beating with a rod. . . . When they be praised, or shamed, or blamed, they set little thereby. . . . Since all children be tatched with evil manners, and think only on things that be, and reck not of things that shall be, they love plays, games, and vanity. . . . And things most worthy they repute least worthy, and least worthy most worthy. . . . And the goodness that is done for them, they let it pass out of mind. They desire all things they see. . . . They love talking and counsel of such children as they be, and void company of old men. They keep no counsel, but they tell all that they hear or see. Suddenly they laugh, and suddenly they weep. . . . When they be washed of filth, anon they defile themselves again. When their mother washeth and combeth them, they kick and sprawl, and put with feet and with hands, and withstand with all their might. . . .


# Insecurity of the Cities **

*Medieval cities, even in peacetime, faced the danger of pillage by outsiders, who were always ready to plunder any city that relaxed its guard. We read first of the precautions taken at London in 1297, which are an example of those of other towns. We then return to London in 1334 to see how that city attempted to preserve order within its walls.*

## WATCH AND WARD AT THE CITY GATES, 1297

It was ordered that every bedel [parish officer] shall make summons by day in his own Ward, upon view of two good men, for setting watch at

* Bartholomew Angicus, *Medieval Lore*, London, Alexander Moring, Ltd., 1905 (translated by Robert Steele).
** Henry T. Riley, *Memorials of London and London Life 1276–1419*, London, Longmans, Green & Co. Ltd., 1898.

the Gates;—and that those so summoned shall come to the Gates in the day-time, and in the morning, at day-light, shall depart therefrom. And such persons are to be properly armed with two pieces; namely, with haketon [a jacket of quilted leather, sometimes worn under the armour, and sometimes used as armour itself] and gambeson [an inner jacket, worn beneath the haketon, or other armour], or else with haketon and corset [or corslet; a light cuirass], or with haketon and plates. And if they neglect to come so armed, or make default in coming, the bedel shall forthwith hire another person, at the rate of twelve pence, in the place of him who makes such default; such sum to be levied on the morrow upon the person so making default.

### Proclamation Made for the Safekeeping of the City, 1334

In the time of Reynald de Conduit, Mayor of London.—This proclamation was made on the Wednesday next after the Feast of St. Lucy the Virgin [13 December], in the 8th year of the reign of King Edward, after the Conquest the Third.—

"Forasmuch as our Lord the king, whom may God save and preserve, is now engaged in his war against his enemies in Scotland, and every man ought to be most tender of keeping and maintaining his peace;—it is ordained and granted by the Mayor, Aldermen, and Commonalty, of the City of London, for maintaining the peace between all manner of folks in the said city, that no person, denizen or stranger, other than officers of the City, and those who have to keep the peace, shall go armed, or shall carry arms, by night or by day, within the franchise of the said city, on pain of imprisonment, and of losing the arms.

"Also, it is agreed that whosoever shall draw sword, or knife, or other arm, in affray of the people, shall be forthwith attached, and shall have imprisonment, without being left to find surety, according to the discretion of the Mayor and of the Aldermen of the City. . . .

"Also, it is ordained and assented to, that no person shall be so daring, on pain of imprisonment, as to go wandering about the City, after the hour of curfew rung out at St. Martin's le Grand; unless it be some man of the City of good repute, or his servant; and that, for reasonable cause, and with light.

"And whereas misdoers, going about by night, commonly have their resort more in taverns than elsewhere, and there seek refuge and watch their time for evil-doing; it is forbidden that any taverner or brewer shall keep the door of his tavern open after the hour of curfew aforesaid, on the pain as to the same ordained; that is to say, the first time, on pain of being amerced in 40 pence; the second time, half a mark; the third time, 10 shillings; the fourth time, 20 shillings; and the fifth time, he is to forswear the trade.

"Also, we do forbid, on the same pain of imprisonment, that any man shall go about at this Feast of Christmas with companions disguised with false faces, or in any other manner, to the houses of the good folks of the City, for playing at dice there; but let each one keep himself quiet and at his ease within his own house."

## Plunder of a City *

SIR JEAN FROISSART

*Preparations made for the protection of cities were not always successful, since their wealth served as a magnet to draw marauding bandits from the countryside. Sir Jean Froissart tells us of an attack on a French town.*

. . . "We have this day," continued the knight, "passed the castle of Ortingas, the garrison of which did great harm to this part of the country. Peter d'Achin had possession of it; he took it by surprise, and by it gained 60,000 francs from France." "How so?" said I. "In the middle of August, on the Feast of Our Lady," replied the knight, "a fair is held at Ortingas, when all the country people assemble, and to which much merchandise is brought. Now Peter d'Achin and his companions at Lourdes had long wanted to gain the town and castle of Ortingas, but could not devise the means. In the beginning of May, however, they instructed two of their men to seek for service in the town, in order that they might have friends within the walls whenever they should find themselves prepared to surprise the place.

"When the fair time came, the town was filled with foreign merchants, and in the houses of the masters of these two servants there was, as usual, much drinking and feasting. Peter d'Achin, thinking this a good opportunity, placed some men in ambush, and sent forward six varlets with two

* Sir Jean Froissart, *Chronicles*, vol. 1, New York, The Colonial Press, 1901 (translated by Thomas Johnes).

ladders to the town, who, with the assistance of the servants, managed to fix the ladders against the walls, which they mounted; one of the servants then conducted them toward the gate, where only two men were on guard, and placing them in concealment, said, 'Do you remain here till you hear me whistle; then sally forth and slay the guards.' The servant then advanced to the gate, and calling the guards by name, said, 'Open the door—I bring you some of the best wine you have ever tasted.' As soon as the door was opened, he gave a whistle, upon which his comrades rushed into the guard-room and slew the guards so suddenly that they could give no alarm; they then let down the drawbridge, and at one blast of their horn all the party in ambush mounted their horses, and came full gallop into the town, where they found all its inhabitants either feasting or in bed, and so gained the town." "But how did they gain the castle?" I asked. "I will tell you," said Sir Espaign du Lyon, for that was the name of my companion. "When the town was taken, as ill-luck would have it, the governor was absent, supping with some merchants, so that he was made prisoner, and the next day Peter d'Achin had him brought before the castle, in which were his wife and children, whom Peter so frightened, by declaring that unless they surrendered the place he should be put to death before their eyes, that they most gladly complied, and by this means Peter d'Achin got possession of the castle, and a very large booty, besides much money."

### Sanitation in Medieval Cities *

> The closely packed houses provided ideal conditions for the spread of fire and disease. A fire could destroy a town in a blazing hour, and epidemics such as typhoid might ravage an entire population in a few short weeks. Sewage systems did not exist, with the result that medieval towns could be smelled miles away. Edinburgh in Scotland became known to Scots as "Auld Reekie" (Old Stinky), but it was no worse than any other large European center in medieval times. We see one attempt to wrestle with the problem in London in 1309.

* Henry T. Riley, *Memorials of London and London Life 1276–1419*, London, Longmans, Green & Co. Ltd., 1898.

Seeing that the people in the town do cause the ordure that has been collected in their homes, to be collected and placed in the streets, and in the lanes of the City, whereas they ought to have it carried to the Thames, or elsewhere out of the town; and that thereby the streets and lanes are more incumbered than they used to be;—we do forbid, on the King's behalf, that from henceforth any person shall have the ordure that has been collected in his house, carried into the King's highways; but let them cause the same to be carried to the Thames, or elsewhere out of the City. . . . And if any one shall do so, he shall be amerced, the first time, 40 pence, and afterwards, an half a mark each time; and nevertheless, he shall have the same removed at his own charges. . . .

## The Charter of a Medieval Guild *

> The members of each trade or occupation in each city banded together for mutual aid and protection. Each craft came to have its own guild (union) which regulated prices, quality of goods, wages, and conditions for apprentices (trainees). It also provided for the sick and for the widows and orphaned children of its members. In later years these guilds came to have distinctive costumes, banners, and halls. In some cities every citizen belonged to a guild, even princes being proud to share membership. Following is an example of a guild charter, that of the Hatters of London, drawn up in 1347.

The points of the Articles touching the trade of Hat-makers, accepted by Thomas Leggy, Mayor, and the Aldermen of the City of London, at the suit, and at the request, of the folks of the said trade.

In the first place,—that six men of the most lawful and most befitting of the said trade shall be assigned and sworn to rule and watch the trade, in such manner as other trades of the said city are ruled and watched by their Wardens.

Also,—that no one shall make or sell any manner of hats within the franchise of the city aforesaid, if he be not free of the same city; on pain of forfeiting to the Chamber the hats which he shall have made and offered for sale.

* Henry T. Riley, *Memorials of London and London Life 1276–1419*, London, Longmans, Green & Co. Ltd., 1898.

Also,—that no one shall be made apprentice in the said trade for a less term than seven years, and that, without fraud or collusion. And he who shall receive any apprentice in any other manner, shall lose his freedom, until he shall have bought it back again.

Also,—that no one of the said trade shall take any apprentice, if he be not himself a freeman of the said city.

Also,—that the Wardens of the said trade shall make their searches for all manner of hats that are for sale within the said franchise, so often as need shall be. And that the aforesaid Wardens shall have power to take all manner of hats that they shall find defective and not befitting, and to bring them before the Mayor and Aldermen of London, that so the defaults which shall be found may be punished by their award.

Also,—whereas some workmen in the said trade have made hats that are not befitting, in deceit of the common people, from which great scandal, shame, and loss have often arisen to the good folks of the said trade, they pray that no workman in the said trade shall do any work by night touching the same, but only in clear daylight; that so, the aforesaid Wardens may openly inspect their work. And he who shall do otherwise, and shall be convicted thereof before the Mayor and Aldermen, shall pay to the Chamber of the Guildhall, the first time 40d., the second time half a mark, and the third time he shall lose his freedom.

Also,—that no one of the said trade shall be admitted to be free of the City, or to work in the said trade, or to sell any manner of hats within the said franchise, if he be not attested by the aforesaid Wardens as being a good and lawful person, and as a proper workman.

Also,—that no one of the said trade shall receive the apprentice or serving-man of another, until he has fully completed his term, or his master has given him a proper dismissal; on pain of paying, for every time, to the said Chamber half a mark, down to the fourth time, when he shall lose his freedom, until he shall have bought it back again.

Also,—that no one of the said trade shall receive the serving-man of another to work, so long as he is in debt to his master; but he is to remain in the service of his master, until he shall have made satisfaction for the debt which he owes him. And he who shall receive such serving-man otherwise, shall pay to the said Chamber for every time 40d.; but only down to the fourth time, when he shall lose his freedom, until he shall have bought it back again.

Also,—whereas foreign folks of divers Counties do bring to the said city divers manners of hats to sell, and carry them about the streets, as well before the houses of freemen of the said trade, as elsewhere; and thereby bar them of their dealings and of their sale, so that the freemen of the said trade in the City are greatly impoverished thereby; it is agreed that no strange person bringing hats to the said city for sale, shall sell them by retail, but only in gross, and that, to the freemen of the City; on pain of losing the same.

## To Become a Master *

> *Membership in a craft guild was not easily gained. An individual became a member only after a long period of thorough training. The first step was for the young boy to learn the trade by serving as an apprentice for from two to ten years, depending on the skill required for the craft. (An average was about seven years.) Next, the person served as a journeyman, a free worker able to hire out for wages. Finally, when and if the journeyman had accumulated a sufficient amount of capital and had passed a rigorous examination (which often included the submission of a "masterpiece"), he was eligible himself to become a master. The following are two thirteenth-century apprenticeship arrangements in Flanders.*

Be it known to present and future aldermen that Ouede Ferconne apprentices Michael, her son, to Matthew Haimart on security of her house, her person, and her chattels, and the share that Michael ought to have in them, so that Matthew Haimart will teach him to weave in four years, and that he (Michael) will have shelter, and learn his trade there without board. And if there should be reason within two years for Michael to default she will return him, and Ouede Ferconne, his mother, guarantees this on the security of her person and goods. And if she should wish to purchase his freedom for the last two years she may do so for thirty-three solidi, and will pledge for that all that has been stated. And if he should not free himself of the last two years let him return, and Ouede Ferconne, his mother, pledges this with her person and her goods. And the said Ouede pledges that if Matthew Haimart suffers either loss or damage

* Roy C. Cave, Herbert H. Coulson, *A Source Book for Medieval Economic History*, New York, The Bruce Publishing Co., 1936.

through Michael, her son, she will restore the loss and damage on the security of herself and all her goods, should Michael do wrong.

April the ninth. I, Peter Borre, in good faith and without guile, place with you, Peter Feissac, weaver, my son Stephen, for the purpose of learning the trade or craft of weaving, to live at your house, and to do work for you from the feast of Easter next for four continuous years, promising you by this agreement to take care that my son does the said work, and that he will be faithful and trustworthy in all that he does, and that he will neither steal nor take anything away from you, nor flee nor depart from you for any reason, until he has completed his apprenticeship. And I promise you by this agreement that I will reimburse you for all damages or losses that you incur or sustain on my behalf, pledging all my goods, etc.; renouncing the benefit of all laws, etc. And I, the said Peter Feissac, promise you, Peter Borre, that I will teach your son faithfully and will provide food and clothing for him.

Done at Marseilles, near the tables of the money-changers.


## *Leagues of Merchant Cities* *

> *Before the new national kingdoms had clearly organized and absorbed the cities into their own system, the cities often entered into leagues among themselves. One of the most famous federations was that of the merchant cities of the North Sea and Baltic Sea. This "Hanseatic League" eventually included such cities as London in England, Hamburg, Cologne, Lübeck, and Bremen in Germany, and Novgorod in Russia, with more than a hundred others in between. The league coined money, maintained a war fleet under its own banners, negotiated treaties, and seemed for a time to represent a new nation of the north in the making.*

### Agreement for Mutual Protection Between Lubeck and Hamburg, 1241

The advocate, council and commune of Lübeck. . . . We have made the following agreement with our dear friends, the citizens of Hamburg.

* Oliver J. Thatcher, Edgar Holmes McNeal, *A Source Book for Mediæval History*, New York, Charles Scribner's Sons, 1905.

1. If robbers or other depredators attack citizens of either city anywhere from the mouth of the Trave river to Hamburg, or anywhere on the Elbe river, the two cities shall bear the expenses equally in destroying and extirpating them.

2. If anyone who lives outside the city, kills, wounds, beats, or mishandles, without cause, a citizen of either city, the two cities shall bear the expenses equally in punishing the offender. We furthermore agree to share the expenses equally in punishing those who injure their citizens in the neighborhood of their city and those who injure our citizens in the neighborhood of our city.

3. If any of their citizens are injured near our city [Lübeck], they shall ask our officials to punish the offender, and if any of our citizens are injured near their city [Hamburg], they shall ask their officials to punish the offender.

### DECREES OF THE HANSEATIC LEAGUE, 1260–64

We wish to inform you of the action taken in support of all merchants who are governed by the law of Lübeck.

(1) Each city shall, to the best of her ability, keep the sea clear of pirates, so that merchants may freely carry on their business by sea. (2) Whoever is expelled from one city because of a crime shall not be received in another. (3) If a citizen is seized [by pirates, robbers, or bandits] he shall not be ransomed, but his sword-belt and knife shall be sent to him [as a threat to his captors]. (4) Any merchant ransoming him shall lose all his possessions in all the cities which have the law of Lübeck. (5) Whoever is proscribed in one city for robbery or theft shall be proscribed in all. (6) If a lord besieges a city, no one shall aid him in any way to the detriment of the besieged city, unless the besieger is his lord. (7) If there is a war in the country, no city shall on that account injure a citizen from the other cities, either in his person or goods, but shall give him protection. (8) If any man marries a woman in one city, and another woman from some other city comes and proves that he is her lawful husband, he shall be beheaded. . . .

### DECREES OF THE HANSEATIC LEAGUE, 1265

We ought to hold a meeting once a year to legislate about the affairs of the cities.

(5) If pirates appear on the sea, all the cities must contribute their share to the work of destroying them.

# Enforcing Obedience to the Church

*Throughout the Middle Ages the Catholic Church was the most powerful single force in Europe. Its strongest weapon in enforcing its decrees was "excommunication," which forbade one the society of all Christians. Civil governments supported the church in this, with the result that the excommunicate could not engage in business, plead in court, marry, or legally bear arms. During the high Middle Ages governments took even stronger action. England imprisoned after forty days of excommunication, France seized all property after a year and a day, while Sweden executed one still excommunicated at the end of a year. But the greatest strength of this weapon lay in the people's faith that excommunication continued in effect after death. We read two decrees of excommunication.*

## A Decree of Excommunication of 988 *

May jaundice seize and blindness smite him. May his present life end miserably in a most wretched death. May he undergo eternal damnation with the devil, where, being bound with red-hot chains, he may lament ceaselessly; and may the worm that never dies consume his flesh, and the flames that cannot be quenched be his food and sustenance through all eternity.

## Excommunication of the Emperor Frederick II, by Innocent IV, at the Council of Lyons, 1245 **

[Innocent recapitulates the efforts of the popes to maintain peace between the church and the empire and dwells upon the sins of the emperor. Then, after charging him with particular crimes of perjury, sacrilege, heresy, and tyranny, he proceeds as follows:]—We, therefore, on account of his aforesaid crimes and of his many other nefarious misdeeds, after careful deliberation with our brethren and with the holy council, acting however unworthily as the vicar of Jesus Christ on earth and knowing how it was said to us in the person of the blessed apostle Peter, *Whatsoever ye shall bind on earth shall be bound in heaven;* We announce and declare

* University of Pennsylvania, *Translations and Reprints from the Original Sources of European History*, vol. 4, no. 4, Philadelphia, 1898.
** University of Pennsylvania, *Translations and Reprints from the Original Sources of European History*, vol. 4, no. 4, Philadelphia, 1898.

the said prince to be bound because of his sins and rejected by the Lord and deprived of all honor and dignity, and moreover by this sentence we hereby deprive him of the same since he has rendered himself so unworthy of ruling his kingdom and so unworthy of all honors and dignity; for, indeed, on account of his iniquities he has been rejected of God that he might not reign or exercise authority. All who have taken the oath of fidelity to him we absolve forever from such oath by our apostolic authority, absolutely forbidding anyone hereafter to obey him or look upon him as emperor or king. Let those whose duty it is to select a new emperor proceed freely with the election. . . .

## The Interdict *

POPE INNOCENT III

> *A weapon used by the church against a region or even a whole nation was the "interdict," which forbade or severely limited church services throughout the area. We read an interdict on France of Pope Innocent III in 1200.*

Let all the churches be closed; let no one be admitted to them except to baptize infants; let them not be otherwise opened except for the purpose of lighting the lamps, or when the priest shall come for the Eucharist and holy water for the use of the sick. We permit mass to be celebrated once a week on Friday early in the morning . . . but only one clerk is to be admitted to them, beware lest the laity hear them; and let them not permit the dead to be interred, or their bodies to be placed unburied in the cemeteries. Let them, moreover, say to the laity that they sin and transgress grievously by burying bodies in the earth, even in unconsecrated ground, for in so doing they arrogate to themselves an office pertaining to others. Let them forbid their parishioners to enter churches that may be open in the king's territory. . . . Let the priest confess all who desire it in the portico of the church; if the church have no portico we direct that in bad or rainy weather, and not otherwise, the nearest door of the church may be opened and confessions heard on its threshold (all being excluded

* University of Pennsylvania, *Translations and Reprints from the Original Sources of European History*, vol. 4, no. 4, Philadelphia. 1898.

except the one who is to confess) so that the priest and the penitent can be heard by those who are outside the church. If, however, the weather be fair, let the confession be heard in front of the closed doors. Let no vessels of holy water be placed outside of the church, nor shall the priests carry them anywhere. . . . Extreme unction, which is a holy sacrament, may not be given.

## Manual of the Inquisitor *

BERNARD GUI

> By the thirteenth century, religion was challenged increasingly by strange cults, some of which secretly worshiped the devil. In 1233 Pope Gregory IX established a permanent commission to root out such teachings wherever they existed. A manual for the investigators ("inquisitors") was drawn up by a monk named Bernard Gui.

. . . It is, indeed, all too difficult to bring heretics to reveal themselves when, instead of frankly avowing their error they conceal it, or when there is not sure and sufficient testimony against them. Under these circumstances difficulties rise on all sides for the investigator. On the one hand his conscience will torment him if he punishes without having obtained a confession or conviction of heresy; on the other hand, all that repeated experience has taught him of the falseness, guile and malice of such people will cause him still greater anguish. If they escape punishment owing to their fox-like craftiness it is to the great harm of the faith. . . .

INSTRUCTIONS CONCERNING THE PROCEDURE TO BE FOLLOWED WITH PERSONS WHO HAVE CONFESSED THE TRUTH IN COURT AND WITH THOSE WHO HAVE BEEN CHARGED AND ARE SUSPECT WHO REFUSE TO DO SO

If having stated in court the truth concerning the infractions committed by himself or by another person, having abjured all heresy and been reconciled with the unity of the Church, an accused shows repentance

* Bernard Gui, "Manual of the Inquisitor," in *Introduction to Contemporary Civilization in the West*, vol. 1, New York, Columbia University Press, 1947, pp. 160–168 *passim*.

that seems sincere; and if, moreover, there is no fear that he may flee, be corrupted or relapse, and if there are no other objections, he shall be released with another person as bond for him until the time of the general sermon in the course of which penance for his crimes will be imposed on him. . . .

On the other hand, when a person who is suspected of, denounced or reported for or accused of the crime of heresy has been charged and refuses to confess, he shall be held in prison until the truth comes to light; the status and station of the person, as well as the nature of the suspicion and of the crime should, however, be taken into account. He may be released with another person as bond for him, especially when proof of his guilt is not conclusive, when the accusation was not direct but incidental and when suspicion was not clearcut. . . . Nevertheless, those who benefit from this leniency shall, instead of imprisonment, take a position before the door of the home of the inquisitor each day . . . and shall not depart therefrom without permission of the inquisitor. . . .

When an accused is strongly suspect and in all likelihood and probability guilty, and when the inquisitor is thoroughly convinced thereof; in such a case, when the person persists in his denials, as I have stated time and time again, he should not be released for any reason whatever, but should be held for a number of years, in order that his trials may open his mind. Many have I seen who, thus subjected for a number of years to this regime of vexations and confinement, end by admitting not only recent but even long-standing old crimes, going back thirty and forty years or more. . . .

### The Manner of Acting toward Heretics Who Repent at the Moment of Execution

Should it happen, as it already has on several occasions, that a condemned person abandoned and handed over to the secular arm, taken by said court and brought to the place of execution, should . . . affirm a desire to repent and renounce the said errors, he should be spared and returned to the inquisitors. And they should receive him, unless he had perhaps already relapsed into heresy, for here equity is to be preferred to severity. . . .

In such a case, the inquisitors should take all necessary precautions, for those who are converted in such an extremity are rightfully suspect of acting in fear of punishment, and the inquisitors should carefully consider whether the conversion is genuine or feigned. . . .

And this may be brought out in several ways and according to several signs: if, for example, he promptly and spontaneously reveals and denounces all his accomplices to the inquisitors; if he attacks his sect in gesture, words and deeds; if he admits his former errors humbly and one by one . . . ; and all of these things can be known with certainty through the questioning he will undergo and the confession he will sign. . . .

As has already been said, this clemency and admission to penance after pronouncement of sentence is not, in truth, in common law; but the office of the Inquisition, holding very broad powers, has introduced this procedure in many cases of this kind. And since what it has in view and seeks above all is the salvation of souls and purity of the faith, it admits to penance, the first time, heretics who wish to be converted and return to the unity of the Church. Moreover, the confessions of these converts frequently lead to the discovery of accomplices and of errors: the truth is brought to light, falsehood is uncloaked, and the office benefits thereby.

Once a conversion of this type appears to the inquisitors probably to be feigned and simulated, everything is brought to a halt and the sentence is carried out.

## The Struggle for Power Between Church and State

*By the thirteenth century the church had reached its position of greatest political power; but its claims were contested by the Holy Roman emperor in Germany and by the emerging national kingdoms of England and France. The struggle focused on the questions of taxation, the extent to which national law could affect the church, and the right to appoint bishops. Because bishops not only were the principal officials of the church but also were often powerful feudal lords whose support was necessary to kings and emperors, disputes as to who should appoint them—called "investiture controversies"—were long and bitter. The quarrels extended over three centuries, from the dispute between Pope Gregory VII and Emperor Henry IV in 1075 to that in which Pope Boniface VIII stated the church's claims in the bull (decree) Unam Sanctam of 1302, which was countered by the emperor's diet (council) of 1338.*

Bishop Gregory, servant of the servants of God, to King Henry, greeting and apostolic benediction:—that is, if he be obedient to the apostolic chair as beseems a Christian king. Considering and carefully weighing with what strict judgment we shall have to render account for the ministry entrusted to us by St. Peter, chief of the apostles, it is with hesitation that we have sent unto you the apostolic benediction. For you are said knowingly to exercise fellowship with those excommunicated by a judgment of the apostolic chair. . . . If this be true, you know yourself that you may receive the favour neither of the divine nor the apostolic benediction. . . . Therefore we counsel your Highness that, if you feel yourself guilty in this matter, you seek the advice of some bishop with speedy confession. Who, with our permission enjoining on you a proper penance for this fault, shall absolve you. . . .

For the rest it seems strange enough to us that, although you transmit to us so many and such devoted letters; and although your Highness shows such humility through the words of your legates—calling yourself the son of holy mother church and of ourselves . . . : you do, however, at heart and in deeds most stubborn, show yourself contrary to the canonical and apostolic decrees. . . . And now, indeed, inflicting wound upon wound, contrary to the establishments of the apostolic chair, you have given the churches of Fermo and Spoleto—if indeed a church could be given or granted by a man—to certain persons not even known to us. . . .

Since you confess yourself a son of the church, it would have beseemed the royal dignity to look more respectfully upon the master of the church,—that is, St. Peter, the chief of the apostles. . . . Inasmuch as in his seat and apostolic ministration we, however sinful and unworthy, do act as the representative of his powers. . . . And at the very time when we are either perusing the letters or listening to the voices of those who speak, he himself is discerning, with subtle inspection, in what spirit the instructions were issued. . . .

. . . It would . . . have been but right that, before you violated apostolic decrees, you should, by negotiation, make demands from us in cases where we oppressed you or stood in the way of your prerogatives. But of how much worth you considered either our commands or the observances of justice, is shown by those things which were afterwards done and brought about by you.

* Ernest F. Henderson, *Select Historical Documents of the Middle Ages,* London, George Bell & Sons, 1896 (adapted).

But since, inasmuch as the still long-suffering patience of God invites you to amend your ways, we have hopes that, your perception being increased, your heart and mind can be bent to the obedience of the mandates of God: we warn you with paternal love, that, recognizing over you the dominion of Christ, you reflect how dangerous it is to prefer your own honour to His. . . .

### HENRY IV TO GREGORY VII, JANUARY 24, 1076 *

Henry, king not through usurpation but through the holy ordination of God, to Hildebrand, not pope but false monk. Such greeting as this have you merited through your disturbances, inasmuch as there is no grade in the church which you have omitted to make a partaker not of honour but of confusion, not of benediction but of malediction. . . . You have looked upon [the bishops] as knowing nothing, and upon your sole self, moreover, as knowing all things. This knowledge, however, you have not used for edification but for destruction; so that with reason we believe that St. Gregory, whose name you have usurped for yourself, was prophesying concerning you when he said: "The pride of him who is in power increases the more, the greater the number of those subject to him; and he thinks that he himself can do more than all." And we, indeed, have endured all this, being eager to guard the honour of the apostolic see; you, however, have understood our humility to be fear, and have not, accordingly, shunned to rise up against the royal power conferred upon us by God, daring to divest us of it. As if we received our kingdom from you! As if the kingdom and the empire were in your and not in God's hand. . . . And from the throne of peace you have disturbed peace, inasmuch as you have armed subjects against those in authority over them. . . . On me also who, although unworthy to be among the anointed, have nevertheless been anointed to the kingdom, you have laid your hand; me who—as the tradition of the holy Father teaches, declaring that I am not to be deposed for any crime unless, which God forbid, I should have strayed from the faith—am subject to the judgment of God alone. . . . The true pope, Peter . . . exclaims: "Fear God, honour the king." But you, who do not fear God, do dishonour in me his appointed one. . . . St. Paul, when he has not spared even an angel of Heaven if he shall have preached otherwise, has not excepted you also, who do teach otherwise upon earth. For he says: "If any one, either I or an angel from Heaven

* Ernest F. Henderson, *Select Historical Documents of the Middle Ages,* London George Bell & Sons, 1896 (adapted).

should preach a gospel other than that which has been preached to you, he shall be accursed." You, therefore, accursed by St. Paul and by the judgment of all our bishops and by our own, descend and relinquish the apostolic chair which you have usurped. Let another ascend the throne of St. Peter, who shall not practice violence under the cloak of religion, but shall teach the sound doctrine of St. Peter. I, Henry, king by the grace of God, do say to you, together with all our bishops: Descend, descend, to be accursed throughout the ages.

## DEMAND OF POPE URBAN IV FOR THE PAYMENT OF THE ENGLISH TRIBUTE, 1262 *

If our dearest son in Christ, the illustrious king of England [Henry III], pays promptly what he owes, he will acquire grace deservedly and the royal highness will deserve to be commended affectionately. Since, therefore, an annual census of 1,000 marks of sterlings is owed by him to the sacrosanct Roman church, and now there will have been a cessation of the payment of it for three years reckoned at the next festival of Michaelmas, we have caused that king by our letters . . . to be asked with paternal affection that, with any obstacle of difficulty removed, with prompt willingness, he pay that census for the aforesaid time to you in the name of us and the aforesaid church. Wherefore . . . we command . . . that, when our letters which we direct to the said king about this have been received, you do not delay the presentation of them to him, and warn him seriously and persuade him that he pay that census in full for the aforesaid term, within a reasonable time . . . to you in behalf of us and that church. Otherwise do you place his chapel under ecclesiastical interdict. . . .

Moreover, all money which you may receive from the census, do you take care to assign with due precaution to Rayner Bonaccursi. . . . What and how much you have assigned to him, the day of assignment, and whatever you have done therein, do you write faithfully to us in your letters. . . .

## THE BULL "UNAM SANCTAM" OF BONIFACE VIII, 1302 **

. . . By the words of the Gospel we are taught that the two swords, namely, the spiritual authority and the temporal, are in the power of the

* William E. Lunt, *Papal Revenues in the Middle Ages*, vol. 2, New York, Columbia University Press, 1934, pp. 50–51.
** Oliver J. Thatcher, Edgar H. McNeal, *A Source Book for Mediæval History*, New York, Charles Scribner's Sons, 1905.

church. . . . Whoever denies that the temporal sword is in the power of Peter does not properly understand the word of the Lord when he said: "Put up thy sword into the sheath." Both swords, therefore, the spiritual and the temporal, are in the power of the church. The former is to be used by the church, the latter for the church; the one by the hand of the priest, the other by the hand of kings and knights, but at the command and permission of the priest. Moreover, it is necessary for one sword to be under the other, and the temporal authority to be subjected to the spiritual. . . . And we must necessarily admit that the spiritual power surpasses any earthly power in dignity and honor, because spiritual things surpass temporal things. . . . For the truth itself declares that the spiritual power must establish the temporal power and pass judgment on it if it is not good. . . . Therefore if the temporal power errs, it will be judged by the spiritual power, and if the lower spiritual power errs, it will be judged by its superior. But if the highest spiritual power errs, it can not be judged by men, but by God alone. For the apostle says: "But he that is spiritual judgeth all things, yet he himself is judged of no man.". . . We therefore declare, say, and affirm that submission on the part of every man to the bishop of Rome is altogether necessary for his salvation.

## The Law "Licet Juris" of the Diet of Frankfurt, August 8, 1338 *

Both the canon and the civil law declare plainly that the dignity and authority of the emperor come of old directly from the Son of God, that God has appointed the emperors and kings of the world to give laws to the human race, and that the emperor obtains his office solely through his election by those who have the right to vote in imperial elections, without the confirmation and approval of anyone else. For in secular affairs he has no superior on earth, but rather is the ruler of all nations and peoples. Moreover, our Lord Jesus Christ has said: "Render unto Caesar the things which are Caesar's, and unto God the things which are God's." Nevertheless, certain persons, blinded by avarice and ambition, and totally ignorant of the Scriptures, have distorted the meaning of certain passages by false and wicked interpretations, and on this basis have attacked the imperial authority and the rights of the emperors. . . . For they wrongfully assert that the emperor derives his position and authority from the pope, and that the emperor elect is not the real emperor until his election is confirmed and approved, and he is crowned by the pope. . . .

* Oliver J. Thatcher, Edgar H. McNeal, *A Source Book for Mediæval History*, New York, Charles Scribner's Sons, 1905.

In order to prevent this we now declare by the advice and with the consent of the electors and other princes of the empire, that the emperor holds his authority and position from God alone . . . and has full power to administer the laws of the empire and to perform all the functions of the emperor, without the approval, confirmation, authorization, or consent of the pope or any other person.

Therefore, we decree by this perpetual edict that the emperor elected by the electors or a majority of them is to be regarded and considered by all to be the true and lawful emperor, by reason of the election alone; that he is to be obeyed by all subjects of the empire; and that he has . . . the complete imperial power of administration and jurisdiction. If anyone contradicts these decrees . . . or agrees with those who contradict them . . . we hereby deprive him and declare him to be deprived, by virtue of his act and of this law, of all fiefs which he holds of the empire, and of all favors, jurisdiction, privileges, and immunities which have been granted to him by us or by our predecessors. Moreover, we declare that he is guilty of offence against the majesty of the emperor, and subject to the penalties incurred by this offence.

## The Rise of Universities *

### EMPEROR FREDERICK I BARBAROSSA

> Just as there were guilds of craftsmen and other occupations, there developed guilds of scholars and of teachers. Some acquired continent-wide reputations and attracted students from all over Europe. Salerno early was famous for its faculty of medicine, Bologna for law, and Paris for theology. These developed into communities of scholarship called "universities," with their own laws and customs. Much friction existed between the cities with their liberties, the universities with their guild rules, and the kings whose laws often stopped at the boundaries of both. For the protection of students and masters within the Holy Roman Empire, Emperor Frederick I issued the following edict in 1158.

* Frederic A. Ogg, A Source Book of Mediæval History, New York, American Book Co., 1907.

After a careful consideration of this subject by the bishops, abbots, dukes, counts, judges, and other nobles of our sacred palace, we, from our piety, have granted this privilege to all scholars who travel for the sake of study . . . that they may go in safety to the places in which the studies are carried on . . . and may dwell there in security. For we think it fitting that, during good behavior, those should enjoy our praise and protection, by whose learning the world is enlightened to the obedience of God and of us, his ministers, and the life of the subject is molded; and by a special consideration we defend them from all injuries.

For who does not pity those who exile themselves through love for learning, who wear themselves out in poverty in place of riches, who expose their lives to all perils and often suffer bodily injury from the vilest of men? This must be endured with vexation. Therefore, we declare by this general and perpetual law, that in the future no one shall be so rash as to venture to inflict any injury on scholars, or to occasion any loss to them on account of a debt owed by an inhabitant of their province—a thing which we have learned is sometimes done by an evil custom. [Greedy creditors sometimes compelled students to pay debts owed by the fellow-countrymen of the latter—a very thinly disguised form of robbery. This abuse was now to be abolished.] And let it be known to the violators of this constitution, and also to those who shall at the time be the rulers of the places, that a fourfold restitution of property shall be exacted from all and that, the mark of infamy being affixed to them by the law itself, they shall lose their office forever. . . .

## *"Town and Gown" Conflict* *

HASTINGS RASHDALL

*The laws and customs of the universities often clashed with those of the cities in or near which the universities took root. As a result, relations between the gown-wearing students and the citizens of the towns were not always cordial, as in this account of events at the University of Paris in the thirteenth century.*

* Hastings Rashdall, *The Universities of Europe in the Middle Ages*, vol. 1, Oxford, Clarendon Press, 1895.

. . . During the Carnival of 1228–1229 some students were taking the air in a suburban region [of Paris] . . . when they entered a tavern and "by chance found good and sweet wine there." A dispute arose with the landlord over the reckoning. From words the disputants rapidly proceeded to blows—to pulling of ears and tearing of hair. The worsted inn-keeper called in his neighbors, who compelled the clerks [students] to retire severely beaten. The next day they returned with strong rein-forcements of gownsmen armed with swords and sticks, who broke into the tavern, avenged their comrades on the host and his neighbors, set the taps running, and then "flown with insolence and wine" sallied forth into the streets to amuse themselves at the expense of peaceable citizens. . . . So [they] continued to disport themselves until the tables were once more turned in favour of "Town" by the appearance on the scene of the Provost and his satellites the savage police of a savage city. . . . [The police] fell upon the offenders or (if we may trust our historian) a party of per-fectly innocent students engaged in their holiday games outside the walls; and several of them were killed in the ensuing *mêlée*. The Masters . . . [then] suspended their Lectures. . . . We may judge of the strength of the feeling against the University on the part of the Bishop and Church of Paris by the fact that . . . the murder of a number of students by a brutal soldiery was welcomed by their official superiors as tending to the humiliation of the upstart University. . . .

Finding the "Cessation" ineffectual the Masters . . . proceeded to a more extreme remedy. They resolved that, if justice were not done them within a month, they would dissolve the University for a period of six years, and would not return even at the expiration of that period unless satisfactory redress had been granted in the interval. And the Masters were as good as their word. The great mass of Masters and scholars left Paris. Many of them no doubt accepted the pressing invitation of Henry III of England, crossed the channel, and reinforced the rising Universities of Oxford and Cambridge. . . . Here they could pursue their studies at their own discretion, without interference from either civil or ecclesiastical authority. . . .

. . . At last, however, the Court was seriously alarmed at the loss of the prestige and of the commercial prosperity which the capital derived from its scholastic population. . . . It is not till the beginning of 1231 that we find the Masters and scholars at work again in their old quarters. The heroic remedy of a dispersion had not been applied in vain. Not only the particular grievance which had immediately provoked it, but others which had no doubt contributed to the disaster now met with effectual redress. . . . By the Bull *Parens Scientiarum* the University received Apostolical sanction for its great engine of warfare, the right of suspending lectures, in case satisfaction for an outrage were refused after fifteen days' notice. . . . The Bishop is required to be moderate in the exercise of his jurisdiction over scholars; he is forbidden to have innocent scholars arrested instead of the guilty (a significant indication of the way in which godly discipline had heretofore been administered at Paris), to imprison for debt or to impose pecuniary penances. The Chancellor is forbidden to have a prison at all; scholars are to be imprisoned in the Bishop's prison only, and bail is to be allowed in all cases. . . .

### The Life of University Students *

> *While students did much as they pleased in the early universities, their welfare was still a matter of concern for their elders. An attempt to protect the inexperienced newcomer to the university is seen in a decree of the University of Paris (1340). Parental worry over two students starting at the University of Toulouse (1315) in France is shown in the letter from a Spanish father.*

. . . No one of whatever faculty he be, shall take any money from a Freshman because of his class or anything else, . . . under penalty of deprivation of any honor now held or to be held from the university. . . .

The university bids the Freshmen . . . that if anyone does any wrong to them by word or deed on account of their class, they shall straightaway secretly reveal this to the proctors and deans of the faculties. . . .

. . . The said university enjoins all those renting lodgings to students that, as soon as they know any violence or threats have been made to a Freshman because of his class, they immediately reveal this. . . .

. . . The university enjoins all who have taken its oaths that, if they know any person or persons to have inflicted bodily violence or insult, threats and any injury upon Freshmen because of their class, they reveal this by their oaths as quickly as they can, as has been said above.

* Lynn Thorndike, *University Records and Life in the Middle Ages*, New York, Columbia University Press, 1944, pp. 154–160 *passim*, 192–193.

## A FATHER'S ADVICE

Choose lodgings removed from all foul smells as of ditches . . . or the like, since in breathing we are continually drawing in air which, if it is infected, infects us more and more forcibly than tainted food and drink do.

Likewise in winter keep your room closed from all noxious wind and have straw on the pavement lest you suffer from cold.

Furthermore, if you can have coals or chopped wood in a clay receptacle of good clay, or if you have a chimneyplace and fire in your room, it is well.

Also, be well clad and well shod, and outdoors wear pattens to keep your feet warm. . . .

And when you got to bed at night, have a white nightcap on your head and beneath your cheeks, and another colored one over it, for at night the head should be kept warmer than during the day.

Moreover, at the time of the great rains it is well to wear outdoors over your cap a bonnet or helmet of undressed skin, that is, a covering to keep the head from getting wet. Indeed, some persons wear a bonnet over the cap in fair weather, more especially when it is cold, so that in the presence of the great they may remove the bonnet and be excused from doffing the cap.

Also, look after your stockings and don't permit your feet to become dirty.

Also, wash the head, if you are accustomed to wash it, at least once a fortnight with hot lye and in a place sheltered from draughts on the eve of a feast day towards nightfall. Then dry your hair with a brisk massage; afterwards do it up; then put on a bonnet or cap.

Also comb your hair daily, if you will morning and evening before eating or at least afterwards, if you cannot do otherwise.

Also look out that a draught does not strike you from window or crack while you study or sleep, or indeed at any time, for it strikes men without their noticing.

Also, in summer, in order not to have fleas or to have no more of them, sweep your room daily with a broom and do not sprinkle it with water, for they are generated from damp dust. But you may spray it occasionally with strong vinegar which comforts heart and brain.

If you will, walk daily somewhere morning and evening. And if the weather is cold, if you can run, run on empty stomach, or at least walk rapidly, that the natural heat may be revived. For a fire is soon extinguished unless the sticks are moved about or the bellows used. However, it is not advisable to run on a full stomach but to saunter slowly in order to settle the food in the stomach.

If you cannot go outside your lodgings, either because the weather does not permit or it is raining, climb the stairs rapidly three or four times, and have in your room a big heavy stick like a sword and wield it now with one hand, now with the other, as if in a scrimmage, until you are almost winded. This is splendid exercise to warm one up and expel noxious vapors through the pores and consume other superfluities. Jumping is a similar exercise. Singing, too, exercises the chest. And if you will do this, you will have healthy limbs, a sound intellect and memory. . . .


## A Controversial Teacher *

PETER ABELARD

> *Peter Abelard won widespread notoriety for his teaching methods, in which he attacked many of the views of his day and encouraged his students to join his challenge of church doctrine. We hear from Abelard in his book* Sic et Non *("Yes and No").*

There are many seeming contradictions and even obscurities in the innumerable writings of the church fathers. Our respect for their authority should not stand in the way of an effort on our part to come at the truth. The obscurity and contradictions in ancient writings may be explained upon many grounds, and may be discussed without impugning the good faith and insight of the fathers. A writer may use different terms to mean the same thing, in order to avoid a monotonous repetition of the same word. Common, vague words may be employed in order that the common people may understand; and sometimes a writer sacrifices perfect accuracy in the interest of a clear general statement. Poetical, figurative language is often obscure and vague. . . .

Doubtless the fathers might err; even Peter, the prince of the apostles, fell into error; what wonder that the saints do not always show themselves inspired? The fathers did not themselves believe that they, or their com-

* Quoted in James H. Robinson, *Readings in European History,* vol. 1, New York, Ginn and Company, 1904.

panions, were always right. Augustine found himself mistaken in some cases and did not hesitate to retract his errors. He warns his admirers not to look upon his letters ás they would upon the Scriptures, but to accept only those things which, upon examination, they find to be true.

All writings belonging to this class are to be read with full freedom to criticise, and with no obligation to accept unquestioningly; otherwise the way would be blocked to all discussion, and posterity be deprived of the excellent intellectual exercise of debating difficult questions of language and presentation. But an explicit exception must be made in the case of the Old and New Testaments. In the Scriptures, when anything strikes us as absurd, we may not say that the writer erred, but that the scribe made a blunder in copying the manuscripts, or that there is an error in interpretation, or that the passage is not understood. The fathers make a very careful distinction between the Scriptures and later works. . . .

In view of these considerations, I have ventured to bring together various dicta of the holy fathers, as they came to mind, and to formulate certain questions which were suggested by the seeming contradictions in the statements. These questions ought to serve to excite tender readers to a zealous inquiry into truth and so sharpen their wits. The master key of knowledge is, indeed, a persistent and frequent questioning. . . .

## Bernard of Clairvaux *

> Bernard (1091–1153), abbot of Clairvaux, through his holy life and unusual eloquence was one of the most influential Europeans of his time. His preaching won royal support for the Second Crusade; his activities as a Cistercian monk promoted a reform movement within the church; he was asked by the pope to create the rules under which the Order of the Knights Templars came into being. He found time in the midst of great matters of church and state to worry about his friends, as we see in his letter to one who has abandoned the religious life.

I am grieved for you my son Geoffrey, I am grieved for you. And not without reason. For who would not grieve that the flower of your youth,

* Some Letters of Saint Bernard, Abbot of Clairvaux, translated by Dr. Eales, selected by Francis A. Gasquet, London, John Hodges, 1904.

which, amid the joy of angels, you offered unimpaired to God *for the odour of a sweet smell* (Phil. iv. 18), should now be trampled under the feet of devils, stained by the filthiness of vice and the uncleanness of the world? How can you, who once were called by God, follow the devil who calls you back? How is it that you, whom Christ began to draw after Himself, have suddenly withdrawn your foot from the very threshold of glory? In you I now have proof of the truth of the Lord's word, when He said: *A man's foes shall be they of his own household* (S. Matt. x. 36). Your friends and kinsfolk have approached and stood against you. They have called you once more in the gates of death. They have placed you in dark places, like the dead of this world; and now it is a matter for little surprise that you are descending into the belly of hell, which is hasting to swallow you up, and to give you over as a prey to be devoured by those who roar in their hunger.

Return, I pray you; return before *the deep swallow thee up and the pit shut her mouth upon thee* (Ps. ixix. 16); before you sink whence you shall never more rise; before you be *bound hand and foot and cast into outer darkness, where there is weeping and gnashing of teeth* (S. Matt. xxii. 13); before you be thrust down to the place of darkness and covered with the gloom of death. Perhaps you blush to return, because you gave way for an hour. Blush, indeed, for your flight, but do not blush to return to the battle after your flight, and to fight again. The fight is not over yet. Not yet have the opposing lines drawn off from each other. Victory is still in your power. If you will, we are unwilling to conquer without you, and we do not grudge to you your share of glory. I will even gladly come to meet you and gladly welcome you with open arms, saying: *It is meet that we should make merry and be glad; for this thy brother was dead and is alive again; he was lost and is found* (S. Luke xv. 32).

## *Bernard and Abelard* *

> *Bernard of Clairvaux was profoundly disturbed by the teachings of Abelard, which seemed to him a challenge to the Christian faith. Bernard's secretary tells of Bernard's meeting with Abelard.*

* From St. Bernard of Clairvaux, the *Vita Prima Bernardi*, translated by Geoffrey Webb and Adrian Walker, copyright Mowbrays, London, by permission.

Peter Abelard was without any doubt a great master, and he was most celebrated for his learning. But with as little doubt his teaching on the Catholic faith was not faithful to tradition—rather was it a "faithless faith." His works were circulating in no time, disseminating profane novelties in word and sense, together with the gravest blasphemies. William of Saint Thierry wrote to Bernard and Geoffrey of Chartres about him. . . .

. . . Bernard answered: ". . . I have not read Abelard's book completely, but what I have read is sufficient to tell me that his doctrine is wrong and dangerous. But as you well know, I am not satisfied with my own judgment alone, particularly in matters of such importance as this. I think we should confer about it. . . ."

Bernard, however, with his usual kindness and gentleness, saw Abelard in secret, so that he might try to correct his errors without humiliating him in public. He did this so humbly and so reasonably that Abelard became contrite to the point of promising to alter everything as Bernard should see fit. But after their meeting Abelard went back on his word, being persuaded by his own great talents and the evil counsels of certain of his confrères, that he could defend his position by the force of his own arguments. He even accused Bernard of having tried secretly to destroy his works. He applied for a hearing to the Bishop of Sens in whose church a great council was to be held. He was ready, he said, to defend his works in public, and if the abbot of Clairvaux had anything against him, he requested that the said abbot should be invited to the Council to make his complaints public.

And so it was done as Abelard wished, but although Bernard was invited, he declined at first to come. He was, however, persuaded . . . lest his absence should lend strength to Abelard's cause. So he agreed, sadly, to be there, as he wrote in his letter to Pope Innocent, summing up Abelard's errors, for, "all the dangers and scandals that occur in the kingdom of God must be referred to the Holy See, but none more urgently than those which concern the faith. . . . The time has come for you to acknowledge your primacy, to prove your zeal and to honour your ministry. In this you will be fulfilling Peter's task, while you sit on his throne, if you confirm the faith that vacillates in the hearts of Christians, and punish those who corrupt the faith, by means of your authority."

The Council was convened, and Bernard offered the offending passages in Abelard's work to the assembly, giving him the option of disclaiming them as his opinions, or humbly correcting them, or answering (if he could) objections put to him from the accepted authority of the fathers.

But Abelard would not admit himself in the wrong, and at the same time he could not resist the way in which Bernard put his arguments, and so in order to gain time, he appealed to Rome. It was made clear to him that he could speak with absolute freedom, and need fear no harm to his person—on the contrary, all were willing to bear with him patiently. But as he said afterwards to his friends (or at least, so we are told) his mind was a blank at the time, his memory and all his wits having forsaken him.

The Council of Sens let him go in peace, while condemning the errors in his works, and the same judgment was passed on him by the Holy See. He was forbidden to teach in future, and his writings burned. How indeed could poor Peter Abelard expect to find an indulgent ear at the see of Peter, when his own faith was so very different from Peter's?


## Science during the Middle Ages *

Bede

> The record of scientific achievement in the Middle Ages is hardly imposing. The thinkers of the period were absorbed in other fields, such as philosophy and theology. The errors as well as the useful information of such ancient scientists as Aristotle and Ptolemy were accepted without question. It is interesting to note that though the men of the Middle Ages believed the sun revolved about the earth, they were aware the earth was a sphere. Bede, from whose On the Nature of Things the selection below is taken, wrote, "We speak of the globe of the earth . . . because, if all its lines be considered, it has the perfect form of a sphere."

On the second day God made the heaven, which is called the firmament, which is visible and corporeal; and yet we may never see it, on account of its great elevation and the thickness of the clouds, and on account of the weakness of our eyes. The heaven incloses in its bosom all the world, and it ever turns about us, swifter than any mill-wheel, all as deep under this earth as it is above. It is all round and entire and studded with stars.

* James H. Robinson, *Readings in European History,* vol. 1, New York, Ginn and Company, 1904.

Truly the sun goes by God's command between heaven and earth, by day above and by night under the earth. She is ever running about the earth, and so light shines under the earth by night as it does above our heads by day. . . . The sun is very great: as broad she is, from what books say, as the whole compass of the earth; but she appears to us very small, because she is very far from our sight. Everything, the further it is, the less it seems. . . . The moon and all the stars receive light from the great sun. The sun is typical of our Saviour, Christ, who is the sun of righteousness, as the bright stars are typical of the believers in God's congregation, who shine in good converse. . . .

. . . We speak of new moon according to the custom of men, but the moon is always the same, though its light often varies. . . . It happens sometimes when the moon runs on the same track that the sun runs, that its orb intercepts the sun's, so that the sun is all darkened and the stars appear as by night. This happens seldom, and never but at new moons. By this it is clear that the moon is very large, since it thus darkens the sun.

Some men say stars fall from heaven, but it is not stars that fall, but it is fire from the sky, which flies down from the heavenly bodies as sparks do from fire. Certainly there are still as many stars in the heavens as there were at the beginning, when God made them. They are almost all fixed in the firmament, and will not fall thence while this world endures. The sun, and the moon, and the evening star, and morning star and three other stars are not fast in the firmament, but they have their own course severally. These seven stars are called planets.

Those stars are called comets which appear suddenly and unusually, and which are rayed so that the ray goes from them like a sunbeam. They are not seen for any long time, and as oft as they appear they foreshadow something new toward the people over whom they shine.


# Thunder and Lightning *

BARTHOLOMEW ANGLICUS

> *In the mid-thirteenth century, Bartholomew Anglicus set forth what he believed to be the nature of thunder and lightning.*

* Bartholomew Anglicus, *Medieval Lore*, London, Alexander Moring, Ltd., 1905 (translated by Robert Steele).

Of impressions that are gendered in the air of double vapour, the first is thunder, the which impression is gendered in watery substance of a cloud. For moving and shaking hither and thither of hot vapour and dry, that fleeth its contrary, is beset and constrained in every side, and smit into itself, and is thereby set on fire and on flame, and quencheth itself at last in the cloud, as Aristotle saith. When a storm of full strong winds cometh in to the clouds, and the whirling wind and the storm increaseth, and seeketh out passage: it cleaveth and breaketh the cloud, and falleth out with a great rese and strong, and all to breaketh the parts of the cloud, and so it cometh to the ears of men and of beasts with horrible and dreadful breaking and noise. And that is no wonder: for though a bladder be light, yet it maketh great noise and sound, if it be strongly blown, and afterward violently broken. And with the thunder cometh lightning, but lightning is sooner seen, for it is clear and bright; and thunder cometh later to our ears, for the wit of sight is more subtle than the wit of hearing. As a man seeth sooner the stroke of a man that heweth a tree, than he heareth the noise of the stroke. . . .

## Medieval Medicine *

BARTHOLOMEW ANGLICUS

> During the Middle Ages, medicine fared somewhat better than the other sciences. Not only did medieval physicians study Greek physicians such as Galen and Hippocrates, but also they gradually became aware of the works of such Arab doctors as Avicenna. We hear again from Bartholomew Anglicus.

These be the signs of frenzy, violence and continual waking, moving and casting about the eyes, raging, stretching, and casting out of hands, moving and wagging of the head, grinding and gnashing together of the teeth; always they will arise out of their bed, now they sing, now they weep, and they bite gladly and rend their keeper and their leech: seldom be they still, but cry much. And these be most perilously sick, and yet they know not then that they be sick. Then they must be soon helped lest

* Bartholomew Anglicus, *Medieval Lore*, London, Alexander Moring, Ltd., 1905 (translated by Robert Steele).

they perish, and that both in diet and in medicine. The diet shall be full scarce, as crumbs of bread, which must many times be wet in water. The medicine is, that in the beginning the patient's head be shaven, and washed in lukewarm vinegar, and that he be well kept or bound in a dark place. . . . All that be about him shall be commanded to be still and in silence; men shall not answer to his nice words. In the beginning of medicine he shall be let blood in a vein of the forehead, and bled as much as will fill an egg-shell. . . . Over all things, with ointments and balming men shall labour to bring him asleep. The head that is shaven shall be plastered with lungs of a swine, or of a wether, or of a sheep; the temples and forehead shall be anointed with the juice of lettuce, or of poppy. If after these medicines are laid thus to, the violence lasts three days without sleep, there is no hope of recovery.

Madness is infection of the foremost cell of the head, with privation of imagination, like as melancholy is the infection of the middle cell of the head, with privation of reason.

Madness comes sometime of passions of the soul, as of business and of great thoughts, of sorrow and of too great study, and of dread: sometime of the biting of a mad hound, or some other venomous beast: sometime of melancholy meats, and sometime of drink of strong wine. And as the causes be diverse, the tokens and signs be diverse. For some cry and leap and hurt and wound themselves and other men, and darken and hide themselves in privy and secret places. The medicine of them is, that they be bound, that they hurt not themselves and other men. And namely, such shall be refreshed, and comforted, and withdrawn from cause and matter of dread and busy thoughts. And they must be gladded with instruments of music, and to some extent be occupied. . . .

The veins have that name for that be the ways, conduits, and streams of the fleeting of the blood, and disperse it into all the body. And Constantine says, that the veins spring out of the liver. . . . And veins are needful as vessels of the blood to bear and to bring blood from the liver, to feed and nourish the members of the body. . . .

The lungs be the bellows of the heart. It beats in opening itself that it may take in breath, and thrusting together may put it out, and so it is in continual moving, in drawing in and out of breath. . . . The lungs by continual moving put off air that is gathered within, clean and purge it. . . . And when the lungs be grieved by any occasion, it speeds to death-ward.

# A Medieval Tragedy *

SIR JEAN FROISSART

*Throughout history man has shown his fear of the unknown and sought ways to pacify that which he did not know or could not control. Even modern man looks for a four-leaf clover, is wary of black cats, and often is afraid to walk under a ladder. Knowing little of the internal workings of the human body, medieval people placed much faith in magic potions. Any sudden death from unknown causes was attributed to secret poisons, which were widely, and incorrectly, believed to exist. Sir Jean Froissart tells a story that reveals belief in such potions and poisons.*

It is well known that the Count and Countess de Foix are not on good terms with each other. This disagreement arose from the King of Navarre, who is the lady's brother. The King of Navarre had offered to pledge himself, in the sum of 50,000 francs, for the Lord d'Albreth, whom the Count de Foix held in prison. The count, knowing the King of Navarre to be crafty and faithless, would not accept his security. . . . The countess went to the King of Navarre to endeavor to settle this business; and when, after much talking, she found she could come to no satisfactory arrangement, she was afraid to return home, knowing her husband to be of a cruel disposition toward those with whom he was displeased. Thus things remained for some time. Gaston, my lord's son, grew up and became a fine young gentleman. . . .

Some time after his marriage he took it into his head to make a journey into Navarre to visit his mother and uncle; but it was an unfortunate journey for him and for this country. In Navarre he was splendidly entertained, and stayed there some time with his mother. On taking leave he could not prevail on her to return, for she had found that the count had bid him convey no such request to her. She consequently remained, and the heir of Foix went to take leave of his uncle . . . who on his departure made him several handsome presents. The last gift he gave to him was the cause of his death, and I will tell you in what way. As the youth was on the point of setting out, the King took him privately into his

* Sir Jean Froissart, *Chronicles*, vol. 1, New York, The Colonial Press, 1901 (translated by Thomas Johnes).

chamber and gave him a bag full of powder, which was of such pernicious quality that it would cause the death of anyone who ate it. "Gaston, my fair nephew," said the King, "will you do what I am about to tell you? You see how unjustly the Count de Foix hates your mother. Now, if you wish to reconcile them, you must take a small pinch of this powder and strew it upon the meat destined for your father's table; but take care no one sees you. The instant he has taken it he will be impatient for your mother's return, and henceforth they will so love each other that they will never again be separated. Do not mention this to anyone, for if you do, it will lose its effect."

The youth, who believed all which his uncle told him, cheerfully agreed to do as he said. . . . On his return, his father received him gladly, and asked what presents he had received. The youth replied, "Very handsome ones;" and then showed him all, except the bag which contained the powder. It was customary in the Hôtel de Foix for Gaston and his brother, Evan, to sleep in the same chamber. . . . It happened one night that their clothes got mixed together; and the coat of Gaston being on the bed, Evan, noticing the powder in the bag, said to him, "What is this, Gaston?" By no means pleased at the inquiry, Gaston replied, "Give me back my coat, Evan; what have you to do with it?" Evan flung him his coat. . . . Three days after this, as if God were interposing to save the life of the Count de Foix, Gaston quarrelled with Evan at tennis, and gave him a box on the ears. Much vexed at this, Evan ran crying into the count's apartment, who immediately said to him, "What is the matter, Evan?" "My lord," replied he, "Gaston has been beating me, but he deserves beating much more than I do." "For what reason?" said the count. "On my faith," said Evan, "ever since his return from Navarre, he wears a bag of powder. . . . I know not what he intends to do with it; but he has once or twice told me that his mother would soon return thither, and be more in your good graces than she ever was." "Ho," said the count; "be sure you do not mention to anyone what you have just told me." The Count de Foix then became very thoughtful on the subject, and remained alone until dinner-time, when he took his seat as usual at the table. It was Gaston's office to place the dishes before him and taste them. As soon as he had served the first dish the count detected the strings of the bag . . . the sight of which made his blood boil, and he called Gaston toward him. The youth advanced to the table, when the count . . . with his knife cut away the bag. Gaston was thunderstruck, turned very pale, and began to tremble exceedingly. The count took some powder from the bag, which he strewed over a slices of bread, and calling to him one of his dogs, gave it to him to eat. The instant the dog had eaten a morsel, his eyes rolled round in his head, and he died.

The count was much enraged . . . "Ho, Gaston," he said, "thou traitor; for thee, and to increase thine inheritance, have I made war, and incurred the hatred of the kings of France and England, Spain, Navarre, and Arragon;" then, leaping over the table, with a knife in his hand, he was about to thrust it into his body, when the knights and squires interfered; and on their knees besought him—. . . . "Let him be confined, and inquiry made into the matter. Perhaps he was ignorant of what the bag contained, and, therefore, may be blameless." "Well, then, confine him in the tower," said the count. . . .

. . . At the count's orders he was confined in a room of the dungeon where there was little light; there he remained ten days, scarcely eating or drinking anything. It is even reported, that after his death all the food that had been brought to him was found untouched; so that it is marvellous how he could have lived so long. From the time he entered the dungeon he never put off his clothes, and the count would permit no one to remain in the room to advise or comfort him.

On the day of his death, the person who waited upon him, seeing the state he was in, went to the count and said, "My lord, for God's sake, do look to your son; he is certainly starving himself." On hearing which the count became very angry, and went himself to the prison. It was an evil hour: the count had in his hand a knife, with which he had been paring his nails, and which he held tight between his fingers, with scarcely the point protruding, when, pushing aside the tapestry that covered the entrance of the prison, through ill luck, he hit his son on a vein of the throat with the point of the knife, as he rushed forward, addressing him, "Ha! traitor! why dost thou not eat?" Then, without saying or doing more, he instantly left the place. . . . The point of the knife, small as it was, had cut a vein, and as soon as he felt it, he turned himself on one side, and died. Scarcely had the count reached his apartment when his son's attendants came to him in haste to inform him that Gaston was dead. "Dead?" cried the count. "Yes; God help me, he is indeed dead, my lord." The count would not believe the report, and sent one of his knights to ascertain the truth. The knight soon returned to confirm the account, when the count wept bitterly, crying out, "Ha, ha, Gaston, how sad a business is this for thee and me! In an evil hour didst thou visit thy mother in Navarre. Never shall I be happy again. . . ."

# The Dawn of Modern Scientific Method *

Roger Bacon

> Scientific progress was slow during the Middle Ages because
> men of that era relied on ancient authorities or upon inter-
> pretations of churchmen that were based on the Scriptures.
> Among the outstanding teachers of the thirteenth century
> was the Franciscan Roger Bacon of Oxford. He insisted
> that true knowledge must bring experimentation to the sup-
> port of reason and authority. He did not challenge the ideas
> of his time so much as the method by which they were es-
> tablished.

. . . I now wish to unfold the principles of experimental science, since
without experience nothing can be sufficiently known. For there are two
modes of acquiring knowledge, namely, by reasoning and experience.
Reasoning draws a conclusion and makes us grant the conclusion, but does
not make the conclusion certain, nor does it remove doubt so that the mind
may rest on the intuition of truth, unless the mind discovers it by the path
of experience; since many have the arguments relating to what can be
known, but because they lack experience they neglect the arguments, and
neither avoid what is harmful nor follow what is good. For if man who
has never seen fire should prove by adequate reasoning that fire burns
and injures things and destroys them, his mind would not be satisfied
thereby, nor would he avoid fire, until he placed his hand on some com-
bustible substance in the fire, so that he might prove by experience what
reasoning taught. But when he has had actual experience of combustion
his mind is made certain and rests in the full light of truth. Therefore
reasoning does not suffice, but experience does. . . .

Since this Experimental Science is wholly unknown to the rank and
file of students, I am therefore unable to convince people of its utility
unless at the same time I disclose its excellence and its proper signification.
This science alone, therefore, knows how to test perfectly what can be done
by nature, what be an effort of art, what by trickery . . . so that all falsity
may be removed and the truth alone of art and nature be retained. This
science alone teaches us how to view the mad acts of magicians, that they
may not be ratified but shunned. . . .

* *The Opus Major of Roger Bacon*, vol. 2, Philadelphia, University of Pennsylvania Press, 1928 (translated by Robert B. Burke).

## Praise for a Scientist [*]

ROGER BACON

> *Bacon not only set forth the principles of experimental science, but also described how a scientist should go about his work. He foresaw, too, some of the achievements of present-day science and technology.*

One man I know, and one only, who can be praised for his achievements in experimental science. . . . What others strive to see dimly and blindly, like bats blinking at the sun in the twilight, he gazes at in the full light of day, because he is a master of experiment. Through experiment he gains knowledge of natural things, medical, chemical, indeed of everything in the heavens and on earth.

He is ashamed that things should be known to laymen, old women, soldiers, plowmen, of which he is ignorant. Therefore he has looked closely into the doings of those who melt metals and who work in gold and silver and other metals and in minerals of all sorts; he knows everything relating to the art of war, the making of weapons, and the chase; he has looked carefully into agriculture, mensuration, and farming work; he has even taken note of remedies, lot casting, and charms used by old women and by wizards and magicians, and of the devices and deceptions of conjurers, so that nothing which deserves investigation should escape him, and in order that he might be able to expose the impostures of the magicians.

If philosophy is to be carried to its perfection and is to be handled with certainty and advantage, his aid is indispensable. As for the reward, he neither receives it nor looks for it. If he frequented the courts of kings and princes he would easily find those who would bestow upon him both honor and wealth. Or if he would show the results of his researches in Paris the whole world would follow him. But since either of these courses would hinder him from pursuing the great experiments in which he takes delight, he puts honor and wealth aside, knowing well that his knowledge would secure him wealth whenever he chose. For the last three years he has been working at the invention of a mirror which should produce combustion at a fixed distance, and he will, with God's aid, soon reach his end.

[*] James H. Robinson, *Readings in European History*, vol. 1, New York, Ginn and Company, 1904.

I will now enumerate the marvelous results of art and nature which will make all kinds of magic appear trivial and unworthy. Instruments for navigation can be made which will do away with the necessity of rowers, so that great vessels, both in rivers and on the sea, shall be borne about with only a single man to guide them and with greater speed than if they were full of men. And carriages can be constructed to move without animals to draw them, and with incredible velocity. Machines for flying can be made in which a man sits and turns an ingenious device by which skillfully contrived wings are made to strike the air in the manner of a flying bird. Then arrangements can be devised, compact in themselves, for raising and lowering weights infinitely great. . . . Bridges can be constructed ingeniously so as to span rivers without any supports.

## The Call for the First Crusade *

URBAN II

> Pilgrimages to holy places were an important aspect of medieval Christian and Islamic life. But they became increasingly dangerous in the tenth and eleventh centuries until pilgrims began to arm themselves for protection against raiders. Islam now threatened Christian Europe on three fronts. In the west the Islamic caliphate of Cordova pressed against the tiny Christian states of northern Spain, and in 997 horrified the Christian world by sacking the great pilgrimage center of Saint James of Compostella. On the long line of the Mediterranean, Islamic rovers menaced the Christian ports of Genoa, Pisa, and Venice, nor were the shrines in Rome itself now safe. In the east a more warlike group of Muslims, the Seljuk Turks, seized Jerusalem in 1071, captured much of Christian Asia Minor, and threatened Constantinople. Appeals for western aid from the Byzantine Emperor Alexius Comnenus were read by Pope Urban II at a gathering of church leaders at Clermont, France, in 1095. Urban urged his followers to end their destructive internal warfare and join together in a great

* Oliver J. Thatcher, Edgar H. McNeal, A Source Book for Mediæval History, New York, Charles Scribner's Sons, 1905.

*crusade to aid Comnenus and to wrest the Holy Land from the infidels. An aroused Europe leaped into action.*

Most beloved brethren: Urged by necessity, I, Urban, by the permission of God chief bishop and prelate over the whole world, have come into these parts as an ambassador with a divine admonition to you, the servants of God. I hoped to find you as faithful and as zealous in the service of God as I had supposed you to be. . . .

Although, O sons of God, you have promised more firmly than ever to keep the peace among yourselves and to preserve the rights of the Church, there remains still an important work for you to do. Freshly quickened by the divine correction, you must apply the strength of your righteousness to another matter which concerns you as well as God. For your brethren who live in the east are in urgent need of your help, and you must hasten to give them the aid which has often been promised them. For, as most of you have heard, the Turks and Arabs have attacked them. . . . They have occupied more and more of the lands of those Christians, and have overcome them in seven battles. They have killed and captured many, and have destroyed the churches and devastated the empire. If you permit them to continue thus for a while with impunity, the faithful of God will be much more widely attacked by them. On this account I, or rather the Lord, beseech you as Christ's heralds to publish this everywhere and to persuade all people of whatever rank, footsoldiers and knights, poor and rich, to carry aid promptly to those Christians and to destroy that vile race from the lands of our friends. I say this to those who are present, it is meant also for those who are absent. Moreover, Christ commands it.

All who die by the way, whether by land or by sea, or in battle against the pagans, shall have immediate remission of sins. This I grant them through the power of God with which I am invested. O what a disgrace if such a despised and base race, which worships demons, should conquer a people which has the faith of omnipotent God and is made glorious with the name of Christ! With what reproaches will the Lord overwhelm us if you do not aid those who, with us, profess the Christian religion! Let those who have been accustomed unjustly to wage private warfare against the faithful now go against the infidels and end with victory this war which should have been begun long ago. Let those who, for a long time, have been robbers, now become knights. Let those who have been fighting against their brothers and relatives now fight in a proper way against the barbarians.

# A Crusader Writes Home *

*In 1097 the First Crusade reached Asia and laid siege to Antioch in northern Syria. No kings accompanied this expedition. During the siege one of the nobles, Count Stephen, wrote home the following account. He kept the promise in his last sentence by deserting the crusade; but he was so disgraced in the eyes of his family that he enlisted in a later crusade, in which he died.*

Count Stephen to Adele, his sweetest and most amiable wife, to his dear children, and to all his vassals of all ranks,—his greeting and blessing.

You may be very sure, dearest, that the messenger whom I sent to give you pleasure left me before Antioch safe and unharmed and, through God's grace, in the greatest prosperity. And already at that time, together with all the chosen army of Christ, endowed with great valor by Him, we have been continually advancing for twenty-three weeks toward the home of our Lord Jesus. You may know for certain, my beloved, that of gold, silver, and many other kind of riches I now have twice as much as your love had assigned to me when I left you. . . .

Doubtless you have heard that after the capture of the city of Nicæa we fought a great battle with the treacherous Turks and, by God's aid, conquered them. Next we conquered for the Lord all Romania, and afterwards Cappadocia. We had learned that there was a certain Turkish prince, Assam, dwelling in Cappadocia; so we directed our course thither. We conquered all his castles by force and compelled him to flee. . . . We also gave the land of that Assam to one of our chiefs, and in order that he might conquer the prince we left there with him many soldiers of Christ. Thence, continually following the wicked Turks, we drove them through the midst of Armenia, as far as the great river Euphrates. Having left all their baggage and beasts of burden on the bank, they fled across the river into Arabia. . . .

We found the city of Antioch very extensive, fortified with the greatest strength and almost impossible to be taken. In addition, more than 5,000 bold Turkish soldiers had entered the city, not counting . . . other different races of whom an infinite multitude had gathered together there. In fighting against these enemies of God and of us we have, by God's grace, endured many sufferings and innumerable hardships up to the present

* Frederick A. Ogg, *A Source Book of Mediæval History*, New York, American Book Co., 1907.

time. . . . Lying before the city of Antioch, indeed, throughout the whole winter we suffered for our Lord Christ from excessive cold and enormous torrents of rain. What some say about the impossibility of bearing the heat of the sun in Syria is untrue, for the winter there is very similar to our winter in the West.

I delight to tell you, dearest, what happened to us during Lent. Our princes had caused a fortress to be built before a certain gate which was between our camp and the sea. For the Turks, coming out of this gate daily, killed some of our men on their way to the sea. The city of Antioch is about five leagues distant from the sea. For this purpose they sent the excellent Bohemond and Raymond . . . to the sea with only sixty horsemen, in order that they might bring mariners to aid in this work. When, however, they were returning to us with these mariners, the Turks collected an army, fell suddenly upon our two leaders, and forced them to a perilous flight. In that unexpected fight we lost more than 500 of our foot-soldiers—to the glory of God. Of our horsemen, however, we lost only two, for certain.

On that same day, in order to receive our brethren with joy, and entirely ignorant of their misfortunes, we went out to meet them. When, however, we approached the above-mentioned gate of the city, a mob of foot-soldiers and horsemen from Antioch, elated by the victory which they had won, rushed upon us in the same manner. Seeing these, our leaders went to the camp of the Christians to order all to be ready to follow us into battle. In the meantime our men gathered together and the scattered leaders, namely, Bohemond and Raymond, with the remainder of their army came up and told of the great misfortune which they had suffered.

Our men, full of fury at these most evil tidings, prepared to die for Christ and, deeply grieved for their brethren, rushed upon the wicked Turks. They, enemies of God and of us, hastily fled before us. . . . We followed them as closely as possible, killed many before they reached the bridge, forced many into the river, all of whom were killed, and we also slew many upon the bridge and very many at the narrow entrance to the gate. I am telling you the truth, my beloved, and you may be assured that in this battle we killed thirty emirs, that is, princes, and three hundred other Turkish nobles, not counting the remaining Turks and pagans. Indeed the number of Turks and Saracens killed is reckoned at 1230, but of ours we did not lose a single man.

On the following day (Easter), while my chaplain Alexander was writing this letter in great haste, a party of our men lying in wait for the

Turks fought a successful battle with them and killed sixty horsemen, whose heads they brought to the army.

These which I write to you are only a few things, dearest, of the many which we have done; and because I am not able to tell you, dearest, what is in my mind, I charge you to do right, to watch carefully over your land, and to do your duty as you ought to your children and your vassals. You will certainly see me just as soon as I can possibly return to you. Farewell.

## The Crusader States in Peril *

AYMERIC OF ANTIOCH

> By 1099 the First Crusade had succeeded in establishing four small states in the Holy Land. But in the years that followed they suffered from the rivalries of the great lords and of merchants from competing Italian cities and from the jealousies of the two orders of knights, the Hospitalers and the Templars. A Second Crusade (1147–1149) failed to deter the Muslim leader Noureddin. Finally in 1187 Jerusalem fell again to the Muslims. The following letter speaks of this troubled time.

Aymeric, by the grace of God, patriarch of the holy Apostolic See of Antioch, to Louis, illustrious king of the French,—greeting and Apostolic benediction.

It would be fitting that we should always write joyful tidings to his royal majesty and should increase the splendor of his heart by the splendor and delight of our words. But the reverse has ever been our lot. The causes for tears . . . are constant, the grief and the groaning are continuous. . . . Nor is there any one who turns his heart towards us and out of pity directs his hand to aid us. But not to protract our words, the few Christians who are here cry out to you, together with us, and implore your clemency, which with God's assistance is sufficient to liberate us and the church of God in the East. . . .

* University of Pennsylvania, *Translations and Reprints from the Original Sources of European History,* vol. 1, no. 4, Philadelphia, 1897.

. . . The great devastator of the Christian people [Noureddin], who rules near us, collected together from all sides the kings and races of the infidels and offered a peace and truce to our prince, and very frequently urged it. His reason was that he wished to traverse our land with greater freedom in order to devastate the kingdom of Jerusalem and to be able to bear aid to his vassal fighting in Egypt. But our prince was unwilling to make peace with him. . . .

When the former saw that he was not able to accomplish what he had proposed, full of wrath, he turned his weapons against us and laid siege to a certain fortress of ours, called Harrenc, twelve miles distant from our city. But those who were besieged—7,000 in number, including warriors, men and women—cried loudly to us, ceasing neither day nor night, to have pity on them, and fixed a day beyond which it would be impossible for them to hold out. Our prince having collected all his forces set out from Antioch on the day of St. Lawrence and proceeded as far as the fortress in entire safety. For the Turks in their cunning gave up the siege and withdrew a short distance from the fortress to some narrow passes in their own country.

On the next day our men followed the enemy to that place and, while they were marching without sufficient circumspection, battle was engaged and they fled. The conflict was so disastrous that hardly any one of ours of any rank escaped . . . ; men, horses and weapons were almost entirely destroyed.

After the slaughter of the Christians the Turks returned to the above-mentioned fortress, captured it, and by compact conducted the feeble multitude of women, children and wounded as far as Antioch. Afterwards they advanced to the city, devastated the whole country as far as the sea with fire and sword and exercised their tyranny . . . on everything which met their eyes.

God is a witness that the remnant which is left us is in no way sufficient to guard the walls night and day, and owing to the scarcity of men, we are obliged to entrust their safety and defense to some whom we suspect. Neglecting the church services, the clergy and presbyters guard the gates. We ourselves are looking after the defense of the walls and, as far as possible, are repairing, with great and unremitting labor, the many portions which have been broken down by earthquakes. And all this in vain, unless God shall look upon us with a more kindly countenance. For we do not hope to hold out longer, inasmuch as the valor of the men of the present day has been exhausted and is of no avail. But we do, in order that whatever can be done may not be left undone by us.

Above all, the only anchor which is left in this extremity for our hope is in you. Because we have heard from everybody of your greatness, because we have understood that you, more than all the other kings of the West, always have the East in mind. From that we are given to understand that your joy will not be full until you accomplish at some time what we are unable through our misdeeds to accomplish. And it is our hope that by your hand the Lord will visit His people and will have compassion on us.

## Disciplining the Crusaders *

RICHARD I OF ENGLAND

> *In spite of their holy mission, the crusaders and their leaders were an unruly, quarrelsome lot. Uncontrollable himself, King Richard I "the Lion-Hearted" of England, who took part in the Third Crusade, tried to maintain order in his army with the following edict—which includes our earliest known example of tarring and feathering.*

Richard by the grace of God king of England, and duke of Normandy and Aquitaine, and count of Anjou, to all his subjects who are about to go by sea to Jerusalem, greeting. Know that we, by the common counsel of upright men, have made the laws here given. Whosoever slays a man on shipboard shall be bound to the dead man and thrown into the sea. But if he shall slay him on land, he shall be bound to the dead man and buried in the earth. If any one, moreover, shall be convicted through lawful witnesses of having drawn a knife to strike another, or of having struck him so as to draw blood, he shall loose his hand. But if he shall strike him down with his fist without drawing blood, he shall be dipped three times in the sea. But if any one shall taunt or insult a comrade or charge him with hatred of God: as many times as he shall have insulted him, so many ounces of silver shall he pay. A robber, moreover, convicted of theft, shall be shorn like a hired fighter, and boiling tar shall be poured over his head, and feathers from a cushion shall be shaken out over his head,—so that he may be publicly known; and at the first land where the ships put in he shall be cast on shore. . . .

* Ernest F. Henderson, *Select Historical Documents of the Middle Ages*, London, George Bell & Sons, 1896.

# A Description of Constantinople *

## Benjamin of Tudela

> *The Fourth Crusade was diverted by Venice into an attack
> on Constantinople, defying the anger of Pope Innocent III,
> who had forbidden an attack on a Christian city by an army
> under the banner of the cross. The avarice of the Venetians
> may have been excited by this account written a few years
> earlier by a western traveler.*

. . . The circumference of the city of Constantinople is eighteen miles.
. . . Great stir and bustle prevails at Constantinople in consequence of the
conflux of many merchants, who resort thither, both by land and by sea,
from all parts of the world for purposes of trade. . . . In this respect the
city is equalled only by Bagdad, the metropolis of the Mohammedans.
At Constantinople is the place of worship called St. Sophia, and the
metropolitan seat of the pope of the Greeks, who are at variance with the
pope of Rome. It contains as many altars as there are days of the year,
and possesses innumerable riches, which are augmented every year by the
contributions of the two islands and of the adjacent towns and villages.
All the other places of worship in the whole world do not equal St. Sophia
in riches. It is ornamented with pillars of gold and silver, and with innumerable lamps of the same precious materials. The Hippodrome is a
public place near the wall of the palace, set aside for the king's sports.
Every year the birthday of Jesus the Nazarene is celebrated there with
public rejoicings. On these occasions you may see there representations
of all the nations who inhabit the different parts of the world. . . .

King Manuel has built a large palace for his residence on the sea-shore,
near the palace built by his predecessors; and to this edifice is given the
name of Blachernes. The pillars and walls are covered with pure gold, and
all the wars of the ancients, as well as his own wars, are represented in
pictures. The throne in this palace is of gold, and ornamented with
precious stones; a golden crown hangs over it, suspended on a chain of the
same material, the length of which exactly admits the emperor to sit under
it. This crown is ornamented with precious stones of inestimable value. . . .

The tribute which is brought to Constantinople every year from all
parts of Greece, consisting of silks, and purple cloths, and gold, fills many
towers. These riches and buildings are equalled nowhere in the world.

* Thomas Wright, ed., "The Travels of Rabbi Benjamin of Tudela, 1160–1173,"
*Early Travels in Palestine*, London, Henry G. Bohn, 1848.

They say that the tribute of the city alone amounts every day to twenty thousand florins, arising from rents of hostelries and bazaars, and from the duties paid by merchants who arrive by sea and by land. The Greeks who inhabit the country are extremely rich, and possess great wealth in gold and precious stones. They dress in garments of silk, ornamented with gold and other valuable materials. They ride upon horses, and in their appearance they are like princes. The country is rich, producing all sorts of delicacies, as well as abundance of bread, meat, and wine. They are well skilled in the Greek sciences. . . . Greeks hire soldiers of all nations, whom they call barbarians, for the purpose of carrying on their wars with the sultan of the Thogarmim, who are called Turks. They have no martial spirit themselves, and . . . are unfit for warlike enterprises. . . .

## Normans in England *

### WILLIAM OF MALMESBURY

> *In 1066 England's King Edward the Confessor died, leaving no immediate heirs. The throne was given to Harold. But across the English Channel a distant relative of Edward, Duke William of Normandy, claimed the throne as rightfully his. William landed an army in England, and in a fierce engagement at Hastings defeated the English and won for himself the nickname "the Conqueror." The Norman Conquest brought England important new elements of government, language, and culture. We read of William at Hastings and of later Norman accomplishments in the account of the twelfth-century chronicler William of Malmesbury.*

. . . The courageous leaders mutually prepared for battle, each according to his national custom. The English, as we have heard, passed the night without sleep, in drinking and singing, and, in the morning, proceeded without delay towards the enemy; all were on foot, armed with battle-axes, and covering themselves in front by the junction of their shields, they formed an impenetrable body. . . .

On the other side, the Normans passed the whole night in confessing their sins, and received the sacrament in the morning: their infantry with

* William of Malmesbury, *Chronicle of the Kings of England,* London, Bell & Daldy, 1866.

bows and arrows formed the vanguard, while the cavalry divided into wings. . . . They fought with ardour, neither giving ground, for the great part of the day. Finding this, William gave a signal to his party, that, by a feigned flight, they should retreat. Through this device, the close body of the English, opening for the purpose of cutting down the straggling enemy, brought upon itself swift destruction; for the Normans, facing about, attacked them thus disordered, and compelled them to fly. In this manner, deceived by a stratagem, they met an honourable death. . . .

Harold, not merely content with the duty of a general in exhorting others, diligently entered into every soldier-like office; often would he strike the enemy when coming to close quarters, so that none could approach him with impunity; for immediately the same blow levelled both horse and rider. Wherefore, as I have related, receiving the fatal arrow from a distance, he yielded to death. One of the soldiers with a sword gashed his thigh, as he lay prostrate; for which shameful and cowardly action, he was branded with ignominy by William, and dismissed from the service.

William too was equally ready to encourage by his voice and by his presence; to be the first to rush forward; to attack the thickest of the foe. Thus everywhere raging, everywhere furious, he lost three choice horses, which were that day pierced under him. The dauntless spirit and vigour of the intrepid general, however, still persisted, though often called back by the kind remonstrance of his body-guard. . . .

. . . The desire after literature and religion had decayed, for several years before the arrival of the Normans. The clergy, contented with a very slight degree of learning, could scarcely stammer out the words of the sacraments; and a person who understood grammar, was an object of wonder and astonishment. . . . The nobility, given up to luxury and wantonness, went not to church in the morning after the manner of Christians, but merely, in a careless manner, heard . . . masses from a hurrying priest in their chambers. . . . The commonality, left unprotected, became a prey to the most powerful, who amassed fortunes, by either seizing on their property, or by selling their person into foreign countries. . . . They were accustomed to eat . . . and to drink till they were sick. These latter qualities they imparted to their conquerors: as to the rest they adopted their manners. . . .

The Normans . . . were at that time, and are even now, proudly apparelled, delicate in their food, but not excessive. . . . They revived by their arrival, the observances of religion, which were everywhere grown lifeless in England. You might see churches rise in every village, and monasteries in the towns and cities, built after a style unknown before. . . .

## A Description of William the Conqueror *

> The Conqueror reorganized his new kingdom along the feudal lines of his Norman duchy. But William introduced in England a far more centralized feudalism than was found on the continent. Insisting that every bit of English soil was his, he made all landholders take an oath of loyalty directly to himself. William's forceful personality and tight reign over England is described in a contemporary account.

If any person wishes to know what kind of man he was . . . then will we write about him as well as we understand him; we who often looked upon him, and lived sometime in his court. . . . He was mild to the good men that loved God, and beyond all measure severe to the men that gainsayed his will. On that same spot where God granted him that he should gain England, he reared a mighty minister [monastery], and set monks therein, and well endowed it. In his days was the great monastery in Canterbury built, and also very many others over all England. . . . So very stern was he also and hot, that no man durst do anything against his will. He had earls in his custody, who acted against his will. Bishops he hurled from their bishoprics, and abbots from their abbacies, and thanes into prison. At length he spared not his own brother Odo, who was a very rich bishop in Normandy. At Baieux was his episcopal stall; and he was the foremost man of all to aggrandise the king. He had an earldom in England; and when the king was in Normandy, then was he the mightiest man in this land. Him he confined in prison. But amongst other things is not to be forgotten that good peace that he made in this land; so that a man of any account might go over his kingdom unhurt. . . . No man durst slay another. . . . He truly reigned over England; and by his capacity so thoroughly surveyed it, that there was not a hide of land in England that he wist not who had it, or what it was worth, and afterwards set it down in his book. . . .

* *The Anglo-Saxon Chronicle,* New York, E. P. Dutton & Co. (translated by Rev. James Ingram).

# England's Great Charter

*Statements of royal intentions in the field of government were made by many English kings. That which is known as the Great Charter (Magna Carta) was wrung from King John by barons seeking to preserve their own feudal position. But in securing their own rights, they strengthened certain principles that grew stronger with time: the idea that the king is not above the law, and that all men have their proper place under it. The fact that the charter was later disallowed by John on the grounds that he was compelled by force to sign it does not prevent it being an important milestone in the development of liberty and good government. Roger of Wendover, a monk, tells us of the events of 1214 and 1215. The king himself then speaks through the Great Charter.*

## THE WINNING OF MAGNA CARTA *

### Of a conference held by the barons against king John

About this time the earls and barons of England assembled at St. Edmund's, as if for religious duties, although it was for some other reason; for after they had discoursed together secretly for a time, there was placed before them the charter of king Henry the First, which they had received, as mentioned before, in the city of London from Stephen archbishop of Canterbury. This charter contained certain liberties and laws granted to the holy church as well as to the nobles of the kingdom besides some liberties which the king added of his own accord. All therefore assembled in the church of St. Edmund. . . . They all swore on the great altar that, if the king refused to grant these liberties and laws, they themselves would withdraw from their allegiance to him, and make war on him, till he should, by a charter under his own seal, confirm to them every thing they required; and finally it was unanimously agreed that, after Christmas, they should all go together to the king and demand the confirmation of the aforesaid liberties to them, and that they should in the meantime provide themselves with horses and arms, so that if the king should endeavour to depart from his oath, they might by taking his castles, compel him to satisfy their demands; and having arranged this, each man returned home. . . .

* Roger of Wendover, *Chronicles*, as quoted in Elizabeth Kendall, *Source-Book of English History*, New York, The Macmillan Company, 1900.

*Of the demand made by the barons of England for their rights*

A.D. 1215; which was the seventeenth year of the reign of king John; he held his court at Winchester at Christmas for one day, after which he hurried to London, and took up his abode at the New Temple; and at that place the above-mentioned nobles came to him in gay military array, and demanded the confirmation of the liberties and laws of king Edward, with other liberties granted to them and to the kingdom and church of England, as were contained in the charter, and above-mentioned laws of Henry the First; they also asserted that, at the time of his absolution at Winchester, he had promised to restore those laws and ancient liberties, and was bound by his own oath to observe them. The king, hearing the bold tone of the barons in making this demand, much feared an attack from them, as he saw that they were prepared for battle; he however made answer that their demands were a matter of importance and difficulty, and he therefore asked a truce till the end of Easter, that he might, after due deliberation, be able to satisfy them as well as the dignity of his crown. . . .

*Of the principal persons who compelled the king to*
*grant the laws and liberties*

In Easter week of this same year, the above-mentioned nobles assembled at Stamford, with horses and arms; for they had now induced almost all the nobility of the whole kingdom to join them, and constituted a very large army; for in their army there were computed to be two thousand knights, besides horse soldiers, attendants, and foot soldiers, who were variously equipped. . . . The king at this time was awaiting the arrival of his nobles at Oxford. On the Monday next after the octaves of Easter, the said barons assembled in the town of Brackley: and when the king learned this, he sent the archbishop of Canterbury, and William Marshal earl of Pembroke, with some other prudent men, to them to inquire what the laws and liberties were which they demanded. The barons then delivered to the messengers a paper, containing in great measure the laws and ancient customs of the kingdom, and declared that, unless the king immediately granted them and confirmed them under his own seal, they would, by taking possession of his fortresses, force him to give them sufficient satisfaction as to their before-named demands. The archbishop with his fellow messengers then carried the paper to the king, and read to him the heads of the paper one by one throughout. The king when he heard the purport of these heads, derisively said, with the greatest indignation, "Why, amongst these unjust demands, did not the barons ask for my kingdom also? Their demands are vain and visionary, and are unsupported by any plea of reason whatever." And at length he angrily declared with an oath, that he would never grant them such liberties as would render him their slave. . . .

### How the city of London was given up to the barons

When the army of the barons arrived at Bedford, they were received with all respect by William de Beauchamp. There also came to them there messengers from the city of London, secretly telling them, if they wished to get into that city, to come there immediately. The barons, inspirited by the arrival of this agreeable message, immediately moved their camp and arrived at Ware; after this they marched the whole night, and arrived early in the morning at the city of London, and, finding the gates open, they, on the 24th of May, which was the Sunday next before our Lord's ascension, entered the city without any tumult whilst the inhabitants were performing divine service; for the rich citizens were favourable to the barons, and the poor ones were afraid to murmur against them. The barons having thus got into the city, placed their own guards in charge of each of the gates, and then arranged all matters in the city at will. They then took security from the citizens, and sent letters through England to those earls, barons, and knights, who appeared to be still faithful to the king, though they only pretended to be so, and advised them with threats, as they regarded the safety of all their property and possessions, to abandon a king who was perjured and who warred against his barons, and together with them to stand firm and fight against the king for their rights and for peace; and that, if they refused to do this, they, the barons, would make war against them all, as against open enemies, and would destroy their castles, burn their houses and other buildings, and destroy their warrens, parks, and orchards. . . . The greatest part of these, on receiving the message of the barons, set out to London and joined them, abandoning the king entirely. . . .

### The conference between the king and the barons

King John, when he saw that he was deserted by almost all, so that out of his regal superabundance of followers he scarcely retained seven knights, was much alarmed lest the barons would attack his castles and reduce them without difficulty, as they would find no obstacle to their so doing; . . . Accordingly, at the time and place pre-agreed on, the king and nobles came to the appointed conference, and when each party had stationed themselves apart from the other, they began a long discussion about terms of peace and the aforesaid liberties. . . . At length, after various points on both sides had been discussed, king John, seeing that he was inferior in strength to the barons, without raising any difficulty, granted the underwritten laws and liberties, and confirmed them. . . .

## MAGNA CARTA *

John, by the grace of God king of England, lord of Ireland, duke of Normandy and Aquitaine, count of Anjou: to the archbishops, bishops, abbots, earls, barons, justices, foresters, sheriffs, provosts, serving men, and to all his bailiffs and faithful subjects, greeting. . . .

1. First of all . . . the English church shall be free and shall have its rights intact and its liberties uninfringed upon. . . .

2. If any one of our earls or barons, or of others holding from us in chief through military service, shall die; and if, at the time of his death, his heir be of full age and owe a relief: he shall have his inheritance by paying the old relief; . . .

3. But if the heir of any of the above persons shall be under age and in wardship,—when he comes of age he shall have his inheritance without relief and without fine.

4. The administrator of the land of such heir who shall be under age shall take none but reasonable issues from the land of the heir, and reasonable customs and services. . . .

5. The administrator, moreover, so long as he may have the custody of the land, shall keep in order, from the issues of that land, the houses, parks, warrens, lakes, mills, and other things pertaining to it. And he shall restore to the heir when he comes to full age, his whole land stocked with ploughs and wainnages [wagons]. . . .

8. No widow shall be forced to marry when she prefers to live without a husband; so, however, that she gives security not to marry without our consent, if she hold from us, or the consent of the lord from whom she holds, if she hold from another.

12. No scutage or aid shall be imposed in our realm unless by the common counsel of our realm; except for redeeming of our body, and knighting our eldest son, and marrying once our eldest daughter. And for these purposes there shall only be given a reasonable aid. . . .

* Ernest F. Henderson, *Select Historical Documents of the Middle Ages*, London, George Bell & Sons, 1896.

14. And, in order to have the common counsel of the realm in the matter of assessing an aid otherwise than in the aforesaid cases, or of assessing a scutage,—we shall cause, under seal through our letters, the archbishops, bishops, abbots, earls, and greater barons to be summoned for a fixed day—for a term, namely, at least forty days distant,—and for a fixed place. And, moreover, we shall cause to be summoned in general, through our sheriffs and bailiffs, all those who hold of us in chief. And in all those letters of summons we shall express the cause of the summons. . . .

20. A freeman shall only be amerced for a small offense according to the measure of that offence. And for a great offence he shall be amerced according to the magnitude of the offence. . . .

21. Earls and barons shall not be amerced save through their peers, and only according to the measure of the offence.

31. Neither we nor our bailiffs shall take another's wood for castles or for other private uses, unless by the will of him to whom the wood belongs.

39. No freeman shall be taken, or imprisoned, or disseized, or out-lawed, or exiled, or in any way harmed—nor will we go upon or send upon him—save by the lawful judgment of his peers or by the law of the land. . . .

. . . Given through our hand, in the plain called Runnimede, between Windsor and Stanes, on the fifteenth day of June, in the seventeenth year of our reign.

## *Summons to the Model Parliament* *

EDWARD I OF ENGLAND

> *Parliaments were called by medieval kings when they wished the advice of the feudal nobles or their consent to unusual taxes. The first English Parliament met in 1265. Thirty years later King Edward I summoned to Parliament not only the great nobles and churchmen, but also representatives of the lesser nobles and of the towns. Because later Parliaments included the same groups, the Parliament of 1295 came to be known as the "Model" Parliament. We hear Edward's call to the Model Parliament.*

* James H. Robinson, *Readings in European History*, vol. 1, New York, Ginn and Company, 1904.

THE KING TO THE SHERIFF OF NORTHAMPTONSHIRE:

Since we intend to have a consultation and meeting with the earls, barons, and other principal men of our kingdom with regard to providing remedies against the dangers which are in these days threatening the same kingdom, and on that account have commanded them to be with us on the Lord's day next after the feast of St. Martin, in the approaching winter, at Westminster, to consider, ordain, and do as may be necessary for the avoidance of those dangers, we strictly require you to cause two knights from the aforesaid county, two citizens from each city in the same county, and two burgesses from each borough, of those who are especially discreet and capable of laboring, to be elected without delay, and to cause them to come to us at the aforesaid time and place.

Moreover, the said knights are to have full and sufficient power for themselves and for the community of the aforesaid county, and the said citizens and burgesses for themselves, and the communities of the aforesaid cities and boroughs separately, then and there, for doing what shall then be ordained according to the common council in the premises; so that the aforesaid business shall not remain unfinished in any way for defect of this power. And you shall have there the names of the knights, citizens, and burgesses, together with this writ.

Witness the king, at Canterbury, on the 3d of October.

## The Battle of Crécy *

SIR JEAN FROISSART

> With the development of the feudal kingdoms of England and France as equal states, feudal relationships between the two countries became unbearable. Ever since the Norman conquest of England in 1066, the kings of England had held French territories such as Normandy as feudal vassals of the French crown. This had led to constant interference of each government in the affairs of the other. Finally in the Hundred Years War (1337–1453) the English attempted to end the situation by the conquest of France. In 1346, early

* Sir Jean Froissart, *Chronicles*, vol. 1, New York, The Colonial Press, 1901 (translated by Thomas Johnes).

*in the war, a great English victory at Crécy demonstrated that medieval knights in armor were rapidly becoming useless as fighting men.*

There is no man, unless he had been present, that can imagine or describe truly the confusion of that day, especially the bad management and disorder of the French, whose troops were out of number. What I know, and shall relate in this book, I have learned chiefly from the English, and from those attached to Sir John of Hainault, who was always near the person of the King of France. The English, who, as I have said, were drawn up in three divisions, and seated on the ground, on seeing their enemies advance, rose up undauntedly and fell into their ranks. . . .

You must know that the French troops did not advance in any regular order, and that as soon as their King came in sight of the English his blood began to boil, and he cried out to his marshals, "Order the Genoese forward and begin the battle in the name of God and St. Denis." There were about 15,000 Genoese cross-bow men; but they were quite fatigued, having marched on foot that day six leagues, completely armed and carrying their cross-bows, and accordingly they told the constable they were not in a condition to do any great thing in battle. . . . When the Genoese were somewhat in order they approached the English and set up a loud shout, in order to frighten them; but the English remained quite quiet and did not seem to attend to it. They then set up a second shout, and advanced a little forward; the English never moved. Still they hooted a third time, advancing with their cross-bows presented, and began to shoot. The English archers then advanced one step forward, and shot their arrows with such force and quickness that it seemed as if it snowed. When the Genoese felt these arrows, which pierced through their armor, some of them cut the strings of their cross-bows, others flung them to the ground, and all turned about and retreated quite discomfited.

The French had a large body of men-at-arms on horseback to support the Genoese, and the King, seeing them thus fall back, cried out, "Kill me those scoundrels, for they stop up our road without any reason." The English continued shooting, and some of their arrows falling among the horsemen, drove them upon the Genoese, so that they were in such confusion they could never rally again.

. . . The valiant King of Bohemia was slain there; he was called Charles of Luxembourg, for he was the son of the gallant King and Emperor, Henry of Luxembourg, and, having heard the order for the battle, he inquired where his son the Lord Charles was; his attendants answered that they did not know, but believed he was fighting. Upon this, he said to them, "Gentlemen, you are all my people, my friends, and brethren at arms this day; therefore, as I am blind, I request of you to lead me so far into the engagement that I may strike one stroke with my sword." The knights consented, and in order that they might not lose him in the crowd, fastened all the reins of their horses together, placing the King at their head that he might gratify his wish, and in this manner advanced toward the enemy. The Lord Charles of Bohemia, who already signed his name as King of Germany, and bore the arms, had come in good order to the engagement; but when he perceived that it was likely to turn out against the French he departed. The King, his father, rode in among the enemy, and he and his companions fought most valiantly; however, they advanced so far that they were all slain, and on the morrow they were found on the ground with all their horses tied together. . . .

The Earl of Blois, nephew to the King of France, and the Duke of Lorraine, his brother-in-law, with their troops, made a gallant defence; but they were surrounded by a troop of English and Welsh, and slain in spite of their prowess. The Earl of St. Pol and the Earl of Auxerre were also killed, as well as many others. Late after vespers, the King of France had not more about him than sixty men, everyone included. Sir John of Hainault, who was of the number, had once remounted the King, for his horse had been killed under him by an arrow; and seeing the state he was in, he said, "Sir, retreat while you have an opportunity, and do not expose yourself so simply; if you have lost this battle, another time you will be the conqueror.". . .

## The Trial of Joan of Arc *

> In the later part of the Hundred Years War, French patriotism was aroused by Joan of Arc, the "Maid of Orleans." After inspiring the French soldiers to several victories, she was captured by the English, condemned as a "sorceress of the devil," and burned as a witch. The following is from the official report of her trial.

* Charles W. Colby, Selections from the Sources of English History, New York, Longmans, Green & Co., 1905.

We next required and admonished Joan, appearing before us in the said place, to take, under penalty of law, the oath which she had taken the day before; and that she should swear simply and absolutely to tell the truth in answer to what was asked her in the matter concerning which the charge had been brought and which was generally known. To this she answered that she had sworn yesterday and that was enough.

Again we required that she should swear; for every one, though he be a prince, when required to take the oath on a point of faith cannot refuse. And she answered again: "I took the oath for you yesterday; that should suffice you quite well. You burden me too much." Finally she swore to tell the truth in whatever related to faith.

Then a distinguished professor of sacred theology, Master John Beaupère, acting by our order and behest, questioned Joan on the points which follow.

And first he urged her to answer his questions truly, just as she had sworn to do. Whereupon she replied: "You might very well ask me one sort of question which I would answer truly, and another sort which I would not answer." And she added: "If you were well informed about me, you should wish that I were out of your hands. I have done nothing save by revelation."

Next asked about her age when she left home: she said that she did not know.

Asked whether in her girlhood she had learned any art: she said yes, that she had learned to sew linen cloth and to knit; and that she did not fear any woman in Rouen when it came to knitting and sewing. She further confessed that, through fear of the Burgundians, she left home and went to the town of Neufchâteau in Lorraine to live with a woman named La Rousse, where she stayed a fortnight; adding furthermore that when she was at home she was exempt from household work nor went with the sheep and other animals to pasture.

Again asked whether she confessed her sins each year: she answered yes, to her own *curé*; and when the *curé* was hindered she with his permission confessed to another priest. Sometimes also, twice or thrice as she believed, she confessed to the friars. . . .

. . . She further confessed that when she was thirteen years old she had a voice from God to aid her in self-discipline. And the first time she was greatly afraid. And this voice came about noon in summer in her father's garden, and she had fasted the day before. And she heard the voice on her right hand toward the church, and she seldom heard it without a light. Which light comes from the same side as the voice, but is usually great. And when she came to France she often heard this voice. Asked how she saw the light which she said was there present when it was on one side; to this she answered nothing, but passed to other things. She moreover said that if she were in a grove she distinctly heard voices coming to her. She also said that the voice seemed to her worthy, and she believes that it was sent by God; and after she had heard it three times she knew that it was the voice of an angel. She also said that it always guarded her well, and that she knew it well.

Asked about the teaching which her voice gave her respecting the salvation of her soul, she said that it taught her to govern herself well, to go often to church, and that it said she must go to France. And Joan added that the questioner would not this time learn from her in what guise the voice had appeared to her. She furthermore confessed that the voice told her twice or thrice a week that she must leave home and go to France; and that her father knew nothing of her departure. [Such was the effect of feudal sub-division, that to a native of Domremy—situated on the confines of Champagne and Lorraine—France seemed a foreign country.] She also said that the voice told her to go to France, and that she could no longer remain where she was, and that the voice told her that she should raise the siege of Orleans. She further said that her voice had told her that she should go to Robert de Baudricourt, Captain of the fortress of Vaucouleurs, and he would give her attendants; and she then answered that she was a poor girl who knew not how to ride a horse nor head a campaign. She also said that she went to her uncle and told him that she wished to stay with him for a little while; and she stayed there about eight days; and she then told her uncle that she must go to the fortress of Vaucouleurs; and he conducted her.

She also said that when she came to Vaucouleurs she recognised Robert de Baudricourt, although she had never seen him before; and she recognised him by the aid of her voice, for the voice told her that it was he; and she told Robert that she must go into France. Twice he denied and withstood her, and the third time he took her and gave her attendants; and so it happened even as her voice had said . . . Moreover she confessed that in leaving Vaucouleurs she put on men's dress, wearing a sword which Robert de Baudricout had given her and no other arms. Accompanied by a knight, a shield-bearer and four servants, she reached the town of St. Urbain, and there passed a night in the abbey. . . . Joan further said that she went to him whom she called her king [Charles VII] without hindrance, and when she reached the town of Ste. Catharine de Fierbois she was sent to Chinon, where he whom she called her king was. She reached this place about noon and lodged in an inn; and after dinner she went to him whom she called her king who was in the castle. She also said that when she entered his chamber she knew him from the rest by the revelation of her voice. And she told her king that she wished to go making war against the English.

Asked if when the voice disclosed the king, there was any light in the place: she answered: "Pass on."

Asked whether she had seen an angel above her king: she answered: "Spare me, pass on." Still she said that before her king gave her a charge she had many beautiful visions and revelations.

Asked how the king regarded the revelations and visions: she answered: "I shall not tell you this. This is not to be answered you; but send to the king himself and he will tell you."

Joan also said that the voice promised her that as soon as she came to her king he would receive her. She said that they on their part well knew that the voice came to her from God, and that they had seen and known her voice, stating that she was confident of it. She further said that her king and several others had heard and seen voices coming to her; . . .

After these things had been thus transacted, because it seemed quite enough for one day, we, the said bishop, postponed the trial until Saturday next following, at eight o'clock in the morning.

## *The Black Death* *

GIOVANNI BOCCACCIO

> *Breaking out in 1348, a great plague returned again and again to Europe for over a century. In some places a third of the population was swept away. The Italian writer Giovanni Boccaccio tells how the plague struck the city of Florence.*

In the year then of our Lord 1348, there happened at Florence, the finest city in all Italy, a most terrible plague; which, whether owing to

* Giovanni Boccaccio, *The Decameron*, in Merrick Whitcomb, ed., *A Literary Source-Book of the Renaissance*, Philadelphia, University of Pennsylvania, 1903.

the influence of the planets, or that it was sent from God as a just punishment for our sins, had broken out some years before in the Levant, and after passing from place to place, and making incredible havoc all the way, had now reached the west. There, in spite of all the means that art and human foresight could suggest, such as keeping the city clear from filth, the exclusion of all suspected persons, and the publication of copious instructions for the preservation of health; and notwithstanding manifold humble supplications offered to God in processions and otherwise; it began to show itself in the spring of the aforesaid year, in a sad and wonderful manner. Unlike what had been seen in the east, where bleeding from the nose is the fatal prognostic, here there appeared certain tumours . . . some as big as a small apple, others as an egg; and afterwards purple spots in most parts of the body; in some cases large and but few in number, in others smaller and more numerous, both sorts the usual messengers of death. To the cure of this malady, neither medical knowledge nor the power of drugs was of any effect; whether because the disease was in its own nature mortal, or that the physicians (the number of whom, taking quacks and women pretenders into the account, was grown very great), could form no just idea of the cause, nor consequently devise a true method of cure; whichever was the reason, few escaped; but nearly all died the third day from the first appearance of the symptoms, some sooner, some later, without any fever or other accessory symptoms. What gave the more virulence to this plague was that, by being communicated from the sick to the hale, it spread daily, like fire when it comes in contact with large masses of combustibles. Nor was it caught only by conversing with, or coming near the sick, but even by touching their clothes, or anything that they had before touched. . . .

These facts, and others of the like sort, occasioned various fears and devices amongst those who survived, all tending to the same uncharitable and cruel end, which was, to avoid the sick and everything that had been near them, expecting by that means to save themselves. And some holding it best to live temperately, and to avoid excesses of all kinds, made parties and shut themselves up from the rest of the world, eating and drinking moderately of the best, and diverting themselves with music, and such other entertainments as they might have within doors, never listening to anything from without to make them uneasy. Others maintáined free living to be a better preservative, and would baulk no passion or appetite they wished to gratify, drinking and revelling incessantly from tavern to tavern, or in private houses (which were frequently found deserted by the owners, and, therefore, common to every one), yet strenuously avoiding, with all this brutal indulgence, to come near the infected. And such, at that time, was the public distress, that the laws, human and divine, were no more regarded; for the officers to put them in force being either dead, sick, or in want of persons to assist them, every one did just as he pleased. . . . Others, with less humanity, but perchance, as they supposed, with more security from danger, decided that the only remedy for the pestilence was to avoid it; persuaded, therefore, of this, and taking care for themselves only, men and women in great numbers left the city, their houses, relations and effects, and fled to the country, as if the wrath of God had been restrained to visit those only within the walls of the city, or else concluding that none ought to stay in a place thus doomed to destruction.

## Economic Effects of the Black Plague *

HENRY KNIGHTON

> The effects of the Black Plague were felt in every phase of life, and the medieval world never recovered from the blow. Church, state, the economy, war, manners, morals, and customs were shaken. Coinciding with the Hundred Years War, it helped close the Middle Ages and introduce the excitement, misery, and splendor of the new age of the Renaissance. Its economic effects in England are reported by Henry Knighton in his History of England, written in the fourteenth century.

. . . Meanwhile the king sent proclamation into all the counties that reapers and other labourers should not take more than they had been accustomed to take, under the penalty appointed by statute. But the labourers were so lifted up and obstinate that they would not listen to the king's command, but if anyone wished to have them he had to give them what they wanted, and either lose his fruit and crops, or satisfy the lofty and covetous wishes of the workmen. And when it was known to the king that they had not observed his command, and had given greater wages to the labourers, he levied heavy fines upon abbots, priors, knights, greater

* Henry Knighton, *History of England,* in Elizabeth Kendall, *Source-Book of English History,* New York, The Macmillan Company, 1900.

and lesser, and other great folk and small folk of the realm, of some 100s., of some 40s., of some 20s., from each according to what he could give. He took from each carucate of the realm 20s., and, notwithstanding this, a fifteenth. And afterwards the king had many labourers arrested, and sent them to prison; many withdrew themselves and went into the forests and woods; and those who were taken were heavily fined. Their ringleaders were made to swear that they would not take daily wages beyond the ancient custom, and then were freed from prison. And in like manner was done with the other craftsmen in the boroughs and villages. . . . After the aforesaid pestilence, many buildings, great and small, fell into ruins in every city, borough, and village for lack of inhabitants, likewise many villages and hamlets became desolate, not a house being left in them, all having died who dwelt there; and it was probable that many such villages would never be inhabited. In the winter following there was such a want of servants in work of all kinds, that one would scarcely believe that in times past there had been such a lack. . . . And so all necessaries became so much dearer that what in times past had been worth a penny, was then worth 4d. or 5d.

Magnates and lesser lords of the realm who had tenants made abatements of the rent in order that the tenants should not go away on account of the want of servants and the general dearness, some half the rent, some more, some less, some for two years, some for three, some for one year, according as they could agree with them. Likewise those who received of their tenants daywork throughout the year, as is the practice with villeins, had to give them more leisure, and remit such works, and either entirely to free them, or give them an easier tenure at a small rent, so that the homes should not be irrecoverably ruined, and the land everywhere remain entirely uncultivated.


## Seeking a Scapegoat *

Jacob R. Marcus

> Some people saw in the Black Death a punishment sent
> them by God for their sins. Others tried to place the blame
> on somebody else. Jews and Gypsies, who throughout the
> Middle Ages had been regarded as strangers living outside

* Jacob R. Marcus, *The Jew in the Medieval World*, Cincinnati, Sinai Press, 1938.

*the law, were in some places accused of causing the plague,*
*and confessions were on occasion extorted from them. We*
*read an account of the persecution of Jews in Germany in*
*1349.*

In the year 1349 there occurred the greatest epidemic that ever happened. Death went from one end of the earth to the other, on that side and this side of the sea, and it was greater among the Saracens than among the Christians. In some lands everyone died so that no one was left. Ships were also found on the sea laden with wares; the crew had all died and no one guided the ship. The bishop of Marseilles and priests and monks and more than half of all the people there died with them. In other kingdoms and cities so many people perished that it would be horrible to describe. The pope at Avignon stopped all sessions of court, locked himself in a room, allowed no one to approach him and had a fire burning before him all the time. [This last was probably intended as some sort of disinfectant.] And from what this epidemic came, all wise teachers and physicians could only say that it was God's will. And as the plague was now here, so was it in other places, and lasted more than a whole year. This epidemic also came to Strasbourg in the summer of the above-mentioned year, and it is estimated that about sixteen thousand people died.

In the matter of this plague the Jews throughout the world were reviled and accused in all lands of having caused it through the poison which they are said to have put into the water and the wells—that is what they were accused of—and for this reason the Jews were burnt all the way from the Mediterranean into Germany, but not in Avignon, for the pope protected them there.

Nevertheless they tortured a number of Jews in Berne and Zofingen [Switzerland] who then admitted that they had put poison into many wells, and they also found the poison in the wells. Thereupon they burnt the Jews in many towns and wrote of this affair to Strasbourg, Freiburg, and Basel in order that they too should burn their Jews. But the leaders in these three cities in whose hands the government lay did not believe that anything ought to be done to the Jews. However in Basel the citizens marched to the city hall and compelled the council to take an oath that they they would burn the Jews, and that they would allow no Jew to enter the city for the next two hundred years. Thereupon the Jews were arrested in all these places and a conference was arranged to meet at Benfeld [Alsace, February 8, 1349]. The bishop of Strasbourg [Berthold II], all the feudal lords of Alsace, and representatives of the three above-mentioned cities came there. The deputies of the city of Strasbourg were asked what they were going to do with their Jews. They answered and said that they knew no evil of them. Then they asked the Strasbourgers why they had closed the wells and put away the buckets, and there was a great indignation and clamour against the deputies from Strasbourg. So finally the bishop and the lords and the Imperial Cities agreed to do away with the Jews. The result was that they were burnt in many cities, and wherever they were expelled they were caught by the peasants and stabbed to death or drowned. . . .

[The town-council of Strasbourg which wanted to save the Jews was deposed on the 9th/10th of February, and the new council gave in to the mob, who then arrested the Jews on Friday, the 13th.]

On Saturday—that was St. Valentine's Day—they burnt the Jews on a wooden platform in their cemetery. There were about two thousand people of them. Those who wanted to baptize themselves were spared. [Some say that about a thousand accepted baptism.] Many small children were taken out of the fire and baptized against the will of their fathers and mothers. And everything that was owed to the Jews was cancelled, and the Jews had to surrender all pledges and notes that they had taken for debts. The council, however, took the cash that the Jews possessed and divided it among the working-men proportionately. The money was indeed the thing that killed the Jews. If they had been poor and if the feudal lords had not been in debt to them, they would not have been burnt. After this wealth was divided among the artisans some gave their share to the cathedral or to the Church on the advice of their confessors.

Thus were the Jews burnt at Strasbourg, and in the same year in all the cities of the Rhine, whether Free Cities or Imperial Cities or cities belonging to the lords. In some towns they burnt the Jews after a trial, in others, without a trial. . . .


## Defiance of the Church *

JOHN WYCLIFFE

> *While war and pestilence were undermining the medieval*
> *way of life, the power of the church as the leading influence*

* University of Pennsylvania, *Translations and Reprints from the Original Sources of European History*, vol. 2, no. 5, Philadelphia, 1902.

*on men was also being weakened. In the fourteenth century the popes for greater security had conducted papal affairs from Avignon, on the border of the kingdom of France. An effort to restore the seat of the papacy to Rome in 1378 led to the Great Schism, in which two popes were elected, one at Rome and another at Avignon. Each claimed to be the rightful head of the church and excommunicated those who would follow the other. The faith of Europeans was shaken, and the way was opened for serious challenges to the church. Critics of the church had always existed, but John Wycliffe set an example for a new generation that would not be silenced.*

### Bull of Pope Gregory XI., against John Wycliffe.

Gregory, bishop, servant of the servants of God, to his beloved sons the chancellor and University of Oxford, in the diocese of Lincoln, grace and apostolic benediction.

We are compelled to wonder and grieve that you, who, in considera-tion of the favors and privileges conceded to your university of Oxford by the apostolic see, and on account of your familiarity with the Scriptures, in whose sea you navigate, by the gift of God, with auspicious oar, you, who ought to be, as it were, warriors and champions of the orthodox faith, without which there is no salvation of souls,—that you through a certain sloth and neglect allow tares to spring up amidst the pure wheat in the fields of your glorious university aforesaid; and what is still more perni-cious, even continue to grow to maturity. . . . By the insinuation of many, if they are indeed worthy of belief, deploring it deeply, it has come to our ears that John de Wycliffe, rector of the church of Lutterworth, in the diocese of Lincoln, Professor of the Sacred Scriptures, (would that he were not also Master of Errors,) has fallen into such a detestable madness that he does not hesitate to dogmatize and publicly preach . . . certain proposi-tions and conclusions which are erroneous and false. He has cast himself also into the depravity of preaching heretical dogmas which strive to sub-vert and weaken the state of the whole church . . . some of which doc-trines, in changed terms, it is true, seem to express the perverse opinions and unlearned learning of Marsilio of Padua of cursed memory, and of John of Jandun, whose book is extant, rejected and cursed by our prede-cessor, Pope John XXII, of happy memory. . . . He has polluted certain of the faithful of Christ by besprinkling them with these doctrines, and led them away from the right paths of the aforesaid faith to the brink of perdition.

Wherefore, since we are not willing, nay, indeed, ought not to be willing, that so deadly a pestilence should continue to exist with our connivance, a pestilence which, if it is not opposed in its beginnings, and torn out by the roots in its entirety, will be reached too late by medicines when it has infected very many with its contagion; we command your university with strict admonition, by the apostolic authority, in virtue of your sacred obedience, and under penalty of the deprivation of all the favors, indulgences, and privileges granted to you and your university by the said see, for the future not to permit to be asserted or set forth to any extent whatever, the opinions, conclusions, and propositions which are in variance with good morals and faith, even when those setting them forth strive to defend them under a certain fanciful wresting of words or of terms. Moreover, you are on our authority to arrest the said John, or cause him to be arrested and to send him under a trustworthy guard to our venerable brother, the Archbishop of Canterbury, and the Bishop of London, or to one of them.

Besides, if there should be, which God forbid, in your university, subject to your jurisdiction, opponents stained with these errors, and if they should obstinately persist in them, proceed vigorously and earnestly to a similar arrest and removal of them, and otherwise as shall seem good to you. . . .

Given at Rome, at Santa Maria Maggiore, on the 31st of May, the sixth year of our pontificate.

### Reply of Wycliffe to His Summons by the Pope to Come to Rome, 1384.

I have joy fully to tell what I hold, to all true men that believe and especially to the Pope; for I suppose that if my faith be rightful and given of God, the Pope will gladly confirm it; and if my faith be error, the Pope will wisely amend it.

I suppose over this that the gospel of Christ be heart of the corps of God's law; for I believe that Jesus Christ, that gave in his own person this gospel, is very God and very man, and by this heart passes all other laws.

I suppose over this that the Pope be most obliged to the keeping of the gospel among all men that live here; for the Pope is highest vicar that

Christ has here in earth. For moreness of Christ's vicar is not measured by wordly moreness, but by this, that this vicar follows more Christ by virtuous living; for thus teacheth the gospel, that this is the sentence of Christ.

And of this gospel I take as believe, that Christ for time that he walked here, was most poor man of all, both in spirit and in having; for Christ says that he had nought for to rest his head on. And Paul says that he was made needy for our love. And more poor might no man be, neither bodily nor in spirit. And thus Christ put from him all manner of worldly lordship. For the gospel of John telleth that when they would have made Christ king, he fled and hid him from them, for he would none such worldly highness.

And over this I take it as believe, that no man should follow the Pope, nor no saint that now is in heaven, but in as much as he follows Christ. For John and James erred when they coveted worldly highness; and Peter and Paul sinned also when they denied and blasphemed in Christ; but men should not follow them in this, for then they went from Jesus Christ. And this I take as wholesome counsel, that the Pope leave his worldly lordship to worldly lords, as Christ gave them,—and move speedily all his clerks to do so. For thus did Christ, and taught thus his disciples. . . .

And if I err in this sentence, I will meekly be amended, yea, by the death. . . . And if I might travel in mine own person, I would with good will go to the Pope. But God has needed me to the contrary, and taught me more obedience to God than to men. . . .


## Christians in the Orient

> Christian interest in Asia did not halt in the Near East. For seventeen years (1275–1292) Venetian merchants of the Polo family lived at the court of the Great Khan in Cathay (China). Marco Polo describes the riches of Japan. John of Monte Corvino, a Franciscan, preached Christianity for thirty years to the Chinese, without much success. His letter speaks of the loneliness of living among strangers. Finally the Englishman Sir John Mandeville claims to have visited Cathay about 1340, although some believe that he wrote of parts of Asia which he did not reach himself.

## The Riches of Japan *

Chipangu [Japan] is an Island towards the east in the high seas, 1500 miles distant from the Continent; and a very great Island it is.

The people are white, civilized, and well-favoured. They are Idolaters, and are dependent on nobody. And I can tell you the quantity of gold they have is endless; for they find it in their own Islands, [and the King does not allow it to be exported.] [Moreover] few merchants visit the country because it is so far from the main land, and thus it comes to pass that their gold is abundant beyond all measure.

I will tell you a wonderful thing about the Palace of the Lord of that Island. You must know that he hath a great Palace which is entirely roofed with fine gold, just as our churches are roofed with lead, insomuch that it would scarcely be possible to estimate its value. Moreover, all the pavement of the Palace and the floors of its chambers, are entirely of gold, in plates like slabs of stone, a good two fingers thick; and the windows also are of gold, so that altogether the richness of this Palace is past all bounds and all belief.

They have also pearls in abundance, which are of a rose colour, but fine, big, and round, and quite as valuable as the white ones. . . . They have also quantities of other precious stones. . . .


## A Letter of John of Monte Corvino **

I, Friar John of Monte Corvino, of the order of Minor Friars, departed from Tauris, a city of the Persians, in the year of the Lord 1291, and proceeded to India. And I remained in the country of India, wherein stands the church of St. Thomas the Apostle, for thirteen months, and in that region baptized in different places about one hundred persons. . . .

I proceeded on my further journey and made my way to Cathay, the realm of the Emperor of the Tartars who is called the Grand Cham. To him I presented the letter of our lord the Pope, and invited him to adopt the Catholic Faith of our Lord Jesus Christ, but he had grown too old in idolatry. However he bestows many kindnesses upon the Christians, and these two years past I am abiding with him. . . .

* Colonel Sir Henry Yule, ed., *The Book of Ser Marco Polo*, vol. 2, London, John Murray, 1903.
** Colonel Henry Yule, ed., "First Letter of John of Montecorvino," *Cathay and the Way Thither*, London, The Hakluyt Society, 1866.

In this mission I abode alone and without any associate for eleven years; but it is now going on for two years since I was joined by Friar Arnold, a German of the province of Cologne.

I have built a church in the city of Cambaliech in which the king has his chief residence. This I completed six years ago; and I have built a bell-tower to it, and put three bells in it. I have baptized there, as well as I can estimate, up to this time some 6,000 persons; . . . And I am often still engaged in baptizing.

Also I have gradually bought one hundred and fifty boys, the children of pagan parents, and of ages varying from seven to eleven, who had never learned any religion. These boys I have baptized and I have also taught them Greek and Latin after our manner. . . . I have the bells rung at all the canonical hours, and . . . the chaunting we do by ear because I have no service book with the notes. . . .

It is twelve years since I have had any news of the Papal court, or of our order, or of the state of affairs generally in the west. Two years ago indeed there came hither a certain Lombard leech, who spread abroad in these parts the most incredible blasphemies about the court of Rome and our Order and the state of things in the west, and on this account I exceedingly desire to obtain true intelligence. . . .

I have myself grown old and grey, more with toil and trouble than with years; for I am not more than fifty-eight. I have got a competent knowledge of the language and character which is most generally used by the Tartars. And I have already translated into that language and character the New Testament and the Psalter, and have caused them to be written out in the fairest penmanship they have; and so by writing, reading, and preaching, I bear open and public testimony to the Law of Christ. . . .

Dated at the city of Cambalec in the kingdom of Cathay, in the year of our Lord 1305. . . .

## THE RICHES OF CATHAY *

Cathay is a great country, fair, noble, rich, and full of merchants. Thither merchants go to seek spices and all manner of merchandises. . . . Merchants who come from Genoa, or from Venice, or from Romania . . . go by sea and by land eleven or twelve months, or more sometimes, before they reach Cathay. . . . Within the palace, in the hall, there are twenty-four pillars of fine gold. . . . At the head of the hall, is the em-

* "The Book of Sir John Maundeville," in Thomas Wright, ed., *Early Travels in Palestine*, London, Henry G. Bohn, 1848.

peror's throne, very high, where he sits. It is of fine precious stones, and great pearls. And the steps up to the throne are of precious stones, mixed with gold. . . . And under the emperor's throne sit four clerks, who write all that the emperor says, be it good or evil; for all that he says must be held good; for he may not change his word nor revoke it.

. . . And all the vessels that men are served with, in the hall, are of precious stones. . . . And the cups are of emeralds, and sapphires, or topazes. . . . Vessel of silver is there none, for they set no value on it, to make vessels of; but they make therewith steps and pillars, and pavements to halls and chambers. . . .

. . . And you shall understand that the emperor, in person, rides not as other great lords do, unless he choose to go privately with a few men, to be unknown. Otherwise he sits in a chariot with four wheels, upon which is made a fair chamber. . . . And it is all covered internally with plates of gold, dubbed with precious stones and pearls. . . .

There is not . . . so great a lord, nor so mighty, nor so rich, as the great chan. . . . All [others], in comparison to the great chan, are neither of might, nobleness, royalty, nor riches; for in all these he surpasses all earthly princes.

## Nomads of Tartary *

MARCO POLO

> Not all the people of the East were living urban lives and enjoying a high state of cultural progress. Marco Polo describes the Tartars, the Mongolian tribes who briefly controlled Europe and Asia from Russia to China.

. . . The Tartars' custom is to spend the winter in warm plains, where they find good pasture for their cattle, whilst in summer they betake themselves to a cool climate among the mountains and valleys, where water is to be found as well as woods and pastures.

Their houses are circular; and are made of wands covered with felts. These are carried along with them whithersoever they go; . . . The

* Colonel Sir Henry Yule, ed., The Book of Ser Marco Polo, vol. 1, London, John Murray (Publishers) Ltd., 1903.

women do the buying and selling, and whatever is necessary to provide for the husband and household; for the men all lead the life of gentlemen, troubling themselves about nothing but hunting and hawking . . . unless it be the practice of warlike exercises. . . .

All their harness of war is excellent and costly. Their arms are bows and arrows, sword and mace; but above all the bow, for they are capital archers, indeed the best that are known. On their backs they wear armour . . . prepared from buffalo and other hides, which is very strong. They are excellent soldiers. . . . They are also more capable of hardships than other nations; for many a time, if need be, they will go for a month without any supply of food, living only on the milk of their mares and on such game as their bow may win them. Their horses also will subsist entirely on the grass of the plains. . . .

When they are going on a distant expedition they take no gear with them except two leather bottles for milk; a little earthenware pot to cook their meat in, and a little tent to shelter them from rain. And in case of great urgency they will ride ten days on end without lighting a fire or taking a meal. On such an occasion they will sustain themselves on the blood of their horses, opening a vein and letting the blood jet into their mouths. . . .

When they come to an engagement with the enemy, they will gain the victory in this fashion. [They never let themselves get into a regular medley, but keep perpetually riding round and shooting into the enemy. And] as they do not count it any shame to run away in battle, they will [sometimes pretend to] do so, and in running away they turn in the saddle and shoot hard and strong at the foe, and in this way make great havoc. Their horses are trained so perfectly that they will double hither and thither, just like a dog, in a way that is quite astonishing. Thus they fight to as good purpose in running away as if they stood and faced the enemy, because of the vast volleys of arrows that they shoot in this way, turning round upon their pursuers, who are fancying that they have won the battle. But when the Tartars see that they have killed and wounded a good many horses and men, they wheel round bodily, and return to the charge in perfect order and with loud cries; and in a very short time the enemy are routed. . . . And you perceive that it is just when the enemy sees them run, and imagines that he has gained the battle, that he has in reality lost it; for the Tartars wheel round in a moment when they judge the right time has come. And after this fashion they have won many a fight.

# PART TWO

# The Renaissance

The period from the fourteenth to the seventeenth century in Europe is called the "Renaissance," or "Rebirth." Historians have disagreed on the true nature of the period. The clue to understanding it lies in realizing that it was an age of contradictions, that it included many conflicting trends. It had its roots in the medieval world; but it scorned the Middle Ages, looking back instead to the days of Greece and Rome. It was not only the daughter of the Middle Ages but also the mother of the modern world. Misery and splendor, beauty and horror, despotism and the urge for free expression, all flourished side by side. Among the few simple things that can be said of it is that it was an age of strong individualism. So we will see some of its achievements here in relation to individuals whose questioning minds were never satisfied.

# Johann Gutenberg *

WILLIAM FICHET

*Without doubt the most important invention of the Renaissance in its influence on the world of the future was that of printing with movable type, invented by Johann Gutenberg of Mainz about 1450. William Fichet, who brought the invention to Paris, writes of Gutenberg to a friend.*

. . . Great light has been thrown by the breed of new makers of books, whom, within our memory, Germany has sent broadcast into every quarter. For they say that there, not far from the city of Mainz, there appeared a certain John whose surname was Gutenberg, who first of all men, devised the art of printing, whereby books are made, not by a reed, as did the ancients, nor with a quill pen, as do we, but with metal letters, and that swiftly, neatly, beautifully. Surely this man is worthy to be loaded with divine honors by all the Muses, all the arts, all the tongues of those who delight in books, and is all the more to be preferred to gods and goddesses in that he has put the means of choice within reach of letters themselves and of mortals devoted to culture. . . .

But that great Gutenberg has discovered things far more pleasing and more divine, in carving out letters in such fashion that whatever can be said or thought can by them be written down at once and transcribed and committed to the memory of posterity.

# Cosimo de Medici Founds a Library **

VESPASIANO DA BISTICCI

*Men of the Renaissance were avid collectors of books, particularly of the classical literature of Greece and Rome. But before the invention of printing, only the wealthiest could afford to establish large libraries, as shown by the account of the founding of the Medici library in Florence.*

* Douglas C. McMurtrie, ed., The Fichet Letter, New York, Press of Ars Typographica, 1927 (translated by Walter A. Montgomery).
** Vespasiano da Bisticci, Life of Cosimo de Medici, in Merrick Whitcomb, ed., A Literary Sourcebook of the Renaissance, Philadelphia, University of Pennsylvania, 1903.

When he had finished the residence and a good part of the church, he fell to thinking how he should have the place peopled with honest men of letters; and in this way it occurred to him to found a fine library; and one day when I happened to be present in his chamber, he said to me: "In what way would you furnish this library?" I replied that as for buying the books it would be impossible, for they were not to be had. Then he said: "How is it possible then to furnish it?" I told him that it would be necessary to have the books copied. He asked in reply if I would be willing to undertake the task. I answered him, that I was willing. He told me to commence my work and he would leave everything to me; and as for the money that would be necessary he would refer the matter to Dom Archangel, then prior of the monastery, who would draw bills upon the bank, which should be paid. The library was commenced at once, for it was his pleasure that it should be done with the utmost possible celerity; and as I did not lack for money I collected in a short time forty-five writers, and finished 200 volumes in twenty-two months; in which work we made use of an excellent arrangement, that of the library of pope Nicholas, which he had given to Cosimo, in the form of a catalogue made out with his own hands. . . .

. . . Cosimo lived to see the library wholly completed, and the cataloguing and the arranging of the books; in all of which he took great pleasure, and the work went forward, as was his custom, with great promptness.

## *The Medici as Patrons of the Arts* *

OLIPHANT SMEATON

> *The artists of the Renaissance were supported by wealthy individuals—bankers, princes, popes, kings. The importance of Florence as one of the greatest art centers was due in large part to her ruling family, the Medici. They had acquired great wealth through trading and banking and used it to gain political power. Some of its members became dukes in Florence; others, popes; and two of its daughters, queens of France.*

* Oliphant Smeaton, *The Medici and the Italian Renaissance*, New York, Charles Scribner's Sons, 1901.

As the friends of learning and the munificent patrons of culture, the house of Medici richly merits remembrance. Condemn as we may their political tyranny . . . their name will be eternally associated with that glorious dawn of modern European scholarship which gilded the fifteenth century. . . .

To name all the painters, sculptors, architects, workers in wood and metals, etc. whom Lorenzo encouraged by his patronage and in many cases supported by his bounty would be impossible. As has been remarked already, no lad whose youth gave promise of a glorious prime ever applied to Lorenzo in vain. But for his encouragement Antonio Pollajuolo could never have pursued his studies into the anatomy of the human frame, which converted painting, from haphazard guesswork, into an intelligent application of scientific principles. . . .

Then as regards oil painting, how much was due to his patronage that the idea really took root among artists, has never really been gauged. Hitherto the work of the leading colourists in Tuscany had been executed in what was called "distemper," namely, with pigments rendered cohesive by the use of glutinous substances. Stimulated, however, by Lorenzo's encouragement, Andrea da Castagna began experimenting in "oils," and finally succeeded in revolutionising his craft. Aided by the Magnifico also, who placed his unrivalled collection of relics of antiquity at his service, the young Filippo Lippi devoted himself to the study of the antique, in order that the backgrounds and minor details in his pictures might be accurate as well as spirited. Luca Signorelli, whose skill in portraying the beauty of the human form and the variations of expression on the human countenance, excited the wonder of his own age; Verrocchio, the apostle of Realism in sculpture and painting, who if he did not invent, at least rendered general the practice of taking casts from the faces of the dead; . . . all owed much to Lorenzo in the way of encouragement, inspiration, and, above all, criticism. For Lorenzo, like his grandfather Cosimo, would only recognise the art of his friends in their best work. To be deemed worthy of a place in one of Lorenzo's villas was the ambition of all his protégés; but as they recognised that only the highest expression of their genius would meet with his approval and win the prize of his praise, his patronage was an important factor in producing those masterpieces which constitute the glory of the Laurentian age.

To Lorenzo's perception of their outstanding genius, amid many other aspirants to his favour, both Leonardo da Vinci and Michael Angelo owed their first step on the ladder of fame. Both were admitted to his house and to his table, while the former was sent by him to Milan, where he speedily rose to eminence. Michael Angelo lived as his son in the Palazzo Medici until Lorenzo's death, when his protégé was but eighteen. Piero, the Magnifico's son and successor, certainly showed the lad great kindness. . . .

Nor was architecture forgotten by Lorenzo. In Giuliano Giamberti, nicknamed "San Gallo," Lorenzo discovered a genius who, if he did not rival Brunelleschi and Ghiberti, showed a "modernness" in his ideas and a power of combining artistic grace with an attention to such practical details as commodiousness and convenience, which rendered him one of the most popular architects of the age. . . .

To name here all the branches of art or industry which enjoyed the Magnifico's fostering care would be impossible. He encouraged gem engraving; majolica-work also received a share of his attention; he subsidised the rearing of silk worms, and brought skilled workmen from Bruges to initiate a Florentine tapestry factory. Even music was a passion with this many-sided patron of the arts. . . .


## A Letter to Posterity *

FRANCESCO PETRARCH

> *The Renaissance began in Italy because of its prosperity, caused by its position as a trading center, and its relative political stability. Wealth and leisure enabled the Renaissance man to study and imitate classical civilizations and to contrast those civilizations with the world around him. Petrarch (1304–1374) is characteristic of the men of the Renaissance, who were concerned with themselves as individuals and with this world more than the next. He found this "humanist" tendency much stronger in Greek and Roman writings than in those of the medieval world. His search for ancient documents, his imitation of their style, his emphasis on secular instead of religious matters became typical of many men of the later Renaissance. His concern with the opinion of others is reflected in his letter to you.*

* Frederic A. Ogg, *A Source Book of Medieval History*, New York, American Book Company, 1907.

Francis Petrarch, to Posterity, greeting:

It is possible that some word of me may have come to you, though even this is doubtful, since an insignificant and obscure name will scarcely penetrate far in either time or space. If however, you should have heard of me, you may desire to know what manner of man I was, or what was the outcome of my labors, especially those of which some description or, at any rate, the bare titles may have reached you. . . .

In my prime I was blessed with a quick and active body, although not exceptionally strong; and while I do not lay claim to remarkable personal beauty, I was comely enough in my best days. I was possessed of a clear complexion, between light and dark, lively eyes, and for long years a keen vision, which, however, deserted me, contrary to my hopes, after I reached my sixtieth birthday, and forced me, to my great annoyance, to resort to glasses. Although I had previously enjoyed perfect health, old age brought with it the usual array of discomforts.

My parents were honorable folk, Florentine in their origin, of medium fortune, or, I may as well admit it, in a condition verging upon poverty. They had been expelled from their native city, and consequently I was born in exile, at Arezzo, in the year 1304 of this latter age, which begins with Christ's birth, July the 20th, on a Monday, at dawn. I have always possessed an extreme contempt for wealth; not that riches are not desirable in themselves, but because I hate the anxiety and care which are invariably associated with them. I certainly do not long to be able to give gorgeous banquets. I have . . . led a happier existence with plain living . . . Nothing displeases me more than display, for not only is it bad in itself and opposed to humility, but it is troublesome and distracting. . . .

I possessed a well-balanced rather than a keen intellect—one prone to all kinds of good and wholesome study, but especially inclined to moral philosophy and the art of poetry. The latter, indeed, I neglected as time went on, and took delight in sacred literature. Finding in that a hidden sweetness which I had once esteemed but lightly, I came to regard the works of the poets as only amenities.

Among the many subjects that interested me, I dwelt especially upon antiquity, for our own age has always repelled me, so that, had it not been for the love of those dear to me, I should have preferred to have been born in any other period than our own. In order to forget my own time, I have constantly striven to place myself in spirit in other ages, and consequently I delighted in history. The conflicting statements troubled me, but when in doubt I accepted what appeared most probable, or yielded to the authority of the writer. . . .

# The Prince *

Niccolò Machiavelli

> *Machiavelli (1469–1527), a Florentine secretary of state and diplomat, is best known to us as an historian and as the author of* The Prince, *an essay on government. From his clear view of practical politics, he concluded that there are two kinds of morality: one for individuals, and another, quite different, for governments. Religious persons were so shocked that they came to call the devil "Old Nick," after Niccolò Machiavelli. He tells us, in* The Prince, *how governments succeed.*

It now remains to be seen what are the methods and rules for a prince as regards his subjects and friends. And as I know that many have written of this, I fear that my writing about it may be deemed presumptuous, differing as I do, especially in this matter, from the opinions of others. But my intention being to write something of use to those who understand, it appears to me more proper to go to the real truth of the matter than to its imagination . . . ; for how we live is so far removed from how we ought to live, that he who abandons what is done for what ought to be done, will rather learn to bring about his own ruin than his preservation. A man who wishes to make a profession of goodness in everything must necessarily come to grief among so many who are not good. Therefore it is necessary for a prince, who wishes to maintain himself, to learn how not to be good, and to use this knowledge and not use it, according to the necessity of the case. . . .

. . . One ought to be both feared and loved, but as it is difficult for the two to go together, it is much safer to be feared than loved, if one of the two has to be wanting. For it may be said of men in general that they are ungrateful, voluble, dissemblers, anxious to avoid danger, and covetous of gain; as long as you benefit them, they are entirely yours; they offer you their blood, their goods, their life, and their children, as I have before said, when the necessity is remote; but when it approaches, they revolt. And the prince who has relied solely on their words, without making other preparations, is ruined; for the friendship which is gained by purchase and not through grandeur and nobility of spirit is bought but not secured, and at a pinch is not to be expended in your service. And

* Niccolò Machiavelli, *The Prince,* London and New York, Oxford University Press, 1960 (translated by Luigi Ricci and revised by E. R. P. Vincent).

men have less scruple in offending one who makes himself loved than one who makes himself feared; for love is held by a chain of obligation which, men being selfish, is broken whenever it serves their purpose; but fear is maintained by a dread of punishment which never fails.

Still, a prince should make himself feared in such a way that if he does not gain love, he at any rate avoids hatred; for fear and the absence of hatred may well go together, and will be always attained by one who abstains from interfering with the property of his citizens. . . .

How laudable it is for a prince to keep good faith and live with integrity, and not with astuteness, every one knows. Still the experience of our times shows those princes to have done great things who have had little regard for good faith, and have been able by astuteness to confuse men's brains, and who have ultimately overcome those who have made loyalty their foundation. . . .

. . . Therefore, a prudent ruler ought not to keep faith when by so doing it would be against his interest, and when the reasons which made him bind himself no longer exist. If men were all good, this precept would not be a good one; but as they are bad, and would not observe their faith with you, so you are not bound to keep faith with them. Nor have legitimate grounds ever failed a prince who wished to show colourable excuse for the non-fulfilment of his promise. Of this one could furnish an infinite number of modern examples, and show how many times peace has been broken, and how many promises rendered worthless, by the faithlessness of princes, and those that have been best able to imitate the fox have succeeded best. But it is necessary to be able to disguise this character well, and to be a great feigner and dissembler; and men are so simple and so ready to obey present necessities, that one who deceives will always find those who allow themselves to be deceived. . . .

. . . And in the actions of men, and especially of princes, from which there is no appeal, the end justifies the means. Let a prince therefore aim at conquering and maintaining the state, and the means will always be judged honourable and praised by every one, for the vulgar is always taken by appearances and the issue of the event; and the world consists only of the vulgar, and the few who are not vulgar are isolated when the many have a rallying point in the prince. A certain prince of the present time, whom it is well not to name, never does anything but preach peace and good faith, but he is really a great enemy to both, and either of them, had he observed them, would have lost him state or reputation on many occasions.

# In Praise of Folly *

Desiderius Erasmus

> At a time when Europe was entering its period of most vio-
> lent religious passions, Desiderius Erasmus (1466–1536), a
> priest of Rotterdam and friend of princes, tried to advance
> the cause of reform in both church and state by the gentler
> weapons of satire and humor. He holds the mirror up to
> mankind in his In Praise of Folly.

. . . I suppose the lawyers . . . of all men have the greatest conceit
of their own abilities. They will argue as confidently as if they spoke
gospel instead of law; they will cite you six hundred precedents, though
not one of them come near to the case at hand; they will muster up the
authority of judgments, deeds, and reports, and tumble over so many
musty records, that they make their employment, though in itself easy,
the greatest slavery imaginable. . . .

To these . . . may be added logicians . . . fellows that talk as much
by rote as a parrot; who shall run down a whole bevy of gossiping old
women, nay, silence the very noise of a belfry, with louder clappers than
those of the steeple; . . .

Next to these come the philosophers, with their long beards and short
cloaks, who esteem themselves as the only favorites of wisdom, and look
upon the rest of mankind as the dirt and rubbish of the creation. . . .
They build castles in the air, and infinite words in a *vacuum*. They will
give you to a hair's breadth the dimensions of the sun, moon, and stars
. . . ;—they will give an elaborate account of the cause of thunder, of
the origin of the winds, of the nature of eclipses . . . without the least
hesitation, as if they had been admitted into the cabinet council of nature, or had been eye-witnesses to all the methods of creation; though in
fact nature does but laugh at all their puny conjectures: for they never
yet made one considerable discovery, as appears from the fact that on no
single point of the smallest moment have they unanimously agreed. . . .

If princes did but seriously consider (and consider they would if they
were but wise), these many hardships of a royal life, they would be so
perplexed in the result of their thoughts thereupon, as scarce to eat or
sleep in quiet. But . . . they leave all these cares to the gods, and mind

* Desiderius Erasmus, In Praise of Folly, New York, The Truth Seeker Company,
1929.

only their own ease and pleasure, and therefore will admit none to their attendance but those who will divert them with sport and mirth. . . . They think they have sufficiently acquitted themselves in the duty of governing, if they do but ride constantly a hunting, breed up good race-horses, sell places and offices to those of the courtiers that will give the most for them, and find out new ways for invading of their people's prosperity, and securing a larger revenue. . . .

And now for some reflections upon popes, cardinals, and bishops, who in pomp and splendor have almost equaled if not outdone secular princes.

[Bishops] . . . are entrusted with a very weighty and difficult office. But, alas, they think it sufficient if they can but feed themselves; and as to their flock, either command them to the care of Christ himself, or commit them to the guidance of some inferior vicars or curates; not so much as remembering what their name of bishop imports, to wit, labor, pains, diligence . . . [instead] they are in a profane sense, *Episcopi*, overseers of their own gain and income.

So cardinals, in like manner, if they did but consider that the church supposes them to succeed in the room of the apostles; that therefore they must behave themselves . . . and so not be lords, but dispensers of spiritual gifts, of the disposal whereof they must one day render a strict account. . . .

Now as to the popes of Rome, who pretend themselves Christ's vicars, if they would but imitate his exemplary life . . . ; if they did but consider the import of the word Pope, which signifies a father; . . . what order or degrees of men would be in a worse condition? . . .

### Leonardo da Vinci States His Qualifications *

> *Typical of the greater minds of the Renaissance, Leonardo da Vinci (1452–1519) explored mechanics, painting, sculpture, architecture, mathematics, landscaping, philosophy, and literature. His genius in probing whatever interested him makes him noteworthy in all of these fields. He speaks for himself in a letter to the duke of Bari and Milan.*

* *The Literary Works of Leonardo da Vinci*, compiled and edited from the original manuscripts by Jean Paul Richter, 2d Ed., Vol. 2, enlarged and revised by Jean Paul Richter and Irma A. Richter, London, Oxford University Press, 1939. Reprinted by courtesy of Gisela M. A. Richter.

Most Illustrious Lord, Having now sufficiently considered the specimens of all those who proclaim themselves skilled contrivers of instruments of war, and that the new inventions and operation of the said instruments are nothing different from those in common use: I shall endeavour, without prejudice to any one else, to explain myself to your Excellency, showing your Lordship my secrets, and then offering them to your best pleasure and approbation to work with effect at opportune moments on all those things which, in part, shall be briefly noted below.

(1) I have a sort of extremely light and strong bridges, adapted to be most easily carried, and with them you may pursue, and at any time flee from the enemy; and others, secure and indestructible by fire and battle, easy and convenient to lift and place. Also methods of burning and destroying those of the enemy.

(2) I know how, when a place is besieged, to take the water out of the trenches, and make endless variety of bridges, and covered ways and ladders, and other machines pertaining to such expeditions.

(3) Item. If, by reason of the height of the banks, or the strength of the place and its position, it is impossible, when besieging a place, to avail oneself of the plan of bombardment, I have methods for destroying every rock or other fortress, even if it were founded on a rock, &c.

(4) Again, I have kinds of mortars, most convenient and easy to carry and with these I can fling small stones almost resembling a storm; and with the smoke of these cause great terror to the enemy, to his great detriment and confusion. . . .

(6) Item. I will make covered chariots, safe and unattackable, which, entering among the enemy with their artillery, there is no body of men so great but they would break them. And behind these, infantry could follow quite unhurt and without any hindrance.

(7) Item. In case of need I will make big guns, mortars, and light ordnance of fine and useful forms, out of the common type. . . .

(10) In time of peace I believe I can give perfect satisfaction and to the equal of any other in architecture and the composition of buildings public and private; and in guiding water from one place to another.

*Item.* I can carry sculpture in marble, bronze, or clay, and also I can do in painting whatever may be done, as well as any other, be he who he may.

And if any of the above-named things seem to any one to be impossible or not feasible, I am most ready to make the experiment in your park, or in whatever place may please your Excellency—to whom I commend myself with the utmost humility, &c.

# Michelangelo Buonarotti *

GIORGIO VASARI

*Another of the great geniuses of many talents was Michelangelo (1474–1563). He was famous as an engineer; as a poet; as a student of anatomy; as sculptor of "David," the "Pietà," and "Moses"; as architect of the dome of the Basilica of St. Peter in Rome; and as painter of the frescoes in the Sistine Chapel. This last task took him some four years to complete. The frescoes, which cover almost an acre of area, show scenes from the Book of Genesis, surrounded by mythological figures and Old Testament prophets. Michelangelo is here described for us by his friend Giorgio Vasari, who was himself a well-known and accomplished painter and architect. Today Vasari is best known, however, for his excellent biographies of the artists of his time. He has left us first-hand accounts of dozen's of the artists of the Renaissance.*

. . . When Michelangelo returned to Rome, he found [Pope] Julius . . . desiring that Michelangelo should paint the ceiling of the chapel. This was a great and difficult labour, and our artist . . . did all he could to excuse himself from undertaking the work, proposing at the same time that it should be confided to Raphael. But the more he refused the more Pope Julius insisted. . . .

. . . The extent of the work compelled Michelangelo to seek assistance; he therefore sent for men to Florence. . . .

These masters having reached the city, the work was begun, and Michelangelo caused them to paint a portion by way of specimen, but what they had done was far from approaching his expectations or fulfilling his purpose, and one morning he determined to destroy the whole of it. He then shut himself up in the chapel, and not only would he never again permit the building to be opened to them, but he likewise refused to see any one of them at his house. . . . Michelangelo then made arrangements for performing the whole work himself, sparing no care nor labour . . . nor would he ever permit himself to be seen, lest he should give occasion for a request to show the work. . . .

When the half was completed, Pope Julius, who had subsequently

* Giorgio Vasari, *Lives of the Most Eminent Painters, Sculptors, and Architects,* vol. 5, London, George Bell and Sons, 1881.

gone more than once to see the work (mounting ladders for that purpose with Michelangelo's aid), and whose temper was hasty and impatient, would insist on having the pictures opened to public view, without waiting until the last touches had been given thereto, and the chapel was no sooner thrown open than all Rome hastened thither. . . . Julius . . . commanded that he should continue the work . . . ; and the master accordingly finished the whole, completing it to perfection in twenty months, without having even the help of a man to grind the colours. It is true that he sometimes complained of the manner in which the Pope hastened forward the work, seeing that he was thereby prevented from giving it the finish which he would have desired to bestow; His Holiness constantly inquiring when it would be completed. On one occasion, therefore, Michelangelo replied, "It will be finished when I shall have done all that I believe required to satisfy Art." "And we command," rejoined the Pontiff, "that you satisfy our wish to have it done quickly"; adding finally, that if it were not at once completed, he would have him, Michelangelo, thrown headlong from the scaffolding.

Hearing this, our artist, who feared the fury of the Pope, and with good cause . . . without taking time to add what was wanting, took down the remainder of the scaffolding, to the great satisfaction of the whole city. . . .

. . . He worked with great inconvenience to himself, having to labour with the face turned upwards, and injuring his eyes so much in the progress of the work, that he could neither read letters nor examine drawings for several months afterwards. . . . I can myself bear full testimony to the effects of such work, having painted the ceilings of five large apartments in the palace of the Duke Cosimo. . . .

Michelangelo found his chief pleasure in the labours of art. . . . For the greater exactitude, he made numerous dissections of the human frame, examining the anatomy of each part. . . . These labours enabled him to complete his works, whether of the pencil or chisel, with perfection, and to give them a grace, a beauty, and an animation, wherein . . . he has surpassed even the antique. . . .

His powers of imagination were such that he was frequently compelled to abandon his purpose, because he could not express by the hand those grand and sublime ideas which he had conceived in his mind, nay, he has spoiled and destroyed many works for this cause; and I know too that some short time before his death he burnt a large number of his designs and sketches . . . that none might see the labours he had endured in his resolve not to fall short of perfection.

# The Movement of the Earth *

Nicolaus Copernicus

> *It was generally believed in medieval and Renaissance Europe that the earth was the center of the universe. But Copernicus (1473–1543), a Polish priest and mathematics teacher, came to believe that the movements of heavenly bodies could be more simply explained. He put forward the theory that the earth and other planets revolve around the sun and explained the rotation of the earth on its axis. On the publication of his thesis in 1543, the year of his death, he was excommunicated for holding beliefs that were felt to be inconsistent with religious views.*

. . . The planetary theories of Ptolemy and most other astronomers, although consistent with the numerical data, seemed . . . to present no small difficulty. For these theories were not adequate unless certain equants were also conceived; it then appeared that a planet moved with uniform velocity neither on its deferent nor about the center of its epicycle. Hence a system of this sort seemed neither sufficiently absolute nor sufficiently pleasing to the mind.

Having become aware of these defects, I often considered whether there could perhaps be found a more reasonable arrangement of circles, from which every apparent inequality would be derived and in which everything would move uniformly about its proper center, as the rule of absolute motion requires. After I had addressed myself to this very difficult and almost insoluble problem, the suggestion at length came to me how it could be solved with fewer and much simpler constructions than were formerly used, if some assumptions (which are called axioms) were granted me. They follow in this order.

1. There is no one center of all the celestial circles or spheres.

2. The center of the earth is not the center of the universe, but only of gravity and of the lunar sphere.

3. All the spheres revolve about the sun as their mid-point, and therefore the sun is the center of the universe.

4. The ratio of the earth's distance from the sun to the height of the firmament is so much smaller than the ratio of the earth's radius to its

* Edward Rosen, ed. and trans., *Three Copernican Treatises*, New York, Columbia University Press, 1939, pp. 57–59.

distance from the sun that the distance from the earth to the sun is imperceptible in comparison with the height of the firmament.

5. Whatever motion appears in the firmament arises not from any motion of the firmament, but from the earth's motion. The earth together with its circumjacent elements performs a complete rotation on its fixed poles in a daily motion, while the firmament and highest heaven abide unchanged.

6. What appear to us as motions of the sun arise not from its motion but from the motion of the earth and our sphere, with which we revolve about the sun like any other planet. The earth has, then, more than one motion.

7. The apparent retrograde and direct motion of the planets arises not from their motion but from the earth's. The motion of the earth alone, therefore, suffices to explain so many apparent inequalities in the heavens.


## The Scientific Method *

FRANCIS BACON

> If the wonders of nature were to be fully explored for the benefit of man, the prejudices and errors of the past would have to be discarded. A call to derive theories from observed facts by what he called the "inductive" method is made by Francis Bacon (1561–1626), an Englishman of the court of Elizabeth I and James I.

Those who have taken upon them to lay down the law of nature as a thing already searched out and understood . . . have therein done philosophy and the sciences great injury. For . . . so they have been effective in quenching and stopping inquiry; and have done more harm by spoiling and putting an end to other men's efforts than good by their own. Those on the other hand who have taken a contrary course, and asserted that absolutely nothing can be known . . . have neither started from true principles nor rested in the just conclusion. . . . The more ancient of the Greeks (whose writings are lost) took up with better judgment a position

* James Spedding, Robert L. Ellis, Douglas D. Heath, eds., *The Works of Francis Bacon*, vol. 8, Boston, Taggard & Thompson, 1863.

between these two extremes . . . ; and though frequently and bitterly complaining of the difficulty of inquiry and the obscurity of things, and like impatient horses champing the bit, they did not the less follow up their object and engage with Nature; thinking (it seems) that this very question,—namely, whether or no anything can be known,—was to be settled not by arguing, but by trying. . . .

Now my method, though hard to practise, is easy to explain; and it is this. I propose to establish progressive stages of certainty. The evidence of the sense, helped and guarded by a certain process of correction, I retain. But the mental operation which follows the act of sense I for the most part reject; and instead of it I open and lay out a new and certain path for the mind to proceed in, starting directly from the simple sensuous perception. . . . There remains but one course for the recovery of a sound and healthy condition,—namely, that the entire work of the understanding be commenced afresh, and the mind itself be from the very outset not left to take its own course, but guided at every step; . . .

There remains simple experience; which, if taken as it comes, is called accident; if sought for, experiment. . . . But the true method of experience . . . first lights the candle, and then by means of the candle shows the way; commencing as it does with experience duly ordered and digested, not bungling or erratic, and from it educing axioms, and from established axioms again new experiments; even as it was not without order and method that the divine word operated on the created mass. Let men therefore cease to wonder that the course of science is not wholly run, seeing that they have gone altogether astray; either leaving and abandoning experience entirely, or losing their way in it and wandering round and round as in a labyrinth; whereas a method rightly ordered leads by an unbroken route through the woods of experience to the open ground of axioms. . . .

## Galileo Galilei *

> Teaching mathematics at Pisa, Padua, and Florence, Galileo (1564–1642) often found himself in trouble with the authorities for asserting "laws of Nature" over the views of

* The Accusation Condemnation & Abjuration of Galileo Galilei before the Holy Inquisition at Rome 1633, London, R. Carlile, 1819.

*medieval scholastic philosophy. Hearing of the invention of the telescope, Galileo made one for himself and with it discovered the sun's spots, Saturn's ring, Jupiter's moons, and the starry nature of the Milky Way. His observations convinced him of the truth of the theories of Copernicus. He was twice obliged to deny these views, due to the religious prejudices aroused by the Reformation struggle, which was then at its peak. We hear the accusation made against him in 1633, and his submission.*

. . . Whereas you, Galileo . . . being 70 years of age, had a charge brought against you in the year 1615, in this Holy Office, that you held as true, an erroneous opinion held by many; namely, *that the Sun is the centre of the World, and immoveable,* and that the *Earth* moves even with a *diurnal motion:* also that you had certain scholars into whom you instilled the same doctrine. . . . Afterwards when a copy of a writing in the form of an Epistle, written by you to a certain late scholar of yours, was presented to you, (it following the hypothesis of Copernicus) you stood up for, and defended certain propositions in it, which are against the true sense, and authority of Holy Scripture.

But whereas we have thought fit in the interim to proceed gently with you, it has been agreed upon in the Holy Congregation . . . on the 25th day of Feb. 1616, that the most Eminent Lord Cardinal Bellarmine should enjoin you entirely to recede from the aforesaid false doctrine; and, on your refusal, it was commanded by the Commissary of the Holy Office, that you should recant the said false doctrine, and should not teach it to others, nor defend it, nor dispute concerning it: to which command if you would not submit, that you should be cast into prison: and in order to put in execution the same decree, on the following day you were gently admonished in the Palace before the abovesaid most eminent Lord Cardinal Bellarmine . . . ; and whereas you promised obedience, you were at that time dismissed.

And to the end, such a *pernicious doctrine* may be entirely extirpated away, and spread no farther, to the grievous detriment of the Catholic verity, a decree was issued by the Holy Congregation *indicis,* prohibiting the printing of books, which treat of such sort of doctrine, which was therein pronounced false, and altogether contrary to Holy and Divine Scripture. And the same book has since appeared at Florence, published in the year last past, the inscription of which shewed that you were its author, as the title was, *"A Dialogue of Galileo Galilei,"* concerning the two principal systems of the World, the Ptolemaic and the Copernican, as the Holy Congregation, recognizing from the expression of the aforesaid book, that the false opinion concerning the motion of the Earth, and the immobility of the Sun prevailed daily more and more: the aforesaid book was diligently examined, when we openly discovered the transgression of the aforesaid command, before injoined you; seeing that in the same book you had resumed and defended the aforesaid opinion already condemned, and in your presence declared to be erroneous, because in the said book by various circumlocutions, you earnestly endeavour to persuade, that it is left by you undecided, and at the least probable which must necessarily be a grievous error, since an opinion can by no means be probable, which hath already been declared and adjudged contrary to divine Scripture.

Wherefore you have by our authority been summoned to this our Holy Office, in which being examined you have on oath acknowledged the said book was written and printed by you. And have also confessed, that about ten or twelve years ago, after the injunction had been given you as above, that the said book was begun to be written by you. Also that you petitioned for licence to publish it, but without signifying to those who gave you such licence, that it had been prohibited you, not by any means to maintain, defend, or teach such doctrine. . . .

And whereas it appeared to us, that the whole truth was not expressed by you, respecting your intention: we have judged it necessary to come to a more accurate examination of the business. . . . Wherefore we having maturely considered the merits of your cause, together with your abovesaid confessions, and defence, and are come to the underwritten definitive sentence against you.

Having invoked the most holy name of our Lord Jesus Christ . . . we, by this our definitive sentence, by the advice and judgment of the most Reverend Masters of Holy Theology . . . on the one part, and you, Galileo Galilei defendant, question examined, and having confessed, as above on the other part, we say, judge and declare, by the present processional writing, you, the abovesaid Galileo, on account of those things, which have been adduced in the written process, and which you have confessed, as above, that you have rendered yourself liable to the suspicion of heresy by this office, that is, you have believed and maintained a false doctrine, and contrary to the Holy and Divine Scriptures, namely, that the Sun is the centre of the orb of the Earth, and that it does not move from the East to the West, and that the Earth moves and is not the centre of the World;

and that this position may be held and defended as a probable opinion, after it had been declared and defined to be contrary to Holy Scriptures, and consequently that you have incurred all the censures and penalties of the Holy Canons, and other Constitutions general and particular, enacted and promulgated against such delinquents from which it is our pleasure to absolve you, on condition that first, with sincere heart and faith unfeigned, you abjure, execrate, and detest the above errors and heresies. . . .

But that your grievous and pernicious error and transgression may not remain altogether unpunished, and that you may hereafter be more cautious, serving as an example to others, that they may abstain from the like offences, we decree, that the book of the Dialogue of Galileo, be prohibited by public edict, *and we condemn yourself to the prison of this Holy Office, to a time to be limited by our discretion; and we enjoin under the title of salutary penitence, that during three years to come you recite once a week the seven penitential Psalms,* reserving to ourselves the power of moderating, changing, or taking away entirely, or in part, the aforesaid penalties and penitences.

## THE ABJURATION OF GALILEO

I, Galileo Galilei, son of the late Vincent Galilei, a Florentine, of the age of 70, appearing personally in judgment, and being on my knees in the presence of you, most eminent and most reverend Lords Cardinals of the Universal Christian Commonwealth, Inquisitors General against heretical depravity, having before my eyes the holy Gospels, on which I now lay my hands, swear that I have always believed, and now believe, and God helping, that I shall for the future always believe, whatever the Holy Catholic and Apostolic Roman Church holds, preaches, and teaches. But because this Holy Office had enjoined me by precept, entirely to relinquish the false dogma which maintains that the sun is the centre of the world, and immoveable, and that the Earth is not the centre, and moves; not to hold, defend, or teach by any means, or by writing, the aforesaid false doctrine; and after it had been notified to me that the aforesaid doctrine is repugnant to the Holy Scripture, I have written and printed a book, in which I treat of the same doctrine already condemned, and adduce reasons with great efficacy in favour of it, not offering any solution of them; therefore I have been adjudged and vehemently suspected of heresy, namely, that I maintained and believed that the Sun is the centre of the world, and immoveable, and that the Earth is not the centre, and moves.

Therefore, being willing to take out of the minds of your eminences, and of every Catholic Christian, this vehement suspicion of right conceived against me, I with sincere heart, and faith unfeigned, abjure, execrate, and detest the aforesaid errors and heresies, and generally every other sect contrary to the abovesaid Holy Church; and I swear that I will never any more hereafter say or assert, by speech or writing, any thing through which the like suspicion may be had of me; but if I shall know any one heretical, or suspected of heresy, I will denounce him to this Holy Office, or to the Inquisitor, and Ordinary of the place in which I shall be. I moreover swear and promise, that I will fulfil and observe entirely all the penitences which have been imposed upon me, or which shall be imposed by this Holy Office. But if it shall happen that I shall go contrary (which God avert) to any of my words, promises, protestations, and oaths, I subject myself to all the penalties and punishments, which, by the Holy Canons, and other Constitutions, general and particular, have been enacted and promulgated against such delinquents: So help me God, and his Holy Gospels, on which I now lay my hands.

I, the aforesaid Galileo Galilei, have abjured, sworn, promised, and have bound myself as above, and in the fidelity of those with my own hands, and have subscribed to this present writing of my abjuration, which I have recited word by word. At Rome, in the Convent of Minerva, this 22d of June, of the year 1633.

I, Galileo Galilei, have abjured as above, with my own hand.

## A Discourse on Method *

RENÉ DESCARTES

> Slowly the idea won support that observation and reason, rather than revelation and authority, must be the basis for belief. Descartes (1596–1650), a contemporary of the English Bacon and the Italian Galileo, speaks in France.

Instead of the great number of precepts on which Logic is composed, I believed that the four following would prove sufficient for me. . . .

* René Descartes, "A Discourse on Method," Charles D. Warner, ed., *Library of the World's Best Literature*, vol. 11, New York, The International Society, 1896.

The *first* was never to accept anything for true which I did not clearly know to be such; that is to say, carefully to avoid precipitancy and prejudice, and to comprise nothing in my judgment than what was presented to my mind so clearly and distinctly as to exclude all ground for doubt.

The *second,* to divide each of the difficulties under examination into as many parts as possible, and as might be necessary for its adequate solution.

The *third,* to conduct my thoughts in such an order that, by commencing with objects the simplest and easiest to know, I might ascend by little and little, and as it were step by step, to the knowledge of the more complex; . . .

And the *last,* to make enumerations so complete, and reviews so general, that it might be assured that nothing was omitted.

[Descartes determines to reject as false all the truths that he had previously taken for granted.] But immediately upon this I observed that whilst I thus wished to think that all was false, it was absolutely necessary that I, who thus thought, should be somewhat; and as I observed that this truth,—"*I think, hence I am,*"—was so certain and of such evidence that no ground of doubt, however extravagant, could be alleged by the skeptics capable of shaking it, I concluded that I might without scruple accept it as the first principle of the philosophy of which I was in search. . . .

. . . As I observed that in the words "*I think, hence I am,*" there is nothing at all which gives me assurance of their truth beyond this, that I see very clearly that in order to think it is necessary to exist,—I concluded that I might take, as a general rule, the principle that all the things which we very clearly and distinctly conceive are true; only observing however that there is some difficulty in rightly determining the objects which we distinctly conceive.

## *The Circulation of the Blood* *

WILLIAM HARVEY

> *While Copernicus, Galileo, and others were observing the heavens, another band of questioners were examining the*

* William Harvey, "On the Motion of the Heart and Blood in Animals," in Charles W. Eliot, ed., *The Harvard Classics,* vol. 38, New York, P. F. Collier & Son Company, 1910 (translated by Robert Willis).

*human body. In 1543 Andreas Vesalius of Brussels described the human body with great accuracy. At about the same time Michael Servetus in Spain claimed that blood moved from heart to lungs and to other parts of the body. But it was left to William Harvey (1578–1657) in England to describe, in 1628, the constant and circular motion of the blood.*

When I first gave my mind to vivisections, as a means of discovering the motions and uses of the heart, and sought to discover these from actual inspection, and not from the writings of others, I found the task so truly arduous, so full of difficulties, that I was almost tempted to think . . . that the motion of the heart was only to be comprehended by God. . . .

At length . . . making frequent inspection of many and various animals, and collating numerous observations, I thought that I had attained to the truth. . . . From that time I have not hesitated to expose my views upon these subjects, not only in private to my friends, but also in public, in my anatomical lectures. . . .

These views as usual, pleased some more, others less; some chid and calumniated me, and laid it to me as a crime that I had dared to depart from the precepts and opinions of all anatomists; others desired further explanations of the novelties, which they said were both worthy of consideration, and might perchance be found of signal use. At length, yielding to the requests of my friends . . . I have moved to commit these things to the press, in order that all may be enabled to form an opinion both of me and my labours. . . .

. . . First of all, the auricle contracts, and in the course of its contraction forces the blood . . . into the ventricle, which, being filled, the heart raises itself straightaway, makes all its fibres tense, contracts the ventricles, and performs a beat, by which it immediately sends the blood supplied to it by the auricle into the arteries. The right ventricle sends its charge into the lungs. . . . The left ventricle sends its charge into the aorta, and through this by the arteries to the body at large. . . .

The motion of the heart, then, is entirely of this description, and the one action of the heart is the transmission of the blood and its distribution, by means of the arteries, to the very extremities of the body; so that the pulse which we feel in the arteries is nothing more than the impulse of the blood derived from the heart. . . .

. . . But what remains to be said upon the quantity and source of the blood which thus passes is of a character so novel and unheard-of that I not only fear injury to myself from the envy of a few, but I tremble lest I have mankind at large for my enemies, so much doth wont and custom become a second nature. Doctrine once sown strikes deep its root, and respect for antiquity influences all men. Still the die is cast, and my trust is in my love of truth. . . . When I surveyed my mass of evidence . . . I frequently and seriously bethought me, and long revolved in my mind, what might be the quantity of blood which was transmitted, in how short a time its passage might be effected, and the like. But not finding it possible that this could be supplied . . . without the veins on the one hand becoming drained, and the arteries on the other getting ruptured through the excessive charge of blood, unless the blood should somehow find its way from the arteries into the veins, and so return to the right side of the heart, I began to think whether there might not be a *motion, as it were, in a circle.* . . .

As the blood vessels . . . are the canals and agents that transport the blood, they are of two kinds . . . ; and this not be reason of there being two sides of the body, as Aristotle has it, but because of the difference of office, not, as is commonly said, in consequence of any diversity of structure, for in many animals, as I have said, the vein does not differ from the artery in the thickness of its walls, but solely in virtue of their distinct functions and uses. A vein and an artery, both styled veins by the ancients, and that not without reason, as Galen has remarked, for the artery is the vessel which carries the blood from the heart to the body at large, the vein of the present day bringing it back from the general system to the heart; the former is the conduit from, the latter the channel to, the heart; the latter contains the cruder, effete blood, rendered unfit for nutrition; the former transmits the digested, perfect, peculiarly nutritive fluid.

# PART THREE

# The Age of
##    Religious Controversy

For a century and a half, from 1500 to 1650, religious controversy dominated European thinking. The bitterness of the struggle left traces that are still visible in some places today. Men of today may look back to it as an age of bigotry, but in its own time it seemed an age of sincerity about the most important things in the universe: God, Christ, salvation or eternal damnation of the soul, the nature of truth here, now, and in all eternity. Men were willing to die for their version of the Christian faith, and they killed and tortured to save the souls of others. Catholic, Lutheran, Calvinist, and Anglican oppressed each other, and all turned in fury on those suspected of witchcraft. Every political, economic, social, and scientific question became entangled in religious issues. The period culminated in the murderous Thirty Years War (1618–1648), which devastated Germany. The war involved every important European state except England, which was absorbed in a revolution that led to a dictatorship by a religious minority.

# *Ridicule of the Pope* *

Desiderius Erasmus

> For many years many Christians, particularly those in north-
> ern Europe, had criticized the popes. In 1514 on the Paris
> stage an anonymous satire was directed at Pope Julius II for
> his taking part in military expeditions to defend the church's
> lands in central Italy. Erasmus of Rotterdam was suspected
> of being the author (although this is still uncertain), since
> he often used satire to attempt to correct political and reli-
> gious practices of which he disapproved. Such gentle wea-
> pons as wit and humor soon disappeared as the issues became
> deadly serious.

## JULIUS II. EXCLUSUS. A DIALOGUE

*Persons.*—Pope Julius II.; Familiar Spirit; St. Peter.

### *Scene.*—Gate of Heaven.

*Julius.* What the devil is this? The gates not opened! Something is
wrong with the lock.

*Spirit.* You have brought the wrong key perhaps. The key of your
money-box will not open the door here. You should have brought both
keys. This is the key of power, not of knowledge.

*Julius.* I never had any but this, and I don't see the use of another.
Hey there, porter! I say, are you asleep or drunk?

*Peter.* Well that the gates are adamant, or this fellow would have
broken in. He must be some giant, or conqueror. Heaven, what a stench!
Who are you? What do you want here?

*Julius.* Open the gates, I say. Why is there no one to receive me?

*Peter.* Here is fine talk. Who are you, I say?

*Julius.* You know this key, I suppose, and the triple crown, and the
pallium?

*Peter.* I see a key, but not the key which Christ gave to me a long
time since. The crown? I don't recognise the crown. No heathen king
ever wore such a thing, certainly none who expected to be let in here. The

---

* James A. Froude, ed., *Life and Letters of Erasmus*, London, Longmans, Green
& Co. Ltd., 1894.

pallium is strange too. And see, there are marks on all three of that rogue and impostor Simon Magus, that I turned out of office.

*Julius.* Enough of this. I am Julius the Ligurian, P.M., as you can see by the letters if you can read.

*Peter.* P.M.! What is that? Pestis Maxima [Greatest Plague]?

*Julius.* Pontifex Maximus, you rascal.

*Peter.* If you are three times Maximus, if you are Mercury Trismegistus, you can't come in unless you are Optimus too.

*Julius.* Impertinence! You, who have been no more than Sanctus all these ages—and I Sanctissimus, Sanctissimus Dominus, Sanctitas, Holiness itself, with Bulls to show it.

*Peter.* Is there no difference between being Holy and being called Holy? Ask your flatterers who called you these fine names to give you admittance. Let me look at you a little closer. Hum! Signs of impiety in plenty, and none of the other thing. . . .

❄

*Julius.* Will you make an end of your talking and open the gates? We will break them down else. You see these followers of mine.

*Peter.* I see a lot of precious rogues, but they won't break in here.

*Julius.* Make an end, I say, or I will fling a thunderbolt at you. I will excommunicate you. I have done as much to kings before this. Here are the Bulls ready.

*Peter.* Thunderbolts! Bulls! I beseech you, we had no thunderbolts or Bulls from Christ.

*Julius.* You shall feel them if you don't behave yourself. . . .

❄

*Peter.* You must show your merits first; no admission without merits.

*Julius.* What do you mean by merits?

*Peter.* Have you taught true doctrine?

*Julius.* Not I. I have been too busy fighting. There are monks to look after doctrine, if that is of any consequence. . . .

❄

*Julius.* Then you won't open the gates?

*Peter.* Sooner to anyone than to such as you. We are not of your communion in this place. You have an army of sturdy rogues behind you, you have money, and you are a famous architect. Go build a paradise of your own, and fortify it, lest the devils break in on you.

*Julius.* I will do better than that. I will wait a few months till I have a larger force, and then if you don't give in I will take your place by storm. They are making fine havoc just now. I shall soon have sixty thousand ghosts behind me.

*Peter.* Oh, wretched man! Oh, miserable Church! You, Spirit, I must speak with you; I can say no more to this monster. Are the bishops generally like this one?

*Spirit.* A good part of them. But he is the top, far and away.

*Peter.* Was it you who tempted him to commit all these crimes?

*Spirit.* Not I. He went too fast. I must have had wings to keep abreast of him.

*Peter.* I am not surprised that so few apply here now for admission, when the Church has such rulers. Yet there must be good in the world, too, when such a sink of iniquity can be honoured, merely because he bears the name of Pope.

*Spirit.* That is the real truth—But my master beckons to me and lifts his stick. Adieu!

## *The Sale of Indulgences* *

### Johann Tetzel

> *Under Catholic doctrine a confessed and repentant sinner was saved from eternal damnation, but the consequences of his sin must still be erased through suffering in Purgatory. For good works the church would sometimes grant indulgences, which would lessen the period of suffering after death. Too often, ignorant persons assumed that such an indulgence was a passport to Heaven and would offer money gifts to secure them. On the occasion of the rebuilding of the Basilica of St. Peter at Rome, the pope asked for donations, and to collect these in Germany he appointed a friar named Johann Tetzel. Tetzel's preaching about indulgences in 1515 was not in accord with church doctrine, and it created a storm of criticism. The criticism soon was extended*

* University of Pennsylvania, *Translations and Reprints from the Original Sources of European History,* vol. 2, no. 6, Philadelphia, 1902.

*to other aspects of the church and finally broadened into
direct attacks on the church. We hear an extract from one
of Tetzel's sermons.*

. . . Know that the life of man upon earth is a constant struggle. We
have to fight against the flesh, the world and the devil, who are always
seeking to destroy the soul. In sin we are conceived,—alas! what bonds of
sin encompass us, and how difficult and almost impossible it is to attain
to the gate of salvation without divine aid; since He causes us to be saved,
not by virtue of the good works which we accomplish, but through His
divine mercy; it is necessary then to put on the armor of God.

You may obtain letters of safe conduct from the vicar of our Lord
Jesus Christ, by means of which you are able to liberate your soul from
the hands of the enemy, and convey it by means of contrition and confession, safe and secure from all pains of Purgatory, into the happy kingdom. For know that in these letters are stamped and engraven all the
merits of Christ's passion there laid bare. Consider, that for each and every
mortal sin it is necessary to undergo seven years of penitence after confession and contrition, either in this life or in Purgatory.

How many mortal sins are committed in a day, how many in a week,
how many in a month, how many in a year, how many in the whole course
of life! They are well-nigh numberless, and those that commit them must
needs suffer endless punishment in the burning pains of Purgatory.

But with these confessional letters you will be able at any time in life
to obtain full indulgence for all penalties imposed upon you, in all cases
except the four reserved to the Apostolic See. Therefore throughout your
whole life, whenever you wish to make confession, you may receive the
same remission, except in cases reserved to the Pope, and afterwards, at
the hour of death, a full indulgence as to all penalties and sins, and your
share of all spiritual blessings that exist in the church militant and all its
members.

Do you not know that when it is necessary for anyone to go to Rome,
or undertake any other dangerous journey, he takes his money to a
broker and gives a certain per cent—five or six or ten—in order that at
Rome or elsewhere he may receive again his funds intact, by means of
the letters of this same broker? Are you not willing, then, for the fourth
part of a florin, to obtain these letters, by virtue of which you may bring,
not your money, but your divine and immortal soul safe and sound into
the land of Paradise?

# The Ninety-five Theses *

MARTIN LUTHER

> *In the forefront of Tetzel's critics was an Augustinian monk named Martin Luther. But to Luther, the issue was far greater than the question of the misuse of indulgences. He had arrived at ninety-five principles, or "theses," which he now proposed for open debate. As was the custom in medieval times, he posted the announcement of these on the church door of Wittenberg, Germany, on October 31, 1517. The theses were widely read and approved by sympathetic Germans, many of whom opposed the movement of funds to Rome.*

In the desire and with the purpose of elucidating the truth, a disputation will be held on the underwritten propositions at Wittenberg, under the presidency of the Reverend Father Martin Luther, Monk of the Order of St. Augustine. He therefore asks those who cannot be present and discuss the subject with us orally, to do so by letter in their absence. In the name of our Lord Jesus Christ. Amen.

1. Our Lord and Master Jesus Christ in saying "Repent ye," etc., intended that the whole life of believers should be penitence.

2. This word cannot be understood as sacramental penance, that is, of the confession and satisfaction which are performed under the ministry of priests.

3. It does not, however, refer solely to inward penitence; nay such inward penitence is naught, unless it outwardly produces various mortifications of the flesh.

4. The penalty thus continues as long as the hatred of self (that is, true inward penitence); namely, till our entrance into the kingdom of heaven.

5. The Pope has neither the will nor the power to remit any penalties except those which he has imposed by his own authority, or by that of the canons.

6. The Pope has no power to remit any guilt, except by declaring and warranting it to have been remitted by God; or at most by remitting cases reserved for himself; in which cases, if his power were despised, guilt would certainly remain.

* University of Pennsylvania, *Translations and Reprints from the Original Sources of European History*, vol. 2, no. 6, Philadelphia, 1902.

7. Certainly God remits no man's guilt without at the same time subjecting him, humbled in all things, to the authority of his representative the priest. . . .

20. Therefore the Pope, when he speaks of the plenary remission of all penalties, does not mean really of all, but only of those imposed by himself.

21. Thus those preachers of indulgences are in error who say that by the indulgences of the Pope a man is freed and saved from all punishment.

22. For in fact he remits to souls in purgatory no penalty which they would have had to pay in this life according to the canons.

23. If any entire remission of all penalties can be granted to any one it is certain that it is granted to none but the most perfect, that is to very few.

24. Hence, the greater part of the people must needs be deceived by this indiscriminate and high-sounding promise of release from penalties.

25. Such power over purgatory as the Pope has in general, such has every bishop in his own diocese, and every parish priest in his own parish, in particular.

26. The Pope acts most rightly in granting remission to souls not by the power of the keys (which is of no avail in this case) but by the way of intercession. . . .

28. It is certain that, when the money rattles in the chest, avarice and gain may be increased, but the effect of the intercession of the Church depends on the will of God alone. . . .

32. Those who believe that, through letters of pardon, they are made sure of their own salvation will be eternally damned along with their teachers. . . .

37. Every true Christian, whether living or dead, has a share in all the benefits of Christ and of the Church, given him by God, even without letters of pardon. . . .

41. Apostolic pardons ought to be proclaimed with caution, lest the people should falsely suppose that they are placed before other good works of charity.

42. Christians should be taught that it is not the wish of the Pope that the buying of pardons should be in any way compared to works of mercy.

43. Christians should be taught that he who gives to a poor man, or lends to a needy man, does better than if he bought pardons. . . .

50. Christians should be taught that, if the Pope were acquainted with the exactions of the Preachers of pardons, he would prefer that the Basilica

of St. Peter should be burnt to ashes rather than that it should be built up with the skin, flesh, and bones of his sheep. . . .

52. Vain is the hope of salvation through letters of pardon, even if a commissary—nay, the Pope himself—were to pledge his own soul for them. . . .

73. As the Pope justly thunders against those who use any kind of contrivance to the injury of the traffic in pardons.

74. Much more is it his intention to thunder against those who, under the pretext of pardons, use contrivances to the injury of holy charity and of truth. . . .

76. We affirm on the contrary that Papal pardons cannot take away even the least of venial sins, as regards its guilt. . . .

81. This license in the preaching of pardons makes it no easy thing, even for learned men, to protect the reverence due to the Pope against the calumnies, or, at all events, the keen questioning of the laity.


## Defiance of the Pope *

MARTIN LUTHER

> Luther's Ninety-five Theses immediately aroused a contro-
> versy in which almost everyone in Germany, and soon in
> other parts of Europe, took sides. By 1521 Luther had been
> declared a heretic. When summoned to recant or be declared
> an outlaw, he replied, "Here I stand. I cannot do otherwise."
> He went into hiding, but continued to write widely-read
> pamphlets against many beliefs, practices, and customs of
> the Catholic Church. Earlier, in 1519, he wrote this letter
> to Pope Leo X.

Necessity once more compels me, the most unworthy and despicable creature upon earth, to address your Holiness. Therefore, would you, in Christ's stead, graciously bend your fatherly ear to the petition of me, your poor sheep. The esteemed Karl von Miltitz, your Holiness's treasurer, has been here and has complained bitterly to the elector Frederick of my

* Margaret A. Currie, The Letters of Martin Luther, London, Macmillan and Company, 1900.

insolence toward the Roman Church and your Holiness, and has demanded a recantation from me.

When I heard this, I felt aggrieved that all my efforts to do honor to the Roman Church had been so misrepresented, and considered foolhardiness and deliberate malice by the head of the Church.

But what shall I do, most holy father? I am quite at sea, being unable to bear the weight of your Holiness's wrath or to escape from it. I am asked to recant and withdraw my theses. If by so doing I could accomplish the end desired, I would not hesitate a moment.

But my writings have become far too widely known and have taken root in too many hearts—beyond my highest expectations—now to be summarily withdrawn. Nay, our German nation, with its cultured and learned men, in the bloom of an intellectual reawakening, understands this question so thoroughly that, on this account, I must avoid even the appearance of recantation, much as I honor and esteem the Roman Church in other respects. For such a recantation would only bring it into still worse repute and make every one speak against it.

It is those, O holy father, who have done the greatest injury to the Church in Germany, and whom I have striven to oppose—those who, by their foolish preaching and their insatiable greed, have brought your name into bad odor, sullying the sanctity of the sacred chair and making it an offense. It is those who, in revenge for my having rendered their godless endeavors abortive, accuse me to your Holiness as the originator of their plots. Now, holy father, I declare before God that I have never had the slightest wish to attack the power of the Roman Church or your Holiness in any way, or even to injure it through cunning. Yes, I declare openly that there is nothing in heaven or on earth which can come before the power of this Church, except Jesus Christ alone—Lord over all. Therefore do not believe those malicious slanderers who speak otherwise of Luther. I also gladly promise to let the question of indulgences drop and be silent, if my opponents restrain their boastful, empty talk. In addition, I shall publish a pamphlet exhorting the people to honor the Holy Church, and not ascribe such foolish misdeeds to her, or imitate my own severity, in which I have gone too far toward her, and by so doing I trust these divisions may be healed. For this one thing I desired, that the Roman Church, our mother, should not be sullied through the greed of strangers, nor the people led into error, being taught to regard love as of less importance than the indulgences. All else, seeing it neither helps nor injures, I regard of less importance.

If I can do anything more in the matter I am willing to do it.

# Economic and Political Issues *

ULRICH VON HUTTEN

> Not all those who took part in the religious dispute were interested in dogma. Many Germans resented the large church landholdings and the flow of German donations to Rome. Some of the nobility saw in the dispute an opportunity to oppose the political power of the Holy Roman emperor in Germany. Ulrich von Hutten, a prominent German nobleman, writes in these terms.

. . . We see that there is no gold and almost no silver in our German land. What little may perhaps be left is drawn away daily by the new schemes invented by the council of the most holy members of the Roman curia. What is thus squeezed out of us is put to the most shameful uses. Would you know, dear Germans, what employment I have myself seen that they make at Rome of our money? It does not lie idle! Leo the Tenth gives a part to nephews and relatives (these are so numerous that there is a proverb at Rome, "As thick as Leo's relations"). A portion is consumed by so many most reverend cardinals (of which the holy father created no less than one and thirty in a single day), as well as to support innumerable referendaries, auditors, prothonotaries, abbreviators, apostolic secretaries, chamberlains and a variety of officials forming the élite of the great head church. These in turn draw after them, at untold expense, copyists, beadles, messengers, servants, scullions, mule drivers. . . . They maintain dogs, horses, monkeys, long-tailed apes, and many more such creatures for their pleasure. They construct houses all of marble. They have precious stones, are clothed in purple and fine linen, and dine sumptuously, frivolously indulging themselves in every species of luxury. In short, a vast number of the worst of men are supported in Rome in idle indulgence by means of our money. . . .

Now, if all these who devastate Germany, and continue to devour everything, might once be driven out, and an end made of their unbridled plundering, swindling and deception, with which the Romans have overwhelmed us, we should again have gold and silver in sufficient quantities, and should be able to keep it. And then this money, in such supply and value as it may be present, might be put to better uses, for example: to put on foot great armaments and extend the boundaries of the Empire;

* University of Pennsylvania, *Translations and Reprints from the Original Sources of European History*, vol. 2, no. 6, Philadelphia, 1902.

also that the Turks may be conquered, if this seems desirable; that many who, because of poverty, steal and rob may honestly earn their living once more, and that those who otherwise must starve may receive from the state contributions to mitigate their need; that scholars may be helped, and the study of the arts and sciences and of good literature be advanced; above all that every virtue may receive its reward; want be relieved at home; indolence banished, and deceit killed.

## A Papal Commission Reports on Church Abuses *

> *Some of the criticism of the Catholic Church by Lutherans was recognized as deserved, but the authorities did not move rapidly enough to still the rising storm. But by the 1530's the rise of Lutheranism and other Protestant groups (such as those led by John Calvin and Huldreich Zwingli) led to the creation of a reform group within the Catholic Church. The goal of these men was to reform the church and rid it of abuses without breaking with it. With the election of Paul III as pope (1534) and the organization of the Society of Jesus, or Jesuits (1540), the reform movement gained momentum. In 1537 Pope Paul appointed a commission of nine cardinals to report to him on abuses that they found within the church. We read an excerpt from their report.*

You [the Pope] have summoned us to yourself, unskilled as we are and unequal to such a great task . . . and with the most serious words you have enjoined that we collect all these abuses and report them to you. . . .

(1) The first abuse is that in the ordination of clerics and even of priests . . . no diligence is employed: the most ignorant men, those born of the most worthless family, reprobates, and adolescents are admitted to Holy Orders and even to the priesthood. . . . In some places the divine worship has not only diminished, but is even already extinct. . . . Your Holiness should not allow anyone to be ordained except by his bishop, or with the permission of his bishop or of the deputies in the city: in addition, each bishop should have in his diocese a teacher to instruct clerics in minor orders in both letters and morals. . . .

* B. J. Kidd, ed., *Documents Illustrative of the Continental Reformation*, Oxford, Clarendon Press, 1921 (translated by Peter Ford).

(2) Another abuse of great seriousness is in the granting of ecclesiastical benefices, especially of parishes, and above all of bishoprics, in which it has become customary that the persons to whom benefices are granted are provided for, and not the flock of Christ and the Church. Therefore benefices, parishes, and especially bishoprics should be granted . . . to holy and learned men: . . .

(3) When benefices are conferred on or granted to others, another abuse has crept in by the fixing of payments on their fruits: . . . A great abuse which should be reformed is the granting of payments to rich clerics, who can live quite comfortably and honestly on the revenues they already have.

(4) Another such abuse is in the exchanging of benefices by simoniacal bargains with no consideration except for profit.

(5) . . . Although the law of the Church prohibits the bequeathing of benefices by will, because they belong not to the testator but to the Church . . . human . . . ingenuity finds many ways of evading this law. . . . .

. . . There is an ancient law . . . that the sons of priests should not inherit the benefices of their parents . . . however (as we hear) dispensations are being given in regard to this venerable law. . . .

(6) Another abuse is in regard to expectations . . . of benefices whereby the occasion is presented that the death of another might be desired and eagerly listened for. . . .

. . . Bishops . . . and curates should not absent themselves from their churches and parishes, except for some serious reason. . . . What more wretched sight is there visible to a Christian man traveling through the Christian world than this desertion of churches? Almost all pastors have left their flocks, almost all [parishes] have been entrusted to hirelings. . . .

(9) Another abuse is that so many . . . cardinals absent themselves from this Curia, and perform no part of their duties. . . .

These, Holy Father, are the abuses . . . which would seem to us ought to be corrected. . . . We have satisfied our consciences, not without a great hope that under your leadership we may see the Church of God purged, beautiful as a dove . . . with the eternal memory of your name. You have taken the name of Paul: we hope that you will imitate the love of Paul: chosen as he was as the vessel to carry the name of Christ to the Gentiles: we hope that you have been chosen, that you might restore the name of Christ which has been so forgotten by the people and us clergy.

# Reform Decrees of the Council of Trent *

> *Far-reaching reforms within the Catholic Church were decreed by the Council of Trent, which met three times between 1545 and 1563. These reforms helped enable Catholicism to retain its strength in Italy, Spain, France, southern Germany, and Poland. But the lands to the north and west were permanently lost to Lutheranism, Calvinism, and other Protestant groups. The religious unity that had marked Europe throughout the Middle Ages was shattered.*

In order that the faithful public may approach the sacraments and accept them with greater reverence and more soulful devotion, this holy Council decrees to all bishops that when they, themselves, are administering the sacraments, they shall first explain to the people, in a way that they can understand, the effectiveness of the sacraments and their usefulness; and also the bishops shall make certain that their parish priests shall do likewise, piously and carefully, and they shall take pains with the ignorant, so that if it is necessary, in order to be better understood, they may make their explanations in the everyday dialect of the people. In like manner, in writing the catechism, the manner of the separate sacraments, as prescribed by this holy Council, may be presented in the people's dialect in order that all the people may be cared for by such exposition by the bishops and the priests. And also for the ritual of the Mass, or the celebration of other holy ceremonies, or the observance of holy days, the sacred precepts shall be explained in the same ordinary everyday language of the people, in order that these may be impressed on the hearts of the people (without confusing them by useless unrelated discussions), so that they [the people] may come to seek further to know the laws of the Lord.

Hopefully those who undertake the bishop's ministry will realize that they are called on not to serve their own convenience, nor to wealth or luxury, but to lives of labor and care for the glory of God. It is not to be doubted that the rest of the faithful will be more easily excited toward religion and innocence if they see those above them in authority intent not on worldly things but on the saving of souls and a heavenly home. Turning its mind especially to the restoring of ecclesiastical discipline, this

* *Canones et decreta sacrosancti concilii Tridentini*, Venice, 1566 (an original translation by James H. Hanscom).

holy Council cautions all bishops so to live, with due meditation, that they can bring together truth and behavior as a kind of perpetual example of frugality, modesty, and decency, and especially of that holy humility that so strongly commends men to God. Therefore, following the example set by our fathers at the Council of Carthage, it is ordered that bishops shall content themselves not only with modest household furniture and simple food, but with regard to the rest of their manner of living and to their whole house, so that nothing appears that is alien to this holy institution of the Church and that does not show simplicity, zeal for God, and contempt for the vanities. It is absolutely forbidden for bishops to enrich their relations or servants out of the Church's revenues, since the rules of the apostles prohibit giving to one's relations the goods of the Church, which belong to God; but if their relations are in need, let them be provided with necessities like the other poor, but let them not dissipate that to which they are not entitled. This holy Council warns as strongly as it can that the bishops must give up human and worldy affection for brothers, nephews, and other relations when this is the cause, as it has been, of many evils in the Church. This, which has been said for bishops, shall also be observed by all who hold ecclesiastical posts, both secular and in church organizations, according to the nature of their rank, even to the cardinals of the Holy Roman Church.


## The Act of Supremacy *

> For centuries Englishmen had quarreled with Rome over the control of the church in England. Reform movements, such as that of Wycliffe, had also come and gone. But at the beginning of the Lutheran movement in Germany, Henry VIII of England remained for a time a stanch defender of the Catholic Church—in return for which the pope awarded him the title "Defender of the Faith," which Henry's successors have retained to this day. But a few years later, Henry broke with Rome because of his desire for a divorce from his wife, Catherine of Aragon, which the pope would not grant. To gain his divorce, Henry determined to make himself head of the Church of England. In 1534 Parliament complied with his demands in the Act of Supremacy.

* University of Pennsylvania, Translations and Reprints of the Original Sources of European History, vol. 1, no. 1, Philadelphia, 1897.

An Act concernynge the Kynges Highnes to be supreme heed of the Churche of Englande and to have auctoryte to reforme and redresse all errours, heresyes and abuses yn the same.

Albeit the Kynges Majestie justely and rightfully is and oweth to be the supreme heed of the Churche of England, and so is recognysed by the clergy of this Realme in theyr convocacions; yet neverthelesse for corroboracion and confirmacion therof, and for increase of vertue in Cristis Religion within this Realme of England. . . . Be it enacted by auctority of this present Parliament that the Kyng our Soveraign Lorde, his heires and successours Kynges of this Realme shall be takyn, acceptyd, and reputed the onely supreme heed in erthe of the Churche of England callyd Anglicana Ecclesia . . . : And that our said Soveraigne Lorde his heires and successours Kynges of this Realme shall have full power and auctorite from tyme to tyme to visite represse redresse reforme order correct restrayne and amende all suche errours heresies abuses offences contemptes and enormyties whatsoever they be whiche by any maner spirituall auctoryte or juristiccion ought or maie lawfullye be reformyd repressyd ordred redressyd correctyd restrayned or amendyd, most to the pleasure of almyghtie God the increase of vertue yn Chrystis Religion and for the conservacy of the peace unyte and tranquylyte of this Realme: Any usage custome foreyne laws· foreyne auctoryte prescripcion or anye other thinge or thinges to the contrarie hereof notwithstandinge.

## Queen Anne Boleyn's Last Letter to King Henry *

> After his divorce from Catherine of Aragon, Henry married Anne Boleyn, a lady of the court. Anne bore Henry a daughter, the future Queen Elizabeth I. But shortly there-after she was accused and convicted of treason, and Henry ordered her executed. Anne writes from her prison.

. . . If, as you say, confessing a truth may indeed procure my safety, I shall with all willingness and duty perform your command.

But let not your Grace ever imagine that your poor wife will ever be brought to acknowledge a fault, where not so much as a thought thereof

* William Oldys, ed., *The Harleian Miscellany*, vol. 3, London, John White, John Murray, and John Harding, 1809.

preceded. And, to speak a truth, never prince has wife more loyal in all duty . . . than you have ever found in Anne Boleyn; with which name and place I could willingly have contented myself, if God and your Grace's pleasure had been so pleased. . . . You have chosen me, from a low estate, to be your Queen and companion, far beyond my desert or desire. If then you found me worthy of such honour . . . let not any light fancy, or bad counsel of mine enemies, withdraw your princely favour from me; . . . Try me, good King; but let me have a lawful trial, and let not my sworn enemies sit as my accusers and judges; . . .

But, if you have already determined of me . . . ; then I desire of God, that he will pardon your great sin thereof . . . ; and that he will not call you to a strict account for your unprincely and cruel usage of me, at his general judgment-seat, where both you and myself must shortly appear; . . .

. . . From my doleful prison in the Tower, this sixth of May [1536].

ANNE BOLEYN

## English Confiscation of Church Lands *

*For various reasons, many Englishmen supported their king's break with Rome. Some approved because of national pride, others through a belief in Protestant ideas. But others were simply hungry for the church's land and wealth, which the king seized and distributed among his favorites. We read first a description of the taking over of a monastery, followed by the request of George, earl of Shrewsbury, for a share of the church lands. The earl's application was not successful in this case; but he persisted in his attempts, and on two later occasions did receive grants of church land.*

### SIR PIERS DUTTON TO SIR THOMAS AUDELEY

Please it your good Lordship to be advised [that] Mr. Combes and Mr. Bolles, the Kings Commissioners within the County of Chester, were lately at Norton within the same county, for the suppressing of the Abby there. And when they had packed up such jewels and stuff as they had

* Sir Henry Ellis, *Original Letters Illustrative of English History*, Third Series, vol. 3, London, Richard Bentley, 1846.

there and thought the next day to depart from there, the Abbot gathered a great company together to the number of two or three hundred persons, so that the said Commissioners were in fear of their lives, and were glad to take [to] a tower there, and thereupon sent a letter unto me, informing me what danger they were in, and desired me to come to assist them or else they were never like to come from there. Which letter came to me about nine of the clock in the night upon Sunday last, and about two of the clock in the same night I came to that place with such of my tenants as I had near about me. . . . I used some bold tactics and came suddenly upon them, so that the company that was there fled. . . . And it was thought [that] if the matter had not been quickly handled it would have grown . . . to what danger God only knows. . . . I took the Abbot and three of his Canons and brought them to the Kings Castle of Halton, and there committed them to confinement to the Constable to be kept as the Kings Rebellious . . . ; and William Parker, the Kings servant who was appointed to be the Kings farmer there was restored to his possession. Wherefore it may please your good Lordship that the King may have knowledge [of this action of mine], and that his pleasure may be further known, which I shall always be ready and glad to do. . . .

### GEORGE, EARL OF SHREWSBURY, TO JOHN SCUDAMORE

Welbiloved frende . . . I understand that for the especyall truste and confydence that the Kyngs Highness has in you he has appoynted you to be one of his Survayors of diverse Abbies within the Countye of Hereforde and others appoynted [scheduled] to be subpressed. Trouth it is [that] in the poore house of Wormseley, within the said Countye of Hereforde, which is of my foundation, many of my ancestors do lye. . . . So that if I myght by any pursute [pleading] to be made unto the Kyngs Grace for the same, I would be very sorye it should be subpressed. And therefore I desyre and heartily pray you to use your lawfull favor, and to be good therein, at this my desyre, so that by your good helpe and meanes I may the soner atteyn that the same may stande and contynewe. And I shalbe glad to do vnto you pleasure at all tymes, as knowth our Lord who have you in his governance.

Yor ffelow
G. SHREWSBURY.

To my hertly biloved fellow, John
Skydmore, oon of the gentylmen vsshers
of the Kyngs most honerable Chamber.

# Protestantism in the Netherlands *

RICHARD CLOUGH

> *For a variety of reasons, economic, social, and political, the Netherlands rose in rebellion against their Spanish rulers. As elsewhere the contest quickly took on a religious form, the rebels identifying themselves with Calvinism and the loyalists with the Catholic Church. A young Englishman writes home from Antwerp of looting by the rebels.*

ANTWERP, 21 August 1566

SIR,

Since I have not received any letters from your Mastership of late, I have the less to write as touching your affairs; all things being in good order hitherto, (God be praised!); but how long it shall so remain, God only knows; for we have had here this past night a terrible thing, all the [Catholic] Churches, chapels and houses of religion utterly defaced, and nothing left whole within them, but broken and utterly destroyed; . . .

. . . About 6 o'clock, they broke up the door, and went and took up all the books; whereof, as it is said, some they saved, and the rest they utterly destroyed and broke.

After that, they began with the large image of our Lady, which had been carried about the town on Sunday last, and utterly defaced her and her chapel; after, the whole church, which was the costliest church in Europe; and have so spoiled it, that they have not left a place to sit on in the church. And from thence, part went to the parish churches, and part to the houses of Religion, and made such dispatch as I think the like was never done in one night; . . . I could not perceive in some churches above 10 or 12 that spoiled—all being boys and rascals; but there were many in the church lookers-on. . . .

. . . So that, after I saw that all was over, I, with about 10 thousand more, went into the churches to see . . . ; and coming into our Lady Church, it looked like a hell: . . . with falling of Images and beating down of costly works; in such sort, that the spoil was so great that a man could not well pass through the church. So that, in fine, I cannot write you in 10 sheets of paper the strange sight I saw there—organs and all, destroyed! . . . They that this did, never looked towards any spoil, but

* John W. Burgon, *The Life and Times of Sir Thomas Gresham*, vol. 2, London, Robert Jennings, 1839 (adapted).

broke everything into pieces, and let it lie underfoot. So that, to be short, they have spoiled and destroyed all the churches. . . . Before it was 3 o'clock in the morning, they had done their work, and all were home again, as if there had been nothing done. . . .

Praying God that all may be well and that you have a good passage and safe arrival here, and then you shall see more than I can write you.

Your servant,
RICHARD CLOUGH

## The Edict of Nantes *

HENRY IV OF FRANCE

*France was so evenly divided between Huguenots (Calvinists) and Catholics that for over fifty years the outcome of their struggle remained in doubt. The massacre of some two thousand Huguenots in Paris on St. Bartholomew's Eve, 1572, was only one incident in the bitterness that plunged France into a prolonged civil war. To bring peace, the Protestant claimant to the throne, Henry of Navarre, became a Catholic and restored the Catholic Church to its position of supremacy in France. To protect his former comrades he, now Henry IV of France, issued the Edict of Nantes in 1598, from whose 148 articles we read these examples. The edict remained in force until revoked by Louis XIV in 1685, who found that he could not centralize his government as long as the Huguenots were holding 200 fortified towns.*

III. We ordain that the Catholic Apostolic and Roman religion shall be restored and reëstablished in all places and localities of this our kingdom and countries subject to our sway, where the exercise of the same has been interrupted, in order that it may be peaceably and freely exercised, without any trouble or hindrance. Forbidding very expressly all persons of whatsoever estate, quality or condition, under the penalties recited above, from troubling, molesting or disturbing ecclesiastics in the celebration of divine service. . . .

* University of Pennsylvania, *Translations and Reprints from the Original Sources of European History*, vol. 3, no. 3, Philadelphia, 1912.

VI. And in order to leave no occasion for troubles or differences be-tween our subjects we have permitted and herewith permit those of the said religion called Reformed to live and abide in all the cities and places of this our kingdom and countries of our sway, without being annoyed, molested or compelled to do anything in the matter of religion contrary to their consciences, nor for this reason to be subject to visitation in houses and places where they desire to dwell, upon condition that they comport themselves in other respects according to that which is contained in this our present edict.

XVIII. We also forbid all our subjects of whatever quality and condi-tion, from carrying off by force or persuasion, against the will of their parents, the children of the said religion, in order to cause them to be baptised or confirmed in the Catholic Apostolic and Roman church: and the same is forbidden to those of the said religion called Reformed, upon penalty of being punished with especial severity.

XXII. We ordain that there shall be no difference or distinction made in respect to the said religion, in receiving pupils to be instructed in universities, colleges and schools; nor in receiving the sick and poor into hospitals, retreats and public charities.

## The Thirty Years War *

### Samuel R. Gardiner

> This struggle, which ravaged the heart of Europe from 1618 to 1648, was at the same time the last of the great religious wars and the first of the modern nationalist wars. The effect of the war on Germany, its principal battleground, was to decimate the population and devastate the land. The char-acter of the war is described by a modern scholar reporting from the original records.

Horrible as the war had been from its commencement, it was every day assuming a more horrible character. On both sides all traces of discipline had vanished in the dealing of the armies with the inhabitants of the

* Samuel R. Gardiner, *The Thirty Years War 1618–48*, New York, Charles Scribner's Sons, 1895.

countries in which they were quartered. Soldiers treated men and women as none but the vilest of mankind would now treat brute beasts. "He who had money," says a contemporary, "was their enemy. He who had none was tortured because he had it not." Outrages of unspeakable atrocity were committed everywhere. Human beings were . . . scalded with boiling water, or hunted with fierce dogs. The horrors of a town taken by storm were repeated every day in the open country. Even apart from its excesses, the war itself was terrible enough. When Augsburg was besieged by the imperialists . . . it contained an industrious population of 70,000 souls. After a siege of seven months, 10,000 living beings, wan and haggard with famine, remained to open the gates to the conquerors and the great commercial city of the Fuggers dwindled down into a country town.

How is it possible to bring such scenes before our eyes in their ghastly reality? Let us turn for the moment to some notes taken by the companion of an English ambassador who passed through the country in 1636. As the party was towed up the Rhine from Cologne . . . they passed "by many villages pillaged and shot down." Further on, a French garrison was in Ehrenbreitstein, firing down upon Coblentz, which had just been taken by the imperialists. "They in the town, if they do but look out of their windows, have a bullet presently presented at their head." More to the south, things grew worse. At Bacharach, "The poor people are found dead with grass in their mouths!". . . At Mentz, the ambassador was obliged to remain "on shipboard, for there was nothing to relieve us, since it was taken by the King of Sweden, and miserably battered. . . . Here, likewise, the poor people were almost starved, and those that could relieve others before now humbly begged to be relieved, and after supper all had relief sent from the ship ashore, at the sight of which they strove so violently that some of them fell into the Rhine, and were like to have been drowned." Up the Main, again, "all the towns, villages and castles be battered, pillaged, or burnt." After leaving Würzburg, the ambassador's train came to plundered villages, and then to Neustadt, "which had been a fair city, though now pillaged and burnt miserably." Poor children were "sitting at their doors almost starved to death," his Excellency giving them food and leaving money with their parents to help them, if but for a time. In the Upper Palatinate, they passed "by churches demolished to the ground, and through woods in danger, understanding that Croats were lying hereabout." Further on they stayed for dinner at a poor little village "which hath been pillaged eight-and-twenty times in two years, and twice in one day." And so on, and so on. . . .

# The Destruction of Magdeburg *

OTTO VON GUERICKE

> *In a war noted for the many atrocities committed by both*
> *sides, one of the greatest was the destruction of the great*
> *city of Magdeburg in May, 1631. We read the eyewitness*
> *account of Otto von Guericke, a native of Magdeburg and*
> *later mayor of the city, who is also noted as the inventor of*
> *the air pump.*

Then, on orders of General Pappenheim, a considerable number of [his] men had been brought from the city walls of the new city into the streets. When von Falckenberg [sent by King Gustavus Adolphus of Sweden to Magdeburg with some aid] was shot, and fires had been set in all parts of the city, all resistance proved to be both futile and too late. Fore even when citizens and soldiers would counter-attack and take up defenses, the imperial troops would always have more and more troops and sufficient cavalry for relief. They finally opened the Krochen Gate and let in the entire army of the imperial and Catholic legions, composed of Hungarians, Croats, Poles, Italians, Spaniards, Frenchmen, Walloons, and North and South Germans. This is how the city with all of its inhabitants fell into the violent hands of its enemies. . . .

Nothing but murder, burning, looting, torture, and beatings were to be the order of the day. Each and every one of the enemy concentrated on exacting great amounts of booty. If such a looting party would come to a house and the owner had anything of value, he could only save himself and those dear to him until another group of looters would arrive. In the end though, after everything had been given away and nothing remained to dispose of, the suffering really began. Then they started with beatings, threats of shooting, spearing, hanging, so that the people would have searched out and turned over what they had, even had it been buried under the ground, or sealed with thousands of locks. Under the heel of this wild rampage, this splendid great city which had stood out like a noble countess in the whole country was steeped in full fiery glow, in great misery and unutterable woe and deep sorrow. Many thousands of innocent men,

---

* Otto von Guericke, *Die Belagerung, Eroberung, und Zerstörung der Stadt Magdeburg am $\frac{10}{20}$ Mai 1631*, Leipzig, R. Voigtländers Verlag, 1912 (an original translation by Joachim M. Schorr).

women, and children were murdered in such pitiful ways, amidst hair-raising and horrendous shrieks, that there are not enough words to describe them nor tears to mourn them.

This widely renowned, distinguished city and showcase of the entire country, then, had in one day gone up in fire and smoke, and her surviving inhabitants with wives and children were driven as captives in front of the enemy so that their outcries, weeping, and howling could be heard far and wide. The flames and ashes of the city were carried by the wind as far as Wanzleben, Egeln, and even more distant places. . . .

In addition to all of this, many splendid and irreplaceable house-furnishings and a great variety of movable property, such as old books, manuscripts, monuments, and paintings, were burned or carried away by the troops as loot. . . .

The rich garments, tapestries, silks, gold and silver, laces, all kinds of linen and other household articles, were bought by the sutlers for next to nothing, and sold throughout the archdiocese of Magdeburg and in Anhalt and Brunswick. Gold chains, rings, gems, and other gold and silverware could be bought for less than a tenth of what they were really worth.


## The Witchcraft Mania *

JOHANNES JUNIUS

> *Catholic, Calvinist, and Lutheran alike thought of himself as the soldier of God in a war with the devil. Each could only see in the successes of the others the terrifying power of Satan. The belief in witchcraft, which had existed for many centuries, blazed up to heights never experienced before. Only when the religious controversy itself slowly subsided did hysteria give way to sanity. Confessions extorted by torture are reported in the letter of Johannes Junius, condemned as a witch and awaiting execution.*

Many hundred thousand good-nights, dearly beloved daughter Veronica. Innocent have I come into prison, innocent have I been tortured, innocent must I die. For whoever comes into the witch prison must

* University of Pennsylvania, *Translations and Reprints from the Original Sources of European History*, vol. 3, no. 4, Philadelphia, 1897.

become a witch or be tortured until he invents something out of his head and—God pity him—bethinks him of something. I will tell you how it has gone with me. When I was the first time put to the torture, Dr. Braun, Dr. Kötzendörffer, and two strange doctors were there. Then Dr. Braun asks me, "Kinsman, how come you here?" I answer, "Through falsehood, through misfortune." "Hear, you," he says, "you are a witch; will you confess it voluntarily? If not, we'll bring in witnesses and the executioner for you." I said "I am no witch, I have a pure conscience in the matter; if there are a thousand witnesses, I am not anxious, but I'll gladly hear the witnesses." Now the chancellor's son was set before me . . . and afterward Hoppfen Elss. She had seen me dance on Hauptsmoor. . . . I answered: "I have never renounced God, and will never do it—God graciously keep me from it. I'll rather bear whatever I must." And then came also—God in highest Heaven have mercy—the executioner, and put the thumb-screws on me, both hands bound together, so that the blood ran out at the nails and everywhere, so that for four weeks I could not use my hands, as you can see from the writing. . . . Thereafter they first stripped me, bound my hands behind me, and drew me up in the torture. Then I thought heaven and earth were at an end; eight times did they draw me up and let me fall again, so that I suffered terrible agony. . . .

And this happened on Friday, June 30, and with God's help I had to bear the torture. . . . When at last the executioner led me back into the prison, he said to me: "Sir, I beg you, for God's sake confess something, whether it be true or not. Invent something, for you cannot endure the torture which you will be put to; and, even if you bear it all, yet you will not escape, not even if you were an earl, but one torture will follow after another until you say you are a witch. Not before that," he said, "will they let you go, as you may see by all their trials, for one is just like another.". . .

And so I begged, since I was in wretched plight, to be given one day for thought and a priest. The priest was refused me, but the time for thought was given. Now, my dear child, see in what hazard I stood and still stand. I must say that I am a witch, though I am not,—must now renounce God, though I have never done it before. Day and night I was deeply troubled, but at last there came to me a new idea. I would not be anxious, but, since I had been given no priest with whom I could take counsel, I would myself think of something and say it. It were surely better that I just say it with mouth and words, even though I had not really done it; and afterwards I would confess it to the priest, and let those answer for it who compel me to do it. . . . And so I made my confession . . . but it was all a lie. . . .

Dear child, keep this letter secret so that people do not find it, else I shall be tortured most piteously and the jailers will be beheaded. So strictly is it forbidden. . . . Dear child, pay this man a dollar. . . . I have taken several days to write this: my hands are both lame. I am in a sad plight. . . . .

Good night, for your father Johannes Junius will never see you more. July 24, 1628.

[And on the margin of the letter he adds:]

Dear child, six have confessed against me at once: the Chancellor, his son, Neudecker, Zaner, Hoffmaisters Ursel, and Hoppfen Elss—all false, through compulsion, as they have all told me, and begged my forgiveness in God's name before they were executed. . . . They know nothing but good of me. They were forced to say it, just as I myself was. . . .

## The Methods of the Witch Persecutions *

FRIEDRICH VON SPEE

> *From Friedrich von Spee in 1631 we have the beginning of a more intelligent attitude toward witchcraft. His book had to be printed anonymously to protect the author from being himself charged with aiding witches.*

*What, now, is the outline and method of the trials against witches to-day in general use?—a thing worthy Germany's consideration.*

I answer: . . .

1. Incredible among us Germans . . . are the popular superstition, envy, calumnies, backbitings, insinuations, and the like, which, being neither punished by the magistrates nor refuted by the pulpit, first stir up suspicion of witchcraft. All the divine judgments which God has threatened in Holy Writ are now ascribed to witches. No longer do God or nature do aught, but witches everything.

* University of Pennsylvania, *Translations and Reprints from the Original Sources of European History*, vol. 3, no. 4, Philadelphia, 1897.

2. Hence it comes that all at once everybody is clamoring that the magistrates proceed against the witches—those witches whom only their own clamor has made seem so many.

3. Princes, therefore, bid their judges and counselors to begin proceedings against the witches.

4. These at first do not know where to begin, since they have no testimony or proofs, and since their conscience clearly tells them that they ought not to proceed in this rashly.

5. Meanwhile they are a second time and a third admonished to proceed. The multitude clamors that there is something suspicious in this delay; and the same suspicion is, by one busybody or another, instilled into the ear of the princes.

6. To offend these, however, and not to defer at once to their wishes, is in Germany a serious matter: most men, and even clergymen, approve with zeal whatever is but pleasing to the princes, not heeding by whom these (however good by nature) are often instigated.

7. At last, therefore, the judges yield to their wishes, and in some way contrive at length a starting-point for the trials.

8. Or, if they still hold out and dread to touch the ticklish matter, there is sent to them a commissioner [*Inquisitor*] specially deputed for this. And, even if he brings to his task something of inexperience or of ardor, as is wont to happen in things human, this takes on in this field another color and name, and is counted only zeal for justice. This zeal for justice is no whit diminished by the prospect of gain, especially in the case of a commissioner of slender means and avaricious, with a large family, when there is granted him as salary so many dollars per head for each witch burned, besides the fees and assessments which he is allowed to extort at will from the peasants. . . .

10. And yet, lest it appear that she is indicted on the basis of rumor alone, without other proofs, as the phrase goes, lo a certain presumption is at once obtained against her by posing the following dilemma: Either [she] . . . has led a bad and improper life, or she has led a good and proper one. If a bad one, then, say they, the proof is cogent against her; for from malice to malice the presumption is strong. If, however, she has led a good one, this also is none the less a proof; for thus, they say, are witches wont to cloak themselves. . . .

21. Then, when [she] . . . has thus been searched and shaved, she is tortured that she may confess the truth, that is to say, that she may simply

declare herself guilty; for whatever else she may say will not be the truth and cannot be. . . .

24. Without any scruples, therefore, after this confession she is executed. Yet she would have been executed, nevertheless, even though she had not confessed; for when once a beginning has been made with the torture, the die is already cast—she cannot escape, she must die. . . .

36. If, now, any under stress of pain has once falsely declared herself guilty, her wretched plight beggars description. For not only is there in general no door for her escape, but she is also compelled to accuse others, of whom she knows no ill, and whose names are not seldom suggested to her by her examiners or by the executioner, or of whom she has heard as suspected or accused or already once arrested and released. These in their turn are forced to accuse others, and these still others, and so it goes on: who can help seeing that it must go on without end? . . .

46. From all which there follows this corollary, worthy to be noted in red ink: that, if only the trials be steadily pushed on with, there is nobody in our day, of whatsover sex, fortune, rank, or dignity who is safe, if he have but an enemy and slanderer to bring him into suspicion of witchcraft. . . .

# PART FOUR

# The Age of
## Oceanic Discovery

During the Middle Ages the Northmen had reached Greenland and had even ventured to America, but none settled there permanently. The great age of exploration dawned in the fifteenth century with Italian, Spanish, and Portuguese sailors in the forefront of a race to explore the oceans of the world. A little later French, English, and Dutch joined in the competition to find new routes to old lands, and new lands in hitherto uncharted seas. Their discoveries resulted in a shift of maritime leadership from the Mediterranean to nations fronting on the Atlantic. Superstitious terrors of sea-monsters, magic islands, broiling suns, and stagnant deadly seas had made the Atlantic fearful since ancient times, when Phoenician and Carthaginian sailors had circulated wild tales of its dangers. It took a combination of missionary zeal, curiosity about the unknown, love of adventure, and desire for wealth to overcome the inherited fears of centuries.

# The Admiral of the Ocean Sea *

CHRISTOPHER COLUMBUS

> The most famous of many hundreds of famous intrepid ex-
> plorers is undoubtedly Christopher Columbus, whose dis-
> coveries won him the title "Admiral of the Ocean Sea" from
> the monarchs of Spain. It is therefore interesting that so
> little is known of his life before his voyages to America. His
> birthplace, nationality, family, appearance, and his very name
> have all been the subject of dispute by historians. Of his
> later life, this much is certain: the discoverer of America
> never knew that he had not reached the East Indies. His
> hopes and disappointments are heard in his letters.

A LETTER SENT BY COLUMBUS TO THE CHANCELLOR OF THE
EXCHEQUER [OF ARAGON], RESPECTING THE ISLANDS IN THE "INDIES,"
ENCLOSING ANOTHER FOR THEIR HIGHNESSES. [WRITTEN FEB. 15, 1493.]

Sir,—Believing that you will take pleasure in hearing of the great success which our Lord has granted me in my voyage, I write you this letter,
whereby you will learn how in thirty-three days' [from the 8th of September when Columbus sailed from the Canaries, to the 11th of October
when he first saw land] time I reached the Indies with the fleet which the
most illustrious King and Queen, our Sovereigns, gave to me, where I
found many islands thickly peopled, of all which I took possession without
resistance for their Highnesses. . . . When I reached *Juana* [Cuba], I
followed its coast to the westward, and found it so large that I thought it
must be the mainland,—the province of *Cathay*; and, as I found neither
towns nor villages on the sea-coast . . . I kept on the same route, thinking that I could not fail to light upon some large cities and towns. At
length, after the proceeding of many leagues, and finding that nothing
new presented itself, and that the coast was leading me northwards . . .
I resolved not to wait for a change in the weather, but returned to a
certain harbour . . . and from which I sent two men ashore to ascertain
whether there was any king or large cities in that part. They journeyed
for three days and found countless hamlets and numberless inhabitants,
but with nothing like order; they therefore returned. In the meantime I

* R. H. Major, ed., *Select Letters of Christopher Columbus*, London, The Hakluyt
Society, 1870.

had learned from some other Indians whom I had seized, that this land was certainly an island. . . . On my reaching the Indies, I took by force, in the first island that I discovered, some of these natives, that they might learn our language and give me information. . . . They are still with me, and, from repeated conversations that I have had with them, I find that they still believe that I come from heaven. . . . I have already said how I had gone one hundred and seven leagues in following the sea-coast of *Juana* in a straight line from west to east; and from that survey I can state that the island is larger than England and Scotland together, because, beyond these one hundred and seven leagues, there lie to the west two provinces which I have not yet visited, one of which is called *Avan,* where the people are born with a tail. . . . Although I have taken possession of all these islands in the name of their Highnesses, and they are all more abundant in wealth than I am able to express; . . . yet there was one large town in *Española* of which especially I took possession, situated in a locality well adapted for the working of gold mines, and for all kinds of commerce, either with the main land on this side, or with that beyond which is the land of the great Khan, with which there will be vast commerce and great profit. . . . Finally, and speaking only of what has taken place in this voyage, which has been so hasty, their Highnesses may see that I shall give them all the gold they require, if they will give me but a very little assistance. . . . Much more I would have done if my vessels had been in as good condition as by rights they ought to have been.

LETTER OF THE ADMIRAL TO THE NURSE OF PRINCE JUAN.
[WRITTEN NEAR THE END OF THE YEAR 1500.]

Most virtuous lady: Although it is a novelty for me to complain of the ill-usage of the world, it is, nevertheless, no novelty for the world to practice ill-usage. Innumerable are the contests which I have had with it, and I have resisted all its attacks until now, when I find, that neither strength nor prudence is of any avail to me: it has cruelly reduced me to the lowest ebb. . . . All proved incredulous; except the Queen . . . to whom the Lord gave the spirit of intelligence and great courage. . . . All sought to cover the ignorance in which they were sunk, by dwelling on the inconveniences and expense of the proposed enterprise. Her Highness held the contrary opinion, and supported it with all her power. Seven years passed away in deliberations, and nine have been spent in accomplishing things truly memorable, and worthy of being preserved in the history of man. . . .

I have now reached that point, that there is no man so vile but thinks it his right to insult me. The day will come when the world will reckon it a virtue to him who has not given his consent to their abuse. If I had plundered the Indies . . . and had given them all to the Moors, they could not have shown toward me more bitter enmity than they have done in Spain.

A LETTER WRITTEN BY DON CHRISTOPHER COLUMBUS, VICEROY AND ADMIRAL OF THE INDIES, TO KING FERDINAND AND QUEEN ISABELLA OF SPAIN. [WRITTEN JULY 7, 1503.]

. . . For seven years was I at your royal court, where every one to whom the enterprise was mentioned, treated it as ridiculous; but now there is not a man, down to the very tailors, who does not beg to be allowed to become a discoverer. . . . The lands in this part of the world . . . are richer and more extensive than those of any Christian power, and yet, after that I had, by the Divine will, placed them under your high and royal sovereignty . . . ; and while I was waiting for ships, to convey me in safety, and with a heart full of joy, to your royal presence . . . I was arrested and thrown, with my two brothers, loaded with irons, into a ship. . . . My body is infirm, and all that was left to me, as well as to my brothers, has been taken away and sold. . . . I cannot but believe that this was done without your royal permission. The restitution of my honour, the reparation of my losses, and the punishment of those who have inflicted them, will redound to the honour of your royal character. . . .

## *Venetian Cabotas Become English Cabots* *

LORENZO PASQUALIGO

> With the decline of Mediterranean shipping, Italian sailors sought jobs in the rising naval powers on the Atlantic. The Genoese Columbus had sailed under the banner of Castile. The Venetians Giovanni and Sebastiano Cabota carried that of Henry VII of England to Newfoundland, laying the basis for the later claims of England to eastern North America. We hear of John (Giovanni) Cabot's first voyage from another Venetian, a resident of London, writing home.

* Rawdon Brown, ed., *Calendar of State Papers—Venetian*, vol. 1, London Longman, Green, Longman, Roberts & Green, 1864.

Lorenzo Pasqualigo to his Brothers Alvise and Francesco.

The Venetian, our countryman, who went with a ship from Bristol in quest of new islands, is returned, and says that 700 leagues hence he discovered land, the territory of the Grand Cham (*Gram Cam*). He coasted for 300 leagues and landed; saw no human beings, but he has brought hither to the King certain snares which had been set to catch game, and a needle for making nets; he also found some felled trees, wherefore he supposed there were inhabitants, and returned to his ship in alarm.

He was three months on the voyage, and on his return he saw two islands to starboard, but would not land, time being precious, as he was short of provisions. He says that the tides are slack and do not flow as they do here. The King of England is much pleased with this intelligence.

The King has promised that in the spring our countryman shall have ten ships, armed to his order, and at his request has conceded him all the prisoners, except such as are confined for high treason, to man his fleet. The King has also given him money wherewith to amuse himself till then, and he is now at Bristol with his wife, who is also Venetian, and with his sons; his name is Zuan [John] Cabot, and he is styled the great admiral. Vast honour is paid him; he dresses in silk, and these English run after him like mad people, so that he can enlist as many of them as he pleases, and a number of our own rogues besides.

The discoverer of these places planted on his new-found land a large cross, with one flag of England and another of S. Mark, by reason of his being a Venetian, so that our banner has floated very far afield.

London, 23 August 1497.

## Spain Claims a Whole Ocean *

Vasco Nuñez de Balboa

> As it came to be realized that America might not be India or China, a frantic search began for a passage through it into the China Seas, which were expected to be just beyond. All the great rivers of eastern North and South America were explored in this search. Meanwhile in 1513 Vasco Nuñez de Balboa found his way through mountains and jungles of

* J. T. Medina, *El Descubriemento del Océano Pacífico*, vol. I. Santiago, Chile, Imprenta Universitaria, 1914 (an original translation by James H. Hanscom).

*Panama to the ocean which lay to his south as he stood on
the isthmus at Darien. Sword in one hand and banner aloft
in the other, he waded into the ocean and claimed it and all
its islands and continents for Spain.*

Long live the very high and most mighty monarchs Don Fernando and
Dona Johanna, sovereigns of Castile, Leon, Aragon, etc., in whose name
and for the royal crown of Castile I do take and hold possession real,
bodily, and actual, of these southern seas, lands, shores, ports, and islands,
with all that adjoins them, and kingdoms and provinces which relate to
them or may come to be related in whatever manner or by whatever right
or title that may be or come to be, ancient or modern, in time past, present,
or future, without any contradiction. And if any other prince or captain,
Christian or infidel, or of whatever law, sect, or status he may claim, shall
assert any right to these lands and seas, I am ready and prepared to defy
him, and to defend in the name of the sovereigns of Castile, present or to
come, their sovereignty and lordship over these Indies, islands, and continents north and south, with their oceans at the Arctic and Antarctic
poles, on both sides the equator, inside or outside the tropics of Cancer
and Capricorn, according to what is most honorable for Their Majesties
and their successors everywhere or in whatever part pertains thereunto
. . . now and forever while the world endures until the final judgment
day of all mortals.

## *The First Voyage Around the Earth* *

Antonio Pigafetta

> *Seven years after Balboa carried Spain's banners overland to
> the Pacific, the search for a sea passage was successful. The
> Portuguese captain Ferdinand Magellan, sailing under the
> banners of Spain, found his way through the raging currents
> of the strait that was henceforth to bear his name and into
> the ocean to which he gave the misleading name of "Pacific."
> After months of suffering from scurvy and starvation, the
> ocean was crossed. Landing in the Philippine Islands, Ma-
> gellan claimed them for Spain (although only later were they*

* Reprinted by permission of the publishers, The Arthur H. Clark Company, from
*Magellan's Voyage around the World* by Antonio Pigafetta, translated by James A.
Robertson, 1906.

*given their name, which honors King Philip II). Magellan*
*was killed in a local quarrel on one of the islands. His*
*lieutenant, Juan Sebastian del Cano, took command of the*
*one remaining ship, the* Victoria, *and found his way to the*
*East Indies. Here he encountered Portuguese sailors and*
*followed their routes across the Indian Ocean and around*
*Africa. Two hundred and fifty of the men who had sailed*
*from Spain did not live to come home. One of the eighteen*
*who did return relates the story of the voyage.*

[After describing the perilous voyage through what is now called the Strait of Magellan, near the tip of South America, Pigafetta describes the ordeal suffered in crossing the Pacific. The journal is dated November 28, 1520.] We were three months and twenty days without getting any kind of fresh food. We ate biscuit, which was no longer biscuit, but powder of biscuit swarming with worms. . . . We drank yellow water that had been putrid for many days. We also ate some ox hides that covered the top of the mainyard. . . . We left them in the sea for four or five days, and then placed them for a few moments on top of the embers, and so ate them; and often we ate sawdust from boards. Rats were sold for one-half ducado apiece, and even then we could not get them. But above all the other misfortunes the following was the worst. The gums of both the lower and upper teeth of some of our men swelled, so that they could not eat under any circumstances and therefore died. Nineteen men died from that sickness. . . . We sailed about four thousand leguas during those three months and twenty days through an open stretch in that Pacific Sea. In truth it is very pacific, for during that time we did not suffer any storm. We saw no land except two desert islets, where we found nothing but birds and trees, for which we called them the Ysolle Infortunate [the Unfortunate Isles]. . . . Daily we made runs of fifty, sixty, or seventy leguas. . . . Had not God and His blessed mother given us so good weather we would all have died of hunger in that exceeding vast sea. . . . I believe no such voyage will ever be made [again]. . . .

[Magellan reached the Philippines and soon became involved in the local tribal rivalries.] On Friday, April twenty-six, Zula, a chief of the island of Matan, sent one of his sons to present two goats to the captain-general. . . . He requested the captain to send him only one boatload of men on the next night, so that they might help him and fight against the other chief. The captain-general decided to go thither with three boat-loads. . . . When morning came forty-nine of us leaped into the water up to our thighs. . . . The boats could not approach nearer because of certain rocks in the water. . . . When we reached land, [the enemy natives] formed in three divisions to the number of more than one thousand five hundred persons. When they saw us, they charged down upon us with exceeding loud cries. . . . So many of them charged down upon us that they shot the captain through the right leg with a poisoned arrow. On that account he ordered us to retire slowly, but the men took to flight, except six or eight of us who remained with the captain. . . . So we continued to retire. . . . Recognizing the captain, so many turned upon him that they knocked his helmet off his head twice, but he always stood firmly like a good knight. . . . Thus did we fight for more than one hour, refusing to retire farther. . . . One of them wounded him on the left leg with a large cutlass. . . . That caused the captain to fall face downward, when immediately they rushed upon him with iron and bamboo spears . . . until they killed our mirror, our light, our comfort, and our true guide. When they wounded him, he turned back many times to see whether we were all in the boats. Thereupon, beholding him dead, we, wounded, retreated, as best we could, to the boats, which were already pulling off. . . . Had it not been for that unfortunate captain, not a single one of us would have been saved in the boats, for while he was fighting the others retired to the boats. . . . That battle was fought on Saturday, April twenty-seven, 1521. . . .

On Saturday, September six, 1522, we entered the bay of San Lucar with only eighteen men and the majority of them sick. . . . From the time we had left that bay until the present day, we had sailed fourteen thousand four hundred and sixty leguas, and furthermore had completed the circumnavigation of the world from east to west.

## The Aztec Empire Falls to Spain *

Bernal Diaz del Castillo

> *Two wealthy American Indian empires, the Aztec and the*
> *Inca, were conquered by Spaniards. The almost incredible*
> *success of the small Spanish bands was due in part to feuds*
> *within the empires, in part to treachery by some of the na-*

* Bernal Diaz del Castillo, *The True History of the Conquest of Mexico*, vol. 1, New York, Robert M. McBride & Company, 1927 (translated by Maurice Keatinge).

*tive population against their rulers, in part to terror inspired
by belief that the Europeans were gods whose coming had
long been prophesied, and in part to the Spanish possession
of firearms. The success of the adventurers would also not
have been possible had they been less daring, stubborn, or
tough in mind and body. Fighting beside Hernando Cortez
in the 1519 campaign against the Aztecs of Mexico was
young Bernal Diaz del Castillo. In his old age he wrote of
the great events of his youth.*

When we approached Iztapalapa [on the outskirts of the Aztec capital,
Mexico City] we were received by several great lords of that country, relations of Montezuma, who conducted us to our lodgings there, in palaces
magnificently built of stone, and the timber of which was cedar, with
spacious courts, and apartments furnished with canopies of the finest
cotton. After having contemplated these noble edifices we walked through
the gardens, which were admirable to behold from the variety of beautiful
and aromatic plants, and the numerous alleys filled with fruit trees, roses,
and various flowers. Here was also a lake of the clearest water, which
communicated with the grand lake of Mexico by a channel cut for the
purpose, and capable of admitting the largest canoes. The whole was
ornamented with works of art, painted, and admirably plaistered and
whitened, and it was rendered more delightful by numbers of beautiful
birds. When I beheld the scenes that were around me, I thought within
myself that this was the garden of the world! . . .

On the next day we set out . . . and proceeded by the grand cause-
way, which is eight yards wide, and runs in a straight line to the city of
Mexico. It was crowded with people, as were all the towers, temples, and
causeways, in every part of the lake, attracted by curiosity to behold men,
and animals, such as never had been before seen in these countries. We
were occupied by very different thoughts; our number did not amount to
four hundred and fifty, we had perfectly in our recollection the accounts
we had received on our march, that we were to be put to death on our
arrival in the city which we saw before us, approachable only by causeways, whereon were several bridges, the breaking of one of which effectu-
ally cut off retreat. And now let who can, tell me, where are men in this
world to be found except ourselves, who would have hazarded such an
attempt? . . .

[The *conquistadores* entered the city peacefully. Diaz del Castillo
gives his reactions to the Aztec capital.]

. . . Cortes at the head of his cavalry, and the principal part of our soldiers under arms, marched to the grand square, attended by many noblemen of the court. When we arrived there, we were astonished at the crowds of people, and the regularity which prevailed, as well as at the vast quantities of merchandise, which those who attended us were assiduous in pointing out. Each kind had its particular place, which was distinguished by a sign. The articles consisted of gold, silver, jewels, feathers, mantles, chocolate, skins dressed and undressed, sandals, and other manufactures of the roots and fibres of nequen, and great numbers of male and female slaves, some of whom were fastened by the neck, in collars, to long poles. The meat market was stocked with fowls, game, and dogs. Vegetables, fruits, articles of food ready dressed, salt, bread, honey, and sweet pastry made in various ways, were also sold here. Other places in the square were appointed to the sale of earthenware, wooden household furniture such as tables and benches, firewood, paper, sweet canes filled with tobacco mixed with liquid amber, copper axes and working tools, and wooden vessels highly painted. Numbers of women sold fish, and little loaves made of a certain mud which they find in the lake, and which resembles cheese. The makers of stone blades were busily employed shaping them out of the rough material, and the merchants who dealt in gold, had the metal in grains as it came from the mines, in transparent tubes, so that they could be reckoned, and the gold was valued at so many mantles, or so many xiquipils of cocoa, according to the size of the quills. The entire square was inclosed in piazzas, under which great quantities of grain were stored, and where were also shops for various kinds of goods. . . .

From the square we proceeded to the great temple. . . . When we approached the gate of the great temple, to the flat summit of which the ascent was by a hundred and fourteen steps, and before we had mounted one of them, Montezuma sent down to us six priests, and two of his noblemen, to carry Cortes up, as they had done their sovereign, which he politely declined. When we had ascended to the summit of the temple, we observed on the platform as we passed, the large stones whereon were placed the victims who were to be sacrificed. Here was a great figure which resembled a dragon, and much blood fresh spilt. . . .

Montezuma then took him [Cortes] by the hand, and pointed out to him the different parts of the city, and its vicinity, all of which were commanded from that place. Here we had a clear prospect of the three causeways by which Mexico communicated with the land, and of the aqueduct of Chapultepeque, which supplied the city with the finest water. We were struck with the numbers of canoes, passing to and from the main land, loaded with provisions and merchandise, and we could now perceive, that in this great city, and all the others of that neighbourhood which were built in the water, the houses stood separate from each other, communicating only by small drawbridges, and by boats, and that they were built with terraced tops. . . . The noise and bustle of the market-place below us could be heard almost a league off, and those who had been at Rome and at Constantinople said, that for convenience, regularity, and population, they had never seen the like. . . .

## *Treatment of the Conquered Americans*

Paul III, Isabella of Castile

> *The Spanish conquerors who seized Aztec and Inca treasure, and who built huge fortunes on great landed estates, felt that the Indians were best treated as slaves. To the missionaries who were giving their lives to spread Christianity in this New World, the Indians were humans with souls to be saved. Conflict between conquerors and missionaries reached the ears of the heads of church and state, who spoke out plainly in reply. But Europe was far away, and in the long run the conquerors ignored the commands of popes and kings. Pope Paul III (1534–1549) replied to a complaint from the Bishop of Tlascala in Mexico with the Bull (Proclamation) Ipsa Veritas.\**

He who is truth itself, and can neither deceive nor be deceived, said to the preachers of His faith, when He sent them to exercise their ministry, "Go and preach to all nations." He said "all nations". . . because all are capable of receiving this teaching. . . . But the Enemy of the human race [Satan] has persuaded some of his ministers to affirm, the better to satisfy their greed, that the Indians and other peoples recently brought to our knowledge ought to be treated as animals and reduced to slavery, since they are incapable of receiving the Catholic Faith. . . .

Wishing to correct this . . . we declare that the Indians . . . even if they are outside the Christian faith cannot and must not. be deprived of their liberty, or their property, and must by no means be reduced to servitude.

\* An original translation by James H. Hanscom.

> *Queen Isabella of Castile had supported Columbus's ex-*
> *plorations because of her interest in missionary work. On*
> *her death she reminded her husband, Ferdinand of Aragon,*
> *and her daughter Joanna, heiress to the Kingdom of Castile,*
> *of the problem of the native Americans.** 

. . . Our principal intention, in soliciting from Pope Alexander VI the concession of the lands discovered and to be discovered, was to convert their peoples to our holy Catholic faith. . . . I beg the King my lord very affectionately, I order and command the Princess my daughter and the Prince my son, to execute and accomplish this intention.

Let it be their principal end, and let them apply all their diligence to it. Let them not permit, or be the cause, that the Indians inhabiting the said islands and mainland suffer any damage in their persons or their property. They shall be vigilant, on the contrary, to see that these peoples be treated with justice and kindness. And if they receive any prejudice, let this prejudice be repaired. . . .

## A Letter from India **

> *While Spain was extending her control westward to America*
> *and the Philippines, the Portuguese were steadily developing*
> *the eastward route to India. By 1580 a series of Portuguese*
> *holdings extended along both coasts of Africa to India,*
> *Ceylon, Malaya, and the Spice Islands in the East Indies.*
> *Although the German states did not enter into the colonial*
> *race, the great German banking house of Fugger was inter-*
> *ested in commercial ventures everywhere. One of its re-*
> *porters in India appraises the situation there.*

FROM COCHIN IN INDIA, the 10th day of January 1580.

HONOURABLE, MOST KINDLY AND DEAR SIGNOR ADELGAIS!

Before my departure from Lisbon I informed you how I with my companions boarded our ships. Upon the 4th day of April 1579 all five

---

* Louis Bertrand and Sir Charles Petrie, *The History of Spain*, 2d ed., London, Eyre & Spottiswoode, 1952. Reprinted by permission of Sir Charles Petrie.
** Victor von Klarwill, ed., *The Fugger News-Letters*, New York, G. P. Putnam's Sons, 1925.

vessels sailed from Lisbon at the same time; but we did not however, keep together for more than six days, but each soon struck out on its own course, since each captain or pilot believes he knows best how to arrive first at the goal. Although these ships are big and powerful, they strive not to stay together. . . . We arrived, thanks and praise be to the Lord Almighty, upon the 10th day of October at the town of Goa, which belongs to the King of Portugal and is the finest capital in this country. Thus we have been on our way here from Lisbon six months and six days, and during that time have seen no land, only the sky and the sea. The Lord God bestows on such journeys His special blessing and mercy, for otherwise it would not be possible to spend half a year between the planks. To sum up, whosoever is well equipped with provisions and a cook, both of which were mine, thanks to the Lord, feels the hardships of such a voyage less than the common people, who suffer great distress from lack of food and drink, especially water, which no money can buy. In such heat one cannot partake of much wine, only water of which, thanks be to God, I had in sufficient quantity with our food. There were about five hundred persons in our ship of whom not more than twenty-five altogether died on the way from Portugal to India. . . .

Our ships have all five arrived from Lisbon, namely, three in Goa and two here. Now all five ships are here in Cochin. I made a sojourn of four weeks in the town of Goa and built me there a house. From thence I travelled one hundred miles onwards by sea. The voyage can be made in ten to twelve days. The ships are loaded with pepper here in Cochin, twenty miles from Calicut, wherefore they all have to come to this place. I shall maintain two establishments, one in Goa and the other here. I have not yet, however, resolved upon which shall fall my choice for remaining definitely. Although Goa is the capital in which the Viceroy of Portugal holds his Court, it is wearisome to journey back and forth every year, as I needs must be present in this our pepper store.

Such a pepper store is a fine business, but it requires great zeal and perseverance. It takes six weeks to receive the pepper from the heathen King of Cochin, who is our friend, and to load it into our ships. After the departure of these ships for Portugal I and my servants have but little to do. The pepper business is profitable indeed; when the Lord God grants by His mercy that none of the ships take damage either in coming or going, then the merchants wax rich. . . .

This year, in my judgment, we shall not dispatch more than four ships with about twenty loads, although we ought to send thirty. We already possess the money, for so large a sum would not be obtainable by loan. What we are lacking this day can be bought, given a good opportunity, after the sailing of these ships for next year. Of all other spices such as cloves, nutmeg, flour and nuts, cinnamon, maces, and various drugs, this year's supplies are going to Portugal. In precious stones little was dispatched this year on account of the war, which the heathen Kings (of which there are many in this country) waged one upon another. Because of this, precious stones cannot come through from inland into our towns since all of them lie upon the shores of the sea.

All that lieth inland belongs to the Indians, heathens and Moors. We boast of the friendship of two or three of these Kings, but the majority are our enemies. Our fleet is continually fighting them at sea. The King of Portugal despite all his power is too weak for this vast country. The King of Spain, if he but took possession of Portugal, would be the right King for these lands. He should take over the whole of India, all the kingdoms and provinces right into China, where it adjoins Tartary, and unite under his rule his Spanish India with the Portuguese municipalities: this he could accomplish with fifty thousand men. Even though the Indian Kings have a goodly number of warriors, and there are many such Kings, they are not good fighters. One Christian can achieve more than six Indians. Besides, these Kings are continually involved in strife and quarrels amongst themselves.


## Hindu Customs *

PIETRO VALLE

> European travelers to India were fascinated by the strange (to them) customs of the people. Pietro Valle, who visited India early in the seventeenth century, took note of some Hindu customs.

[The Hindus] believe that there is a Paradise in Heaven with God, but that thereinto go only the Souls of their own Nation, more pure and without any sin, who have liv'd piously in this world; or in case they have sin'd, after divers Transmigrations [rebirths] into various bodies of Animals and Men, having by often returning into the world undergone many

* Edward Grey, ed., *The Travels of Pietro Valle in India*, London, The Hakluyt Society, 1892.

pains, they are at length purg'd, and at last dye in the body of some man of Indian and noble Race, as the Brachmans, who amongst them are held the noblest and purest; . . .

. . . With people of other Religion they never eat nor will have any communication of food, and as much as possible they avoid even to touch them; conceiving themselves polluted by communication with others. And herein they are so scrupulous that even amongst the Indians themselves one of more noble Race not only neither eats, nor makes use of the same Clothes or Vessels, nor communicates in anything with one less noble, but also endures not to be touch'd by him; which if it fall out by chance that he be, he must purifie himself from the defilement by washings and other arrogant Ceremonies. And hence 'tis a pretty sight to behold the great respect which upon this account the ignoble bear to the more noble then themselves, and how upon meeting in the street the ignoble not onely give place, but dance wildly up and down for fear of rushing against the noble, and polluting them in any measure; which, if they should not do, the Noble, and especially the Souldiers, would make them do it to the Musick of blows.

From this averseness to communicate one with another, particularly in the use of eating and drinking vessels, concerning which they are most strict, is sprung a strange Custom, which I was delighted not only to see, but also sometimes out of gallantry to imitate in conversation. It happens very often during hot weather, both in Travelling and in Towns, that people have need of refreshing themselves and drinking of a little water; but because every one hath not a drinking-vessel of his own ready, to avoid defiling or being defil'd by his companion's cup, there's a way found out whereby any person may drink in that, or any other whatever, without scruple or danger of any either active or passive contamination. This is done by drinking in such manner that the vessel touches not the lips or mouth of him who drinks; for it is held up on high with the hand over the mouth, and he that lifts it up highest, and holds it furthest from his mouth, shows himself most mannerly; and thus pouring the liquor out of the cup into the mouth, they drink round while there is any left, or so long as they please. So accustom'd are the Indians to drink in this manner that they practice it almost continually with their own vessels for delight, without the necessity of shunning communication with others; and they are so dextrous at it, that I remember to have seen one of them take with both hands a vessel as big as a basin, and lifting it up above a span higher than his mouth, poure a great torrent of water into his throat and drink it all off. . . .

# Chinese Reaction to Europeans *

MATTEO RICCI

> *Increasing contact with Europe brought a hostile response from the Chinese government. The emperors of the Ming dynasty used their waning power to suppress Christianity and to limit the movements of all foreigners. In 1601 Matteo Ricci won a friendly reception, however, by presenting the emperor with his first map of Europe. He was permitted to establish a mission in Peking, was able later to introduce Christianity to other Chinese cities, and wrote several books on Christianity in Chinese. Ricci here describes China in his diary.*

The Chinese will not permit a foreigner to live at large within the confines of the kingdom if he has any intention of ever leaving it or if he has any communication with the outside world. Under no conditions will they permit a stranger to penetrate to the interior of the country. I have never heard of a law to this effect, but it seems quite clear that this custom has developed through the ages from an innate fear and distrust of outside nations. This suspicion exists not only of people who live overseas or at a great distance and are practically unknown to the Chinese. They are also suspicious of friendly as well as of enemy aliens, and even of those with whom they trade, such as the neighboring Koreans, who make use of Chinese laws. . . . If a foreigner should get into China secretly, he would not be put to death or kept in slavery, but he could be prevented from leaving China, lest he should stir up excitement outside to the detriment of the Chinese Government. Hence, the severest punishments are meted out to those who deal with outsiders without the direct consent of the sovereign.

When necessity demands that someone be sent beyond the borders, even though he will be supplied with the proper credentials and a mandate, it is difficult to get anyone to accept the commission. When such a legate is leaving, his whole family bewail his departure as though he were being sent to certain death. It is quite different, however, when he returns, because he is generally rewarded by being appointed to some kind of a judgeship.

* *China in the Sixteenth Century: The Journals of Matthew Ricci:* 1583–1610, New York, Random House, Inc., 1953 (translated by L. J. Gallagher).

# The Age of Absolutism

By 1500 national territorial states had begun to emerge more clearly, although feudalism and other aspects of medievalism died slowly. For the next three hundred years larger units than in medieval times tended to emerge. For example, England, Scotland, and Wales merged into the United Kingdom of Great Britain; Aragon, Leon, and Castile merged into Spain; and France reached its present size. In all European states, power came to rest in the person of a monarch—usually a king, although in some countries there was an occasional reigning queen. The political theory of the states was royal absolutism, justified by a theory that monarchs were divinely blessed and authorized. Economically the new centralization was expressed through the theory of mercantalism, which held that the economy should be in the interest of the state and subject to state controls. Philosophically the era was fascinated with the idea of balance: balance of power in diplomacy between nations, balance of trade in mercantalism, balance of design in painting and of space in architecture, balance of matter and energy in science, and so on.

Since human affairs never fit neatly into periods, there were exceptions to all the generalizations above. Germany and Italy failed to unite at this time in centralized forms. Queens were accepted in England two centuries before one could rule in Austria. Feudalism persisted in Poland throughout the three centuries. The divine-right theory was challenged and overthrown in England while it was still growing elsewhere. Mercantalism was never put into total practice anywhere. Many conditions from before 1500 continued into the era, many conditions after 1800 were born during it. Nevertheless the generalizations stated have enough reality to serve as guides into the history of 1500–1800.

## Political Satire in an Age of Despotism

*Under despotic governments freedom of speech did not exist, and criticism of rulers was severely punished. In England fun was poked at rulers in language that was deliberately left vague, so that the singer could not be accused of ridiculing the crown—although all of the listeners would know who was being derided. Hundreds of these jingles came into being, from "Humpty Dumpty," aimed at King Richard III in 1485, through "Georgy Porgy," poking fun at George I about 1720. In later times, when the political meaning had often been forgotten, collections were published for children's entertainment under the name of "Mother Goose Rhymes." A few examples follow.*

> *Robin the bobbin, big-bellied Ben*
> *Ate more meat then fourscore men,*
> *Ate the church, and ate the steeple,*
> *Ate the priests, and ate the people,*
> *And still his belly wasn't full.*

The first line had long been a popular reference against greedy priests in general. Here it was directed at King Henry VIII (1509–1547), who had Parliament declare him the head of the English Church. He then proceeded to seize lands and buildings of more than three thousand religious orders ("Ate the church," etc.) and still could not satisfy his financial appetite. Henry became grossly overweight in middle life, so the phrase "big-bellied" also had a personal application.

> *Mary, Mary, quite contrary,*
> *How does your garden grow*
> *With silver bells and cockle shells*
> *And pretty maids all in a row?*

Queen Mary I (1553–1558) whose poor body was "contrary," or twisted by arthritis or possibly tuberculosis, tried to restore England to the Catholic faith. This Protestant jingle jeers at this twice. The "silver bells" were a reminder of the emblem worn in the hats of Catholic pilgrims to Canterbury, and the "cockle shells" of those worn by pilgrims to the shrine of Saint James of Compostella, Spain. The Spanish reference also points to Mary's love for her husband, Philip II of Spain. The "pretty maids all in a row" is a phrase which appeared in other poems about Mary's sister, Elizabeth, and raises the question whether this satire may not have been written by the Protestant Elizabeth.

> *Ride a cock horse to Banbury Cross*
> *To see an old lady on a white horse,*
> *With rings on her fingers and bells on her toes*
> *She shall have music wherever she goes.*

Queen Elizabeth I (1558–1603) was inordinately proud of her beautiful hands and her collection of rings. In her old age she toured England taking her attendants on visits to great estates. With the bells on her bridle and stirrups and her court musicians, she attracted crowds of country folk to see her pass as at the medieval cross on the Banbury highway.

> *Rock-a-bye, baby, on the tree top,*
> *When the wind blows thy cradle will rock,*
> *If the bough breaks the cradle will fall*
> *And down will come baby, and cradle, and all!*

The birth of a son to King James II (1685–1688) aroused a Protestant fear that the new prince of Wales would be reared a Catholic like his mother, and so brought on the English Revolution of 1688 (called "bloodless" or "Glorious"). Down came baby from the top of the social tree as the royal family fled into exile.

*Wee Willie Winkie runs through the town*
*Upstairs and downstairs in his nightgown,*
*Calling at the window, crying at the lock,*
*"Are the children all abed? It's now eight o'clock."*

Invited to England to replace the exiled James II, William III (1689–1702) was heartily disliked by many people. His nickname recalls his small stature. Here he is being ridiculed for giving his personal attention to laws such as that which established a curfew forbidding young people to be on the streets late at night.

## An Exhausted Emperor Abdicates *

CHARLES V

> The greatest example of the uncentralized collections of territories which were to give way to closely organized national states was that held by Charles of Habsburg (1500–1558). As Emperor Charles V he presided over the Holy Roman Empire of the Germanies and Italy. As King Charles I he ruled Aragon, Navarre, Naples, and Sicily, all inherited from his grandfather Ferdinand of Aragon. As King Charles I he held Castile, Leon, and the Indies (America) as regent for his insane mother, Joanna, who was legally the heiress of Isabella of Castile. The Castilians hated Charles's identification with the Netherlands, where he was born, and tried to prevent his accepting the imperial title in Germany, threatening to release Mad Joanna from the castle at Tordesillas and place her on the throne. Aragon hated Charles as regent in Castile. The hundreds of German states were jealous of his power as their emperor. The Italian lands hated him as a German. Nationalism was growing in all quarters, and Charles was its victim.
>
> On Charles fell the added burdens of defending Christendom against the aggressive expansion of the Ottoman Turks, of trying in vain to contain Lutheranism in Germany and Calvinism in the Netherlands, of administering newly

* University of Pennsylvania, *Translations and Reprints from the Original Sources of European History*, vol. 3, no. 3, Philadelphia, 1912.

*acquired empires in Mexico, Peru, and the Philippines, of opposing Henry VIII of England, and of containing the imperialistic moves of France.*

*In 1555 the ravings at Tordesillas were silenced by death and the mad old woman ceased to be a possible political pawn of Castilian malcontents. In the same year the Peace of Augsburg gave the Lutheran princes in Germany legal status. At Brussels Charles then gave the Netherlands to his son Philip II in the words we hear next. The next year he made over to Philip also the crowns of Spain, Sicily, and the Indies. In 1558 Charles completed the transfer of the Holy Roman Empire to his brother, Ferdinand. On September 21, 1558, Charles's overburdened life ended.*

. . . You will remember that upon the 5th of February of this year there had elapsed forty years since my grandfather the emperor Maximilian, in the same place and at the same hour declared my majority at the age of fifteen, withdrew me from the guardianship under which I had remained up to that time and made me master of myself. The following year, which was my sixteenth, king Ferdinand died, my mother's father and my grandfather, in the kingdom over which I then commenced to reign, because my beloved mother, who has but lately died, was left, after the death of my father, with disordered judgment and never sufficiently recovered her health to become mistress of herself.

At that time I went to Spain, by way of the sea. Soon came the death of my grandfather Maximilian, in my 19th year, and although I was still young they conferred upon me in his stead the imperial dignity. I had no inordinate ambition to rule a multitude of kingdoms, but merely sought to secure the welfare of Germany, to provide for the defence of Flanders, to consecrate my forces to the safety of Christianity against the Turk and to labor for the extension of the Christian religion. But although such zeal was mine, I was unable to show so much of it as I might have wished, on account of the troubles raised by the heresies of Luther and the other innovators of Germany, and on account of serious war into which the hostility and envy of neighboring princes had driven me, and from which I have safely emerged, thanks to the favor of God. . . .

To-day I feel so exhausted that I should not be of any aid to you, as you see yourselves. In my present state of dejection and weakness, I should have to render a great and serious account to God and man, if I did not lay aside authority, as I have resolved to do, since my son, king Philip, is of an age sufficiently advanced to be able to govern you, and he will be, I hope, a good prince to all my beloved subjects.

I am determined then to retire to Spain, to yield to my son Philip the possession of all my states, and to my brother, the king of the Romans, the Empire. I particularly commend to you my son, and I ask of you in remembrance of me, that you extend to him the love which you have always borne towards me; moreover I ask you to preserve among yourselves the same affection and harmony. Be obedient towards justice, zealous in the observance of the laws, preserve respect for all that merits it, and do not refuse to grant to authority the support of which it stands in need.

Above all, beware of infection from the sects of neighboring lands. Extirpate at once the germs, if they appear in your midst, for fear lest they may spread abroad and utterly overthrow your state, and lest you may fall into the direst calamities. As to the manner in which I have governed you I confess that I have been more than once deceived, led astray by the inexperience of youth, by the hasty conclusions of young manhood, or by some other fault of human weakness. Nevertheless I make bold to assert, that never of my knowledge or by my will has wrong or violence been done to any of my subjects. If then any can complain of having suffered such, I aver that it is unknown to me and against my will; I declare before all the world that I regret it from the bottom of my heart, and I beseech all present, and those who are not here as well, to wish me well and to pardon me.


## Despots Could Be Popular *

Sebastian Giustiniani

> Worn out with the Wars of the Roses, which wrecked the power of the feudal nobility, in 1485 England accepted the seizure of the throne by Henry VII (Tudor) with relief. Henry liquidated all nobles opposed to himself and by careful economy amassed a full treasury. In 1509 the young Henry VIII inherited the absolute power of his father and

* University of Pennsylvania, *Translations and Reprints from the Original Sources of European History*, vol. 1, no. 1, Philadelphia, 1897.

*proceeded to make it stronger by breaking the religious ties which bound England to the continent. His father's wealth and his own boyish good looks did not last forever, but while they did, Henry was idolized by England. In his younger days he appears as a typical glamorous Renaissance prince, as reported by a Venetian observer.*

His majesty is twenty-nine years old and extremely handsome. Nature could not have done more for him. He is much handsomer than any other sovereign in Christendom; a great deal handsomer than the King of France; very fair and his whole frame admirably proportioned. On hearing that Francis I wore a beard, he allowed his own to grow, and as it is reddish, he has now a beard that looks like gold. He is very accomplished, a good musician, composes well, is a most capital horseman, a fine jouster, speaks good French, Latin and Spanish, is very religious, hears three masses daily, when he hunts, and sometimes five on other days. He hears the office every day in the queen's chamber, that is to say vesper and compline. He is very fond of hunting, and never takes his diversion without tiring eight or ten horses, which he causes to be stationed beforehand along the line of country he means to take, and when one is tired he mounts another, and before he gets home they are all exhausted. He is extremely fond of tennis, at which game it is the prettiest thing in the world to see him play, his fair skin glowing through a shirt of the finest texture. He gambles with the French hostages, to the amount occasionally, it is said of from 6,000 to 8,000 ducats in a day. [A Venetian ducat was equal to about $2.30.] He is affable and gracious, harms no one, does not covet his neighbor's goods, and is satisfied with his own dominions, having often said to me, "Sir Ambassador, we want all potentates to content themselves with their own territories; we are satisfied with this island of ours." He seems extremely desirous of peace.

He is very rich. His father left him ten millions of ready money in gold, of which he is supposed to have spent one-half in the war against France, when he had three armies on foot; one crossed the Channel with him, another was in the field against Scotland, and the third remained with the queen in reserve.

His revenues amount to about 350,000 ducats annually, and are derived from estates, forests and meres, the customs, hereditary and confiscated property, the duchies of Lancaster, York, Cornwall and Suffolk, the county palatine of Chester, and others, the principality of Wales, the export duties, the wool staple, the great seal, the annates yielded by Church benefices, the Court of Wards, and from New Year's gifts; for on the first day of the year it is customary for his majesty to make presents to everybody, but the value of those he receives in return greatly exceeds his own outlay. . . . His robes are very rich and superb, and he puts on new clothes every holiday.

## Despots Could Be Unpopular *

### Ivan IV of Russia

> In the year of the death of Henry VIII of England (1547), Ivan IV was crowned tsar of Russia. To western Europeans his country was as strange and distant as Cathay itself, but the same forces of history were at work there. In his centralizing of power in himself as king, Ivan was opposed by the local lords, called "boyars" in Russia. He strengthened and expanded his country, formed commercial ties with the west, introduced arts. But he was remembered less for these things than for his ruthlessness in suppressing rebellion and for slaying his own son in a mad fit of rage. So he entered history as Ivan "the Terrible." One of his letters to a rebel noble follows.

You have written that I am "corrupt in understanding to a degree unparalleled even among the [godless] peoples." And yet I will again place you as judge over myself; are you corrupt or am I, in that I wished to rule you and you did not wish to be under my power, and that for this I inflicted disgrace upon you? Or are you corrupt, in that not only did you [not] wish to be obedient and subordinate to me, but you even ruled over me, and took all my power from me, and ruled yourselves as you wanted and took all the sovereign authority from me: in word I was sovereign, but in fact I ruled nothing. How many evils I received from you, how many insults, how many injuries and rebukes! And for what? . . .

. . . And why did you want to place Prince Vladimir on the [throne of the] kingdom and to remove me and my children? Did I ascend the

* J. L. I. Fennel, ed., and trans., *The Correspondence Between Prince A. M. Kurbsky and Tsar Ivan IV of Russia, 1564–1579*, Cambridge, Cambridge University Press, 1955.

throne by robbery or armed force of blood [shed]? I was born to rule by the grace of God; and I do not even remember my father bequeathing the kingdom to me and blessing me—I grew up upon the throne. . . . And I could not endure such vexations; I stood up for myself. And you began still more to revolt against me and to betray [me]; and I therefore began to stand up against you still more harshly. I wanted to subdue you to my will; and you, in recompense—how you defiled and outraged the sanctity of the Lord! Having fallen into wrath against man, you have given offence to God. How many churches and monasteries and holy places have you utterly outraged and defiled! You yourselves will answer to God for this. In this too shall I again be silent; [but] now I will write to you on matters of the present. Behold, O Prince, the decrees of God; [namely] that God gives power to whom he will. But you, like the devil, with the priest Sylvester and Aleksey Adashev have said, (like he [the devil] boasting in [the book of] Job), " 'I have gone to and fro in the earth and walked up and down on that which is below the heaven, and that which is below the heaven have I brought beneath my feet,' and the Lord said unto him: 'hast thou considered my servant Job?' " Thus too did you think that the whole Russian land would be under your feet; but all your [evil] wisdom was of no avail, thanks to the will of God. For this reason have we sharpened our quill to write to you. . . .

## Despots Could Be Devious in Their Ruthlessness

ELIZABETH I OF ENGLAND

> *Whether it came naturally to her, or whether she consciously adopted policies that were ruthless and deceitful, will never be known about Elizabeth I, queen of England from 1558 to 1603. But there is no question that this queen, under whom England flourished, was expert in double-dealing and double-talk. Typical is her behavior in the execution by her command of Mary, queen of Scots. Having ordered it because of the plots against her own throne, Elizabeth flew into a rage when it was done, had her secretary arrested, and wrote to her cousin James, son of Mary of Scots, denying all responsibility. We read her letter, and then hear the other*

*side of the story in her secretary's "True Relation." Regardless of the reasons, the execution shocked Europe.*

QUEEN ELIZABETH TO JAMES VI OF SCOTLAND (1587)\*

MY DEAR BROTHER,—

I would you knew (though not felt) the extreme dolor that overwhelms my mind, for that miserable accident which (far contrary to my meaning) hath befallen. I have now sent this kinsman of mine whom ere now it hath pleased you to favour, to instruct you truly of that which is too irksome for my pen to tell you. I beseech you that as God and many more know, how innocent I am in this case: so you will believe me that if I had bid [directed] ought I would have bid [abided] by it. I am not so base minded that fear of any living creature or prince should make me afraid to do that were just, or don [make me] to deny the same. I am not of so base a lineage, nor carry so vile a mind. But, as not to disguise, fits not a King, so will I never dissemble my actions, but cause them show even as I meant them. Thus assuring yourself of me, that as I know this was deserved, yet if I had meant it I would never lay it on others' shoulders; no more will I not damnify myself, that thought it not.

The circumstance it may please you to have of this bearer. And for your part, think you have not in the world a more loving kinswoman, nor a more dear friend than myself; nor any that will watch more carefully to preserve you and your estate. And who shall otherwise persuade you, judge them more partial to others than you. And thus in haste I leave to trouble [cease troubling] you: beseeching God to send you a long reign. The 14th of Feb., 1586.

Your most assured loving sister and cousin,

ELIZAB. R.

A TRUE RELATION OF THAT WHICH PASSED BETWIXT HER MAJESTY
AND ME IN THE CAUSE OF THE LATE SCOTTISH QUEEN,
BY SIR WILLIAM DAVISON \*\*

After that the meeting at Fotheringay, about the cause of the late Scottish Queen, was dissolved, the Commissioners returned their sentence, revisited and signed, approved in Parliament, and notified to the world by proclamation, her Majesty being moved with the earnest suit and petitions

\* Charles W. Colby, *Selections from the Sources of English History,* New York, Longmans, Green & Co., 1905.
\*\* Nicholas H. Nicolas, *Life of William Davison,* London, John Nichols and Son, 1823.

of her subjects in the said Parliament assembled, to proceed against the said Queen according to the sentence, did at length give order to the Lord Treasurer to draw the warrant for her execution; which having performed and imparted to her Majesty, his Lordship, the next morning, sent for me to his chamber in Court, then at Richmond, and in the presence of Mr. Treasurer Knollys (whom I found with him) acquainted me therewith, and told me that, himself being to go presently to London, her Highness' pleasure was, that he should leave the same with me to cause it to be engrossed and brought unto her to sign; and so delivered it into my hands. Some few days after the warrant being ready I acquainted her Majesty withal, and desired to know her pleasure therein, who at that time thought good to forbear the signing thereof, because the French and Scotch Ambassadors were here intercessors for the S. Q. [Scottish Queen's] life, willing me to reserve it to a fitter season. By that occasion I retained it in my hands unpresented for the space of some 5 or 6 weeks at the least; . . .

Upon my coming in, her Majesty, descrying some papers in my hand, required what I had there. I answered they were things to be signed that concerned her service. She then demanded whether I had not met with the Lord Admiral, and whether he had said any thing to me touching the warrant for the Sc. Q. My answer was, that I had spoken with his Lordship in the privy chamber, and understood by him that it was her Highness' pleasure I should bring the same unto her to sign. Whereupon, she asking me for it, I delivered it into her hands, who, calling immediately for pen and ink, signed it, and laid it down by her upon the mats; and after some little speech, shewing the reasons why she had so long deferred it, as, namely, that the world might see she had not been violently carried thereunto by any humours of malice or revenge against her, however provoked by her offence, and how loth she was to take this course if she had seen any other way to secure her own person and state. She finally willed me to take up the said warrant, and to carry it immediately to the great seal, commanding me expressly to dispatch and send it down unto the Commissioners with all the expedition I might, appointing the Hall of Fotheringay for the place of execution, misliking the Court-yard for divers respects she alleged; and, in conclusion, absolutely forbade me to trouble her any further, or let her hear any more thereof till it was done. . . .

After dinner I repaired to the Lord Chancellor, according to my directions, having first visited Mr. Secretary Walsingham on my way, and acquainted him with those things her Majesty had given me in charge; and between three and four of the clock that afternoon passed the said warrant under seal; which done, I went home to my own house, where I stayed all that night. . . .

[The next morning] immediately upon my coming thither I went up into the privy chamber, where I found her Majesty, who presently calling me to her, asked me whether the warrant were sealed? I answered that it was dispatched the evening before, and shewed the same unto her; "but (said she) what needed that haste?" I replied, that I had made no more haste than both she herself had commanded me, and my duty in such a case required. And thereupon, taking occasion to ask her Majesty whether she continued in her purpose to proceed therein according to her former directions, or no, she answered she did, albeit she thought it might have been better handled, because this course threw the whole burthen upon herself. . . .

### Elizabethan Sea Dogs *

Francis Pretty

> Under mercantilist theory, the territories seized by Spain and Portugal around the world must not trade with anyone except the mother country. But the England of Elizabeth had produced a generation that was bold, daring, adventurous, and ambitious. Such English gentlemen as Raleigh, Hawkins, Drake and Cavendish became smugglers and pirates, scolded publicly and rewarded privately by Elizabeth for their raids on Spanish ports and their seizure of Spanish treasure ships. Sir Francis Drake of Plymouth was especially feared and hated by the Spanish. His sailing around the world, the next after Magellan's ill-fated voyage, is recounted by Francis Pretty, one of Drake's "gentlemen-at-arms."

The 15. day of November, in the year of our Lord 1577, Master *Francis Drake,* with a fleet of five ships and barks, and to the number of 164 men, gentlemen and sailors, departed from *Plymouth,* giving out his pretended voyage for *Alexandria.* . . .

* Edward J. Payne, *Voyages of the Elizabethan Seamen,* Oxford, Clarendon Press, 1907.

To *Lima* [Peru] we came the 13. of February; and, being entered the haven, we found there about twelve sail of ships lying fast moored at an anchor, having all their sails carried on shore; for the masters and merchants were here most secure, having never been assaulted by enemies, and at this time feared the approach of none such as we were. Our General rifled these ships, and found in one of them a chest full of reals of plate, and good store of silks and linen cloth; and took the chest into his own ship, and good store of the silks and linen. In which ship he had news of another ship called the *Cacafuego,* which was gone towards *Payta,* and that the same ship was laden with treasure. Whereupon we stayed no longer here, but, cutting all the cables of the ships in the haven, we let them drive whither they would, either to sea or to the shore; and with all speed we followed the *Cacafuego* toward *Payta.* . . . And about six of the clock we came to her and boarded her, and shot at her three pieces of ordnance, and strake down her mizen; and, being entered, we found in her great riches, as jewels and precious stones, thirteen chests full of reals of plate, fourscore pound weight of gold, and six-and-twenty ton of silver. The place where we took this prize was called *Cape de San Francisco,* about 150 leagues [south] from *Panama.* . . .

And while we were here we espied a ship and set sail after her, and took her, and found in her two pilots and a Spanish governor, going for the islands of the *Philippinas.* We searched the ship, and took some of her merchandises, and so let her go. Our General at this place and time, thinking himself, both in respect of his private injuries received from the Spaniards, as also of their contempts and indignities offered to our country and prince in general, sufficiently satisfied and revenged; and supposing that her Majesty at his return would rest contented with this service, purposed to continue no longer upon the Spanish coast, but began to consider and to consult of the best way for his country.

He thought it not good to return by the Straits, for two special causes; the one, lest the Spaniards should there wait and attend for him in great number and strength, whose hands, he, being left but one ship, could not possibly escape. The other cause was the dangerous situation of the mouth of the Straits in the South Sea; where continual storms reigning and blustering, as he found by experience, besides the shoals and sands upon the coast, he thought it not a good course to adventure that way. . . .

[Drake thereupon decided to return home to England by way of the Pacific.]

. . . From *Java Major* we sailed for the Cape of *Good Hope,* which was the first land we fell withal; neither did we touch with it, or any other land, until we came to *Sierra Leona,* upon the coast of *Guinea;* notwithstanding we ran hard aboard the cape, finding the report of the Portugals to be most false, who affirm that it is the most dangerous cape of the world, never without intolerable storms and present danger to travellers which come near the same. This cape is a most stately thing, and the fairest cape we saw in the whole circumference of the earth, and we passed by it the 18. of June. From thence we continued our course to *Sierra Leona,* on the coast of *Guinea,* where we arrived the 22. of July, and found necessary provisions. . . .

We arrived in *England* the third of November, 1580, being the third year of our departure.

## The Battle of Lepanto *

MIGUEL DE CERVANTES SAAVEDRA

> *Most despotic rulers took their responsibilities seriously. When Cyprus, a possession of Venice, was seized by the Turks, the pope called for a crusade, and Philip II of Spain responded. On October 5, 1571, the Spanish and Venetian fleets, commanded by Philip's half-brother Don Juan of Austria, defeated the 300 ships of the Turkish navy at Le-panto in the Gulf of Corinth. It was the Turks' first defeat at sea, and for a time they were checked. Miguel de Cervantes Saavedra describes the battle, in which he lost a hand. In later years Cervantes used his other hand to write* Don Quixote, *poking fun at those who still believed in medieval chivalry.*

And on that happy day, when dubious Fate
   Look'd on the foeman's fleet with baleful eye,
   On ours with smiling glance and fortunate,
Inspired with mingled dread and courage high,
   In thickest of the direful fight I stood,

* Henry Edward Watts, *Life of Miguel de Cervantes,* London, Walter Scott, 1891.

My hope still stronger than my panoply
I marked the shatter'd host melt like a flood,
    And thousand spots upon old Neptune's breast
    Dyed red with heathen and with Christian blood;
Death, like a fury, running with foul zest
    Hither and thither, sending crowds in ire
    To lingering torture, or to speedy rest;
The cries confused, the horrid din and dire,
    The mortal writhings of the desperate,
    Who breath'd their last 'mid water and 'mid fire;
The deep-drawn sighs, the groanings loud and great
    That sped from wounded breasts in many a throe,
    Cursing their bitter and detested fate;
The blood that still was left them ceased to flow,
    What time our trumpets, pealing far and near,
    Proclaimed our glory and their overthrow;
The sounds triumphant, ringing loud and clear,
    Bore through the smitten air, in jubilant flood,
    The Christians' victory, from ear to ear!
At that sweet moment I, unlucky, stood
    With one hand buckled firmly to my blade,
    The other dripping downward streams of blood;
Within my breast a cruel thrust had made
    A deep and gaping wound, and my left hand
    Was bruised and shatter'd, past all human aid.

## *The Destruction of the Invincible Armada* *

> For years Elizabeth continued her undercover war against
> Spain while talking about good relations. By 1587 the
> patience of Philip II was exhausted. English raids had in-
> creased, even into Spain's home ports; the Dutch rebels
> against Spain in the Netherlands were being supplied with
> English money; the execution of the Catholic queen of
> Scots had ended the hope that she might succeed to the

* Victor von Klarwill, ed., *The Fugger News-Letters*, New York, G. P. Putnam's
Sons, 1925.

*English throne. In 1588 the "navy that could not be de-*
*feated" sailed against England. Sir Francis Drake, bowling*
*on the high green lawn of the Ho at Plymouth, refused to*
*interrupt his game when the Armada was sighted in the*
*Channel, saying, "We have time to finish the game and still*
*whip the Spaniards." Storms, English seamanship in sailing*
*their small craft into the wind, daring, and good luck all*
*helped prove Drake right. The world-shaking news was*
*reported to the Fugger bankers in Germany in the following*
*dispatch.*

The Armada of the King of Spain set sail from Portugal with one hundred and thirty-five ships, to wit: four galleasses from Naples, four galleons from Portugal, ten vessels with victuals, fourteen Venetian ships, among them several galleons. The remainder was made up of other large and small craft. The Armada arrived in Corunna on the 5th day of July, from whence it intended to sail for Flanders, there to join forces with the Duke of Parma and invade England. At that time the English Armada was in Plymouth Port.

After they had been under sail from Corunna eight days they arrived in Ostend and thereupon lay south of the shores of England, where for four or five days they had various skirmishes with the English Armada. On that occasion the English took two ships. On one of these there was Don Pedro di Mendoza, whom they took prisoner and so to England. Storms south of England caused them the loss of four Portuguese galleons which remained stranded on the French coast. They then proceeded and cast anchor off Calais, since they could no longer get as far as Dunkirk. They wished to wait for the Duke of Parma in Calais, but he sent word that he could not be ready under eight days. Thereupon the admiral sent reply that he would again set sail for Spain. Meanwhile the English sent forth against the Spanish Armada several burning ships, so that they were forced to cut their moorings and to retire hastily. Each ship left two anchors behind and four of the largest galleasses were stranded and wrecked off Calais. The following day at eight o'clock, the two Armadas had a further encounter, heavily bombarding each other for eight hours. In this battle the Spanish lost four ships, namely two Portuguese galleasses, a vessel from Biscay and one other. All four went to the bottom of the sea. Three large Venetian craft remained behind off the coast of Flanders and were in great peril of going under. The inhabitants of Flushing took two of these ships, and the third was shipwrecked. One of them had on board the Colonel commanding the garrison of Seville. According to the prisoners' report the Spaniards lost four thousand men in the battle off Calais, amongst them the Commander-in-Chief of the cavalry at Naples and Seville. The Spaniards are said to have left one hundred and twenty ships, although others could count only one hundred and ten. The big galleon, which the Duke of Florence had sent, was not to be seen anywhere after the battle.

Hereafter the Armada made off and was pursued by the English for five days as far as Scotland. When they counted their men there they found that they had already lost eight thousand, most of whom had been killed or died of disease. From thence they set sail for Ireland without taking provisions on board. Off Ireland they lost two ships, the San Sebastian and the San Mathias, which had four hundred and fifty-six men on board. Lacking fresh water, the fleet threw many horses and mules overboard off Ireland. When they sailed away from Ireland, the Commander-in-Chief, the Duke of Medina Sidonia, ordered each one of his captains to set his course for Corunna or the first Spanish port. They thus sailed together throughout ten days. Then the storm separated the Duke of Medina Sidonia with twenty-seven of his ships from them and no one knew where they had gone. The last time the Armada was assembled it counted no more than seventy-eight ships. Of the big galleasses not one was left. Two of the Duke of Medina Sidonia's ships ran ashore. Only two or three of the men were saved. They say that the Chief Admiral had left on board only five-and-twenty more barrels of wine, but little bread and no water. His masts had been so weakened by firing that he could not carry full canvas. . . . On the 10th day of September a further large ship of five hundred tons, Maria della Rosa, ran ashore off Ireland. . . . The vessel carried fifty cannon and twenty-five other metal pieces, as well as 15,000 ducats and silver reals and much gold. The same day two big vessels put eight hundred and fifty men ashore in Ireland, seven hundred of whom died, and the remainder were taken prisoner. The vessels were cast ashore. On the 12th day of September another big ship was wrecked. Thirteen noblemen were taken prisoner and four hundred men reached land. From yet another ship seventy-eight bodies were washed ashore. From a further wrecked vessel three noblemen, a bishop and seventy-nine mercenaries were taken prisoner. The others perished. On the 17th day of September two large vessels, the St. Joaquim and the St. Martin, sank. The admiral was de Ricaldo, and his ship was almost the largest in the whole fleet. There were on it eight hundred soldiers, sixty Portuguese and forty Biscay fishermen. They had starved for almost four days. . . . On the 18th day of September there arrived news from Ireland that very many bodies had been washed ashore.

## Time Out for Football *

> Great sea battles might be fought and plots against thrones provoke civil war, but not everybody was concentrating on "big issues" in the 1580's, as we see in this complaint about the violence of football.

As concerning football playing, I protest unto you it may rather be called a friendly kinde of fight than a play or recreation; a bloody and murthering practise, than a felowly sporte or pastime. For dooth not every one lye in waight for his adversarie, seeking to overthrowe him, and to pitch him on his nose, though it be upon hard stones? in ditch or dale, in valley or hil, or what place soever it be, hee careth not, so he have him down. And he that can serve the most of this fashion, he is counted the only felow; and who but he? So that by this means, sometimes their necks are broken, sometimes their backs, sometime their legs, sometime their arms; sometime one part thrust out of joynt, sometime another; sometime the noses gush out with blood, sometime their eyes start out, and sometimes hurt in one place, sometimes in another. But whosoever scapeth away the best, goeth not scot free, but is either sore wounded, craised, and bruseed, so as he dyeth of it, or else scapeth very hardly. And no mervaile, for they have the sleights to meet one betwixt two, to dashe him against the hart with their elbowes, to hit him under the short ribbes with their griped fists, and with their knees to catch him upon the hip, and to pick him on his neck, with a hundred such murdering devices; and hereof groweth envy, malice, rancour, choler, hatred, displeasure, enmitie, and what not els: and sometimes fighting, brawling, contention, quarrel-picking, murther, homicide, and great effusion of blood, as experience daly teacheth.

* R. B. Morgan, *Readings in English Social History,* Cambridge, At the University Press, 1923.

Is this murthering play, now, an exercise for the Sabath day? is this a Christian dealing, for one brother to mayme and hurt another, and that upon prepensed malice or set purpose? is this to do to another as we would wish another to doo to us? God make us more careful over the bodyes of our brethren!

## The Beginnings of Colonialism *

ELIZABETH I

> *Permission for individuals or groups to engage in business was granted in royal "patents" or "charters," which frequently granted the right to maintain military forces and enact local laws. Some of these came to be looked upon as political constitutions, contrary to their original intention. Part of the English East India Company charter follows.*

Whereas our most dear and loving cousin, Earl of Cumberland [and two hundred and fifteen others] have been Petitioners unto us, for our Royal Assent and licence to be granted unto them, that they, at their own costs and charges, as well as for the honour of this our Realm of England, as for the increase of our navigation and advancement of trade and merchandize . . . might set forth on one or more voyages . . . to the East Indies, [and] in the countries and parts of Asia and Africa. . . . KNOW YE THEREFORE, that we greatly tendering the honour of our Nation, and the wealth of our people . . . do give and grant unto our said loving subjects . . . that they from henceforth shall be one body corporate . . . by the name of *The Governor and Company of Merchants of London, Trading into the East Indies.* . . . They shall have succession, and that they and their successors . . . shall be, at all times hereafter, persons able and capable in law, and a body corporate and politic, and capable in law to have, purchase, receive, possess, enjoy and retain, lands rents, priviledges. . . . And that they and their successors . . . may plead and be impleaded [sue or be sued], answer and be answered, defend and be defended, in whatsoever courts and places. . . .

* East India Company, *Charters Granted to the East India Company, from 1601,* London, 1773.

The said [Company] and their successors, may have a Common Seal, to serve for all the causes and business. . . . Henceforth twenty-four of the said Company, be elected . . . which shall be called *The Committee of the Said Company,* who together with the Governor . . . shall have the direction [of the Company]. . . . The said *Governor and Committee* . . . may have authority and power, yearly, on the first day of July, or at any time within six days after that day, to assemble and meet together, in some convenient place, to be appointed from time to time by the Governor . . . elect and nominate one of the said Company, which shall be Governor of the said Company for one whole Year. . . . [and] to elect and nominate twenty-four of the said Company, which shall be the Committee of the said Company, for one whole year. . . .

[The Company may] constitute such, and so many reasonable laws . . . [it] shall deem necessary and convenient, for the good government of the same Company . . . and at their pleasure to revoke or alter the same, as occasion shall require . . . and may lawfully impose, ordain, limit and provide such pains, punishments and penalties, by imprisonment of body, or by fines . . . against all offenders [of the laws] . . . ; so [long] always as [the] said laws, orders . . . imprisonments and fines be reasonable, and not contrary or repugnant to the laws, statutes, or customs of this our Realm. . . .

[The Company] shall for a term of fifteen years, have, use, and enjoy, the whole entire and only trade and traffic . . . to and from the said East Indies and to and from all the islands, ports, cities, towns and places aforesaid [in the Charter]. . . .

## New Aids To Business *

ELIZABETH I

> *A popular new device became the selling of shares in a venture; the buyers were given certificates for their share of the "stock in trade." Another device to encourage business ventures was insurance against loss. In 1601 Elizabeth appointed a commision to supervise insurance activities.*

* Adam Anderson, *Origins of Commerce,* vol. 1, London, A. Millar, J. and R. Tonson, etc., 1764.

Whereas it hath been usage amongst merchants, both of this realm and of foreign nations, when they make any adventure, (especially into remote parts) to give some consideration of money to other persons, (which commonly are in no small number) to have from them Assurance made of their goods, merchandizes, ships, and things . . . at such rates, and in such sort, as the parties *assurers* and the parties assured, can agree; which course of dealing is commonly termed *A Policy of Assurance:* By means of which, it cometh to pass, upon the loss or perishing of any ship, there followeth not the undoing of any man, but the loss lighteth rather *easily upon many,* than *heavily upon few;* . . . . And whereas heretofore, such assurers have used to stand to so justly and precisely upon their credits, as few or no controversies have risen thereupon; and if any have grown, the same have from time to time been ended and ordered by certain grave and discreet merchants, appointed by the Lord Mayor of London.—Until of late years, that divers persons have withdrawn themselves from that course; and have . . . suits commenced in her Majesty's Courts, to their great charges and delays.

[For remedy, it is now enacted] that the Lord Chancellor do award one general or standing yearly Commission, for the determining of causes on policies of assurances. . . . Which Commission shall have authority to determine all causes concerning policies of assurance . . . ; who shall summon the parties;—examine witnesses upon oath, and imprison disobeyers of their decrees. . . .


## *This Stinking Smoke* *

JAMES I

> *Not everything brought to Europe from the colonies was looked on with favor. South America's potato was considered safe only for animal consumption. North America's tobacco was accepted by the public, which by 1618 was chewing, smoking, and snuffing it at the rate of 50,000 pounds a year. Some people looked askance at the "filthy novelty," among them King James I of England.*

* Edward Arber, ed., "A Counterblast to Tobacco," *English Reprints*, London, 1870.

. . . Surely Smoke becomes a kitchen far better than a Dining chamber, and yet it makes a kitchen also oftentimes in the inward parts of men, foiling and infecting them, with an unctuous and oily kind of Soot, as hath been found in some great Tobacco takers, that after their death were opened. . . . The public use whereof, at all times, and in all places, hath now so far prevailed, as divers men very sound both in judgment, and complexion, have been at last forced to take it also without desire, partly because they were ashamed to seem singular, (like the two Philosophers that were forced to duck themselves in that rain water, and so become fools as well as the rest of the people) and partly, to be as one that was content to eat Garlic . . . that he might not be troubled with the smell of it, in the breath of his fellows. And is it not a great vanity, that a man cannot heartily welcome his friend now, but straight they must be in hand with Tobacco? No it is become in place of a cure, a point of good-fellowship, and he that will refuse to take a pipe of Tobacco among his fellows . . . is accounted peevish and no good company. . . . But herein is not only a great vanity, but a great contempt of Gods good gifts, that the sweetness of mans breath, being a good gift of God, should be willfully corrupted by this stinking smoke. . . .

Moreover, which is a great iniquity, and against all humanity, the husband shall not be ashamed to reduce thereby his delicate, wholesome, and clean complexioned wife, to that extremity, that either she must corrupt her sweet breath therewith, or else resolve to live in a perpetual stinking torment.

Have you not reason then to be ashamed, and to forbear this filthy novelty, so basely grounded, so foolishly received and so grossly mistaken in the right use thereof?

### Reasons for Migrating to America *

JOHN WINTHROP, GEORGE FOX

*Men left Europe and migrated to the New World for a variety of reasons. Some sought wealth, in the form of either*

* First selection from John Winthrop, *Life and Letters of John Winthrop*, Boston, Ticknor and Fields, 1864; second selection from George Fox, *Journal*, Philadelphia, Kimber and Sharpless, Uriah Hunt, and Nathan Kite, 1832.

*land or treasure. Others were missionaries who traveled the length and breadth of the new lands seeking converts. And increasingly, men left their old lives and endured the hardships of a long sea voyage in order to find a haven from the turmoil they had known. Religious intolerance, political revolution, and hard times combined during the seventeenth century to encourage thousands of Englishmen to migrate to the American colonies. John Winthrop, a wealthy Puritan who later was chosen governor of the Massachusetts Bay Colony, gives some typical reasons for his decision to settle in America. In the account of George Fox, founder of the Society of Friends (Quakers), no mention is made of America; but one can readily understand why many Quakers later went to settle there.*

1. It will be a service to the Church of great consequence to carry the Gospell into those parts of the world, to helpe on the comminge of the fullnesse of the Gentiles, & to raise a Bulworke against the kingdome of AnteChrist which the Jesuites labour to reare up in those parts.

3. This Land growes weary of her Inhabitants, soe as man, whoe is the most pretious of all creatures, is here more vile & base then the earth we treade upon, & of lesse prise among us then an horse or a sheepe: masters are forced by authority to entertaine servants, parents to mainetaine there owne children, all townes complaine of the burthen of theire poore. . . .

4. The whole earth is the Lords garden & he hath given it to the Sonnes of men with a generall Commission: Gen: 1: 28: increace & multiplie, & replenish the earth & subdue it, which was againe renewed to Noah: the end is double & naturall, that man might enioy the friuts of the earth, & God might have his due glory from the creature: why then should we stand striving here for places of habitation, etc., (many men spending as much labour & coste to recover or keepe sometimes an acre or twoe of Land, as would procure them many & as good or better in another Countrie) & in the meane time suffer a whole Continent as fruitfull & convenient for the use of man to lie waste without any improvement?

6. The ffountaines of Learning & Religion are soe corrupted as (besides the unsupportable charge of there education) most children (even the best witts & of fairest hopes) are perverted, corrupted, & utterlie overthrowne by the multitude of evill examples & the licentious government.

7. What can be a better worke, & more honorable & worthy a Christian then to helpe raise & supporte a particular Church while it is in the Infancy, & to ioyne his forces with such a company of faithfull people, as by a timely assistance may growe stronge & prosper . . . ?

On a lecture-day I was moved to go to the steeple-house at Ulverstone, where were abundance of professors, priests, and people. I went near to priest Lampitt, who was blustering on in his preaching. After the Lord had opened my mouth to speak, John Sawrey the justice came to me, and said, "If I would speak according to the scriptures, I should speak." I admired at him for speaking so to me, and told him, "I would speak according to the scriptures, and bring the scriptures to prove what I had to say; for I had something to speak to Lampitt and to them." Then he said, I should not speak; contradicting himself, who had said just before, "I should speak, if I would speak according to the scriptures." The people were quiet, and heard me gladly, till this justice Sawrey (who was the first stirrer up of cruel persecution in the north) incensed them against me, and set them on to hale, beat, and bruise me. . . . At last he came and took me from the people, led me out of the steeple-house, and put me into the hands of the constables and other officers; bidding them whip me, and put me out of the town. They led me about a quarter of a mile, some taking hold by my collar, some by my arms and shoulders, who shook and dragged me along. Many friendly people being come to the market, and some to the steeple-house to hear me, divers of these they knock'd down also, and broke their heads, so that the blood ran down from several; and judge Fell's son running after to see what they would do with me, they threw him into a ditch of water; some of them crying, "Knock the teeth out of his head." When they had haled me to the common moss side, a multitude following, the constables and other officers gave me some blows over my back with their willow rods, and thrust me among the rude multitude; who, having furnished themselves with staves, hedge-stakes, holm or holly bushes, fell upon me, and beat me on my head, arms, and shoulders, till they had deprived me of sense; so that I fell down upon the wet common. When I recovered again, and saw myself lying in a watery common, and the people standing about me, I lay still a little while, and the power of the Lord sprang through me, and the eternal refreshings revived me; so that I stood up again in the strengthening power of the eternal God, and stretching out my arms amongst them, I said, with a loud voice, "Strike again; here are my arms, my head, and my cheeks.". . . .

# Mercantilism Finds A Spokesman *

## THOMAS MUN

> *Side by side with the growing political power of kings went the economic practices of "mercantilism," a system which held that business should be controlled by the state in order to insure the continuing accumulation of gold. Mercantilism appeared in all European countries, although in differing degree and at different times. As a theory, mercantilism was clearly explained by Thomas Mun, a merchant who looked back over mercantilist practices of a century in writing his book.*

Although a Kingdom may be enriched by gifts received, or by purchase taken from some other Nations, yet these are things uncertain and of small consideration when they happen. The ordinary means therefore to encrease our wealth and treasure is by *Forraign Trade*, wherein wee must ever observe this rule; to sell more to strangers yearly than wee consume of theirs in value. For suppose that when this Kingdom is plentifully served with the Cloth, Lead, Tinn, Iron, Fish and other native commodities, we doe yearly export the overplus to forraign Countries to the value of twenty two hundred thousand pounds; by which means we are enabled beyond the Seas to buy and bring in forraign wares for our use and Consumptions, to the value of twenty hundred thousand pounds; By this order duly kept in our trading, we may rest assured that the Kingdom shall be enriched yearly two hundred thousand pounds, which must be brought to us in so much Treasure; because that part of our stock which is not returned to us in wares must necessarily be brought home in treasure. . . .

1. First, although this Realm be already exceeding rich by nature, yet might it be much encreased by laying the waste grounds (which are infinite) into such employments as should no way hinder the present revenues of other cultivated lands, but hereby to supply our selves and prevent the importations of Hemp, Flax, Cordage, Tobacco, and divers other things which now we fetch from strangers to our great impoverishing.

2. We may likewise diminish our importations, if we would soberly refrain from excessive consumption of forraign wares in our diet and rayment, with such often change of fashions as is used. . . .

* Thomas Mun, *England's Treasure By Forraign Trade,* Oxford, published for The Economic History Society by Basil Blackwell, 1928.

3. In our exportations we must not only regard our own superfluities, but also we must consider our neighbours necessities, that so . . . we may . . . gain so much of the manufacture as we can. . . .

4. The value of our exportations likewise may be much advanced when we perform it our selves in our own Ships. . . .

## Absolutism Grows in France *

### CARDINAL RICHELIEU, LOUIS XIII

> The country that eventually became the strongest of the absolute monarchies was France. The architects of French royal supremacy were Cardinals Richelieu and Mazarin, the advisers to King Louis XIII and the young Louis XIV. These statesmen directed French involvement in the Thirty Years War and strengthened the throne against its enemies at home. First we hear Cardinal Richelieu tell how he strengthened the power of Louis XIII. Then we read an edict of Louis XIII, from 1626, designed to weaken his enemies at home and increase his hold on France.

When Your Majesty resolved to admit me both to your council and to an important place in your confidence for the direction of your affairs, I may say that the Huguenots shared the state with you; that the nobles conducted themselves as if they were not your subjects, and the most powerful governors of the provinces as if they were sovereigns in their offices. . . .

I may say that everyone measured his own merit by his audacity; that in place of esteeming the benefits which they received from Your Majesty at their proper worth, they all valued them only as they satisfied the demands of their imaginations; that the most scheming were held to be the wisest, and often found themselves the most prosperous.

I may further say that foreign alliances were scorned, private interests being preferred to those of the public, and in a word, the dignity of the royal majesty was so disparaged, and so different from what it should be, because of the misdeeds of those who conducted your affairs, that it was

* First selection reprinted with permission of the copyright owners, The Regents of the University of Wisconsin, from Henry Bertram Hill, ed., *The Political Testament of Cardinal Richelieu*, Madison, The University of Wisconsin Press, 1961; second selection from Athanase J. L. Jourdan, *Recueil des anciennes lois françaises*, vol. 16, Paris, Librairie de Plon Frères, 1822 (an original translation by Judith Harnick).

almost impossible to recognize it. It was impossible, without losing all, to tolerate longer the conduct of those to whom Your Majesty had intrusted the helm of state; and yet everything could not be changed at once without violating the laws of prudence, which do not permit the passing from one extreme to another without preparation. . . .

The best minds did not think that it would be possible to pass without shipwreck all the rocks in such uncertain times. . . . So few people, consequently, expected good results from the change which it was announced I wished to make, that many held my fall assured even before Your Majesty had elevated me.

Notwithstanding these difficulties which I explained to Your Majesty, knowing how much kings may do when they make good use of their power, I dared to promise you, with assurance, that you would soon find remedies for the disorders in your state, and that your prudence, your courage, and the benediction of God would give a new aspect to this realm. I promised Your Majesty to employ all my industry and all the authority which it should please you to give me to ruin the Huguenot party, to abase the pride of the nobles, to bring all your subjects back to their duty, and to restore your reputation among foreign nations to the state it ought to occupy.

Whereas formerly the assemblies of the states of this realm and those of notable persons chosen to advise us and the late king, our very honored lord and father, on the important affairs of this realm . . . having constantly required and very humbly begged our said late lord and father and us to destroy several strongholds in various places of this realm, which, being neither on enemy frontiers nor in places of consequence, serve only to augment our expense under the name of useless garrisons, and serve as a retreat for various people who, on the least provocation, greatly trouble the provinces where they are located. . . .

For these reasons, we announce, declare, proclaim, and will, that all the strongholds, either towns or castles, which are in the interior of our realm . . . not situated in places of importance either for frontier protection or for other reasons of weight, shall be razed and demolished; even ancient walls shall be destroyed so far as it shall seem necessary for the well-being and peace of our subjects and the security of this state, so that our said subjects henceforth need not fear that the said places will cause them any inconvenience, and so that we shall be freed from the expense of supporting garrisons in them.

# The Most Successful Absolutist of Them All *

Louis XIV

> On the death of Cardinal Mazarin in 1661, Louis XIV took
> the direction of French affairs into his own hands, where they
> remained until his own death in 1715. Under him France
> rose to the position of first place among the nations of
> Europe, and in him royal absolutism, based on the theory of
> divine right of kings, found its most successful practitioner.
> Louis forced the nobles of France into a position of depend-
> ence on his favors, and he developed a group of professional
> administrators that was responsible solely to him. As a result
> of his unceasing efforts, the last half of the seventeenth
> century became known as the "Age of Louis XIV"; his
> armies, clothes, palaces, manners, and actions were copied by
> rulers of other states, large or small, as far as their finances
> would permit. Although the statement "The state is me!"
> (L'état c'est moi) probably was never made by Louis, it
> would have been literally true if he had said it. Louis gives
> us a glimpse of his ideas and attitudes as we read his instruc-
> tions to his son concerning government and the role of a
> sovereign.

### THE IMPORTANCE OF BEING WELL INFORMED

In a word, my son, it is most necessary to have your eyes open, watch-
ful over all parts of the world. It is essential to learn the news of all the
provinces and nations, the secrets of every court, the temper and weakness
of each prince and of all the foreign ministers. We must be informed of
an infinite number of things that people generally believe we do not know
and see that which is hidden with great care from us. . . .

### USE OF MINISTERS

As regards the persons who must assist me in my work, I was resolved
above all things not to secure a first minister [such as Richelieu and Mazarin
had been]. If you take my advice, my son, and all your successors after
you, the office of first minister shall be abolished forever in France, there
being nothing more unworthy than visualizing on one side the executive

* From *Pageant of Europe* by Raymond P. Stearns, copyright, 1947, © 1961, by
Harcourt, Brace & World, Inc., and reprinted with their permission.

head, and on the other the sale of kingly offices. For this plan it was absolutely necessary that I share my confidence and the execution of orders with others without giving full authority in anything to a single person. I placed various persons in different kinds of work and directed their special skills, which is, perhaps, the first and greatest talent of princes.

In order that I might better succeed as king, as there were a great many affairs where our occupations and dignity did not ordinarily permit us to descend, I resolved, when I had made choice of my ministers, to confer several times with each one. When he expected the least to happen he suddenly found matters of business thrust upon him. . . .

In regard to the art of knowing your men, which is so important to you, I tell you, my son, that it is possible to learn but more difficult to teach it. In general, it is undoubtedly right to consider their general reputation and established place in society, because the public has no interest in these and is greatly imposed on in these matters. It is wise to listen to everybody, but believe nobody other than the good which they are constrained to recognize in their enemies, which they are loath to admit, or the bad qualities which they see in their friends, which they try to excuse. . . . But in arriving at conclusions, one learns the talents, the inclinations, and the courage of each one by studying each one and pleasing each one. . . .

### ON ARRIVING AT DECISIONS

The most clever persons, in their own interest, take advice from other clever persons. What would kings be like who, having the public interest in their hands and possessing the power of good or evil throughout the earth, did not take advice? One must not form any important decisions without having called upon, if possible, all the sources of knowledge, wisdom, and reason of our subjects. . . .

Our rank, my son, estranges us in a certain manner from our people, to which our ministers are the nearest which we are capable of consulting. They attend to a thousand details which we ignore—for which, however, we must make decisions and take action. We must not overlook the age, experience, study, and liberty of them that have been greater than all our capacities. This wisdom of our inferiors we must borrow and accept from persons of highest to lowest degree.

But in the important occasions, when all evidence and contrary reasons have been brought to our attention, the decisive action, my son, is up to us; for we decide that which we must enforce. And in this choice, I tell you that we must lack neither sense nor courage.

# Criticism of Louis XIV *

François de Fénelon

*Not everybody in France was happy with conditions under the "Sun King," but most of them were afraid to show it. When a word of criticism did reach Louis, it was made anonymously, as was this unsigned letter from Archbishop Fénelon, tutor of one of the royal children.*

Sire, the person who takes the liberty to write this letter to you has no ax to grind. . . . If he speaks strongly to you, do not be astonished; for the truth is free and strong. You have not been accustomed to hear it. . . .

For nearly thirty years, your principal Ministers have destroyed and reversed all the ancient maxims of the state in order to raise your authority to its highest pitch, an authority which has become theirs because they have it in their own hands. They no longer speak of the state and of its constitution; they only speak of the King and of his royal pleasure. They have pushed your revenues and your expenses to unprecedented heights. They have raised you up to the sky in order, they say, to outshine the grandeur of all your predecessors; that is to say, in order to impoverish the whole of France for the introduction of monstrous and futile luxuries at the court. They have wished to establish you upon the ruin of all the state, as if you could be great in ruining all your subjects, upon whom your true greatness rests. It is true that you have been jealous of authority, perhaps even too much so in little things; but, at bottom, each Minister has been master in the conduct of his own administration. You have believed yourself governor because you have regulated the limits of those who govern. They have well demonstrated their power to the public, and they have done it only too completely. They have been harsh, haughty, unjust, violent, of bad faith. They have recognized no other rule, either in the administration of internal affairs or in foreign relations, but to threaten, to crush, and to destroy all who resist them. . . . They have caused almost twenty years of bloody wars. . . .

Meanwhile, your people, whom you should love as your children, and who until now have been so eager to support you, die of hunger. The cultivation of the soil is almost abandoned; the towns and the countryside

* From *Pageant of Europe* by Raymond P. Stearns, coypright, 1947, © 1961, by Harcourt, Brace & World, Inc., and reprinted with their permission.

are depopulated; all business enterprise is stagnant, and no longer offers employment to workingmen. All commerce is destroyed. As a result, you have ruined half of the real forces within your state in order to make and defend vain conquests outside. Instead of taking money from these poor people, one should give them alms and feed them. All France is nothing more than a great poorhouse, desolate and without provisions. . . .

The people themselves, it should be said, who hitherto have loved you and had confidence in you, are beginning to lose love, confidence, and even respect. Your victories and your conquests no longer cause them to rejoice; they are full of bitterness and despair. Sedition is kindled little by little everywhere. They believe that you love only your authority and your glory. . . .

There, Sire, is the state of things. You live as one whose eyes are fatally blinded.

## Letters from a "Persian" *

CHARLES DE MONTESQUIEU

> *The Baron Charles de Montesquieu, a widely read writer on government, had great influence on later political thinkers, including the framers of the United States Constitution. He did not particularly admire Louis XIV; even in Louis's old age, he thought it safer to publish his description of the king under the makeshift of calling it a letter from a Persian.*

The king of France is an old man. We have no instance in our history of a monarch that has reigned so long. They say he possesses to an extraordinary degree the talent of making himself obeyed. . . .

I have made a study of his character, and I find contradictions which I am unable to reconcile: . . . he is devoted to religion, and he cannot endure those who say it must be rigorously observed; although he flees the tumult of the city and has . . . [contact] with few, yet he is occupied from morning until night in making himself talked about; he loves trophies and victories, but he is afraid of seeing a good general at the head of his

* University of Pennsylvania, *Translations and Reprints from the Original Sources of European History,* vol. 6, no. 1, Philadelphia, 1899.

troops, lest he should have cause to fear the chief of a hostile army. He is the only one, I believe, to whom it has ever happened that he was at the same time overwhelmed with more riches than a prince might hope to possess and burdened with a poverty that a private person would be unable to bear.

He loves to gratify those that serve him; but he rewards the efforts, or rather the indolence, of his courtiers more liberally than the arduous campaigns of his captains. Often he prefers a man whose duty it is to disrobe him or hand him his napkin when he seats himself at dinner, to another who takes cities or wins him battles. He believes that the sovereign grandeur ought not to be limited in the distribution of favors; and without investigating as to whether the one upon whom he heaps benefits is a man of merit, he believes that his choice renders him such; so that he has been seen to give a small pension to a man who had run two leagues, and a fine government to another who had run four.

He is magnificent, especially in his buildings. There are more statues in the gardens of his palace than there are citizens in a great city. His guard is as strong as that of the prince before whom all thrones are overturned; his armies are as numerous, his resources are as great and his finances as inexhaustible.

*Paris, the 7th of the moon of Maharram, 1713.*

## Colbert's Commercial Policy *

Louis XIV

> *Until his death in 1683, Jean Baptiste Colbert served as controller-general of finance for Louis XIV. This honest and hard-working administrator made every effort to promote mercantilist doctrine in France. In addition, Colbert brought a degree of honesty to tax-collecting and tried to reform the tax system. Although he was unable to impose the direct land tax, the* taille, *on the nobility, he did oppose adding any further tax exemptions for them. In a letter Louis XIV wrote in August, 1664, Colbert's economic policy is clearly shown.*

* Jean Baptiste Colbert, "Memoires sur les affaires de finances de France pour servir à l'histoire," *Lettres, instructions et memoires de Colbert,* vol. 2, part 2, Paris, Imprimerie Impériale, 1863 (an original translation by Judith Harnick).

Having considered how useful it would be to this realm to reestablish domestic and foreign commerce . . . we have decided to hold, with this end in mind, every two weeks in our presence a special commerce council, in which the merchants' interests and the means of arriving at this reestablishment will be examined and resolved, as well as everything concerning manufactures. We also inform you that we are setting aside . . . a million livres per year for the reestablishment of manufactures and the increase of navigation, not counting more considerable sums that we are raising to furnish the companies of the East and West Indies;

That we are constantly working to abolish all tolls levied on navigable rivers;

That more than a million livres has already been spent to repair public roads, on which we will continue to work;

That we will aid with funds from the royal treasury all those who wish to undertake the reestablishment of old manufactures or who propose new ones;

That we order all our ambassadors or residents at the courts of the princes our allies, to make, in our name, all the proper efforts to have justice rendered on all complaints of merchants, and to assure for them an entire freedom of commerce;

That we will have lodged comfortably, at our court, each and every merchant who has business here, for the entire time that they are obliged to stay there, having ordered the grand marshal of our palace to indicate a proper place for that purpose, which will be called the House of Commerce. . . .

That all merchants and traders by sea who buy ships or build new ones for trade or commerce will receive subsidies from us to help them in these purchases or the construction of these vessels;

And all those who undertake long voyages will receive from us, if they bring back certification in the form we have prescribed, subsidies for each ton of merchandise that they carry or bring back from these voyages.

In this letter, we have wanted to inform you of all these things, and as soon as you have received it, you are to assemble all the merchants and traders of your town of Marseilles and explain particularly well our intentions in all the matters mentioned above, so that, being thus informed of the favorable treatment we wish to give them, they may be more eager to apply themselves to commerce. Have them understand that for everything that concerns the welfare and advantage of the same, they are to address themselves to Sieur Colbert. . . .

# France Enters the Colonial Race[*]

JACQUES MARQUETTE

> *With the mercantilist idea in mind that colonial sources of supplies would benefit a state, France under Louis XIV joined the race for colonies in earnest. Although a permanent settlement had been made at Quebec as early as 1608, fifty years later New France had only 2,500 settlers. But thereafter New France grew rapidly. French explorers pushed westward into the Great Lakes region, where Indians told of a great river, the Mississippi, which the French hoped might lead to the Pacific. In 1673 Louis Jolliet set out to find and explore this river, accompanied by Jacques Marquette, a Jesuit priest. Father Marquette describes the venture.*

I embarked with M. Jolliet, who had been chosen to conduct this enterprise, on the 13th May, 1673, with five other Frenchmen, in two bark canoes. We laid in some Indian corn and smoked beef for our voyage. . . . The first nation we came to was called the Folles-Avoines, or the *nation of wild oats.* I entered their river to visit them, as I had preached among them some years before. The wild oats, from which they derive their name, grows spontaneously in their country. . . .

I acquainted them with my design of discovering other nations, to preach to them the mysteries of our holy religion, at which they were much surprised, and said all they could to dissuade me from it. They told me I would meet Indians who spare no strangers, and whom they kill without any provocation or mercy; . . . That the Great River was exceedingly dangerous, and full of frightful monsters who devoured men and canoes together, and that the heat was so great that it would positively cause our death. I thanked them for their kind advice, but told them I would not follow it, as the salvation of a great many souls was concerned in our undertaking, for whom I should be glad to lose my life. . . .

Before embarking we all offered up prayers to the Holy Virgin, which we continued to do every morning, placing ourselves and the events of the journey under her protection, and after having encouraged each other, we got into our canoes. The river upon which we embarked is called

[*] Albert B. Hart, ed., *American History Told by Contemporaries*, vol. 1, New York, The Macmillan Company, 1897.

Mesconsin [Wisconsin]; the river is very wide, but the sand bars make it very difficult to navigate, which is increased by numerous islands covered with grape vines. The country through which it flows is beautiful; the groves are so dispersed in the prairies that it makes a noble prospect; and the fruit of the trees shows a fertile soil. . . . After having navigated thirty leagues we discovered some iron mines, and one of our company who had seen such mines before, said these were very rich in ore. They are covered with about three feet of soil, and situate near a chain of rocks, whose base is covered with fine timber. After having rowed ten leagues further, making forty leagues from the place where we had embarked, we came into the Mississippi on the 17th of June [1673].

. . . We slowly followed its course to the south and south-east to the 42° N. lat. Here we perceived the country change its appearance. There were scarcely any more woods or mountains. . . .

As we were descending the river we saw high rocks with hideous monsters painted on them, and upon which the bravest Indians dare not look. They are as large as a calf, with head and horns like a goat; their eyes red; beard like a tiger's; and a face like a man's. Their tails are so long that they pass over their heads and between their fore legs, under their belly, and ending like a fish's tail. They are painted red, green, and black. They are so well drawn that I cannot believe they were drawn by the Indians. And for what purpose they were made seems to me a great mystery. As we fell down the river, and while we were discoursing upon these monsters, we heard a great rushing and bubbling of waters, and small islands of floating trees coming from the mouth of the *Pekitanoni* [Missouri], with such rapidity that we could not trust ourselves to go near it. The water of this river is so muddy that we could not drink it. It so discolors the Mississippi as to make the navigation of it dangerous. This river comes from the north-west, and empties into the Mississippi, and on its banks are situated a number of Indian villages. We judged by the compass, that the Mississippi discharged itself into the Gulf of Mexico. It would, however, have been more agreeable if it had discharged itself into the South Sea or Gulf of California. . . .

Having satisfied ourselves that the Gulf of Mexico was in latitude 31° 40', and that we could reach it in three or four days' journey from the *Akansea* [Arkansas River], and that the Mississippi discharged itself into it, and not to the eastward of the Cape of Florida, nor into the California Sea, we resolved to return home. . . . We then ascended the Mississippi with great difficulty against the current, and left it in the latitude of 38°

north, to enter another river [Illinois], which took us to the lake of the Illinois [Michigan], which is a much shorter way than through the River Mesconsin [Wisconsin], by which we entered the Mississippi. . . .

## A Cloudy Sunset for the Sun King *

### DUC DE SAINT-SIMON

> *In the course of his long reign, Louis XIV succeeded in making France Europe's greatest power in the seventeenth century, as Spain had been in the sixteenth. But the splendor at home and an endless series of wars were burdens that even the wealth of France could not support. In his old age Louis brought on the "War of the Spanish Succession" by claiming the Spanish empire for a French prince. The financial problems he left behind him foreshadowed evil days to come for the French monarchy. A French noble, the duke de Saint-Simon, speaks.*

. . . [The War of the Spanish Succession] as I have said, still continued, but without bringing us any advantages. On the contrary, our losses in Germany and Italy by sickness, rather than by the sword, were so great that it was resolved to augment each company by five men; and, at the same time, twenty-five thousand militia were raised, thus causing great ruin and great desolation in the provinces. The King was rocked into the belief that the people were all anxious to enter this militia, and, from time to time, at Marly, specimens of those enlisted were shown to him, and their joy and eagerness to serve made much of. I have heard this often; while, at the same time, I knew from my own tenantry, and from everything that was said, that the raising of this militia carried despair everywhere, and that many people mutilated themselves in order to exempt themselves from serving. Nobody at the Court was ignorant of this. People lowered their eyes when they saw the deceit practiced upon the King. . . . I saw quite plainly toward what rock we were drifting. We had met losses at Hochstedt, Gibraltar and Barcelona; Catalonia and the neighboring countries were in revolt; Italy yielding us nothing but miserable successes;

* Saint-Simon, *Memoires of Louis XIV and the Regency*, vol. 1, New York, M. Walter Dunne, 1901 (translated by Bayle St. John).

Spain exhausted; France failing in men and money, and with incapable generals, protected by the Court against their faults. . . . I thought that it was time to finish the war before we sank still lower.

Nevertheless, the King, as if to mock at misfortune and to show his enemies the little uneasiness he felt, determined, at the commencement of the new year, 1706, that the Court should be gayer than ever. He announced that there would be balls at Marly every time he was there this winter, and he named those who were to dance there; and said he should be very glad to see balls given . . . at Versailles. Accordingly, many took place there, and also at Marly, and from time to time there were masquerades. One day, the King wished that everybody, even the most aged, who were at Marly should go to the ball masqued; and, to avoid all distinction, he went there himself with a gauze robe above his habit; but such a slight disguise was for himself alone; everybody else was completely disguised. . . .

The difficulty of finding money to carry on the affairs of the nation continued to grow so irksome that Chamillart, who had both the finance and the war departments under his control, was unable to stand against the increased trouble and vexation which this state of things brought him. More than once he had represented that this double work was too much for him. But the King had in former times expressed so much annoyance from the troubles that arose between the finance and war departments, that he would not separate them, after having once joined them together. At last, Chamillart could bear up against his heavy load no longer. . . . He wrote again to the King, begging to be released from his duties, and frankly stated that, in the state he was, if some relief was not afforded him, everything would go wrong and perish. He always left a large margin to his letters, and upon this the King generally wrote his reply. Chamillart showed me this letter when it came back to him, and I saw upon it with great surprise, in the handwriting of the King, this short note: "Well! let us perish together."

The necessity for money had now become so great, that all sorts of means were adopted to obtain it. Among other things, a tax was established upon baptisms and marriages. This tax was extremely onerous and odious. The result of it was a strange confusion. Poor people, and many of humble means, baptized their children themselves, without carrying them to the church, and were married at home by reciprocal consent and before witnesses, when they could find no priest who would marry them without formality. . . .

From public cries and murmurs the people in some places passed to sedition. Matters went so far at Cahors, that two battalions which were there had great difficulty in holding the town against the armed peasants; . . . In the end it was found necessary to drop this tax upon baptism and marriages, to the great regret of the tax gatherers, who, by all manner of vexations and rogueries, had enriched themselves cruelly.

## A Royal Scholar Writes of Royal Absolutism *

JAMES I

> In England, the attempt to impose absolutism did not succeed as it had in France. James Stuart (King James I of England, King James VI of Scotland) was not content to be an absolute ruler in practice, like the Tudors before him. He must also show his learning by lecturing the people and Parliament on the theory of royal absolutism. As is often the case, many who would have accepted the practice refused to support it when it was expressed in extreme form in writing. In spite of the splendid work of his commissions, such as that which translated the Bible into English, it became the fashion to jeer at James. Englishmen lampooned him as "Simple Simon." King Henry IV of France called him "the wisest fool in Christendom." James tells us his ideas of absolute monarchy.

There is not a thing so necessary to be known by the people of any Land, next the knowledge of their God, as the right knowledge of their allegiance, according to the forme of government established among them, especially in a *Monarchie,* which forme of government, as resembling the Divinity, approcheth nearest to perfection. . . .

In brief . . . the duty, and allegiance of the people to their lawful King, their obedience, I say, ought to be to him, as to Gods Lieutenant in earth, obeying his commands in all things, except directly against God, as the commands of Gods Minister, acknowledging him a Judge set by

* James I, *The True Law of Free Monarchies,* London, Printed by T. C. according to the copy Printed at Edinburgh, 1603 (adapted).

*God* over them, having power to judge them but to be judged only by *God,* whom to only he must give count of his judgment: fearing him as their judge; loving him as their father; praying for him as their protector; for his continuance, if he be good; for his amendment, if he be wicked; following and obeying his lawful commands. . . .

I have at length proved, that the King is above the Law, as both the author, and giver of strength thereto: yet a good King will, not only delight to rule his subjects by the Law; but even will conform himself in his own actions thereto, always keeping that ground, that the health of the common-wealth be his chief law. And where he sees the law doubt-some or rigorous, he may interpret or mitigate the same. . . . And therefore general laws, made publicly in Parliament, may . . . by his authority, be mitigated, and suspended upon causes only known to him.

Although I have said, a good King will frame all his actions to be according to the law: yet he is not bound thereto but of his good will, and for good example-giving to his Subjects. . . . So, as I have already said, a good King, although he be above the Law, will subject and frame his actions thereto, for example sake to his Subjects, and of his own free will, but not as subject or bound thereto. . . .

And the proper office of a King towards his subjects agrees very well with the office of the head towards the body. . . . For from the head, being the seat of judgment, proceeds the care and foresight of guiding, and preventing all evil that may come to the body. . . . The head cares for the body, so does the King for his people. As the discourse and direction flows from the head, and the execution . . . belongs to the rest of the members, every one according to their own office: so it is between a wise Prince, and his people. . . .

If the children may, upon any pretext that can be imagined, lawfully rise up against their Father, cut him off, and choose any other whom they please . . . ; and if the body, for the weale of it, nay for any infirmity that can be in the head, strike it off: then I can not deny that the people may rebel, control, and displace, or cut off the King at their own pleasure. . . .

The further a King is preferred by God above all other ranks and degrees of men, and the higher that his seat is above theirs, the greater is his obligation to his maker. And therefore, in case he forgets himself . . . the sadder and sharper will his correction be: and according to the greatness of the height he is in, the weight of his fall will recompence the fame. . . .

# The Petition of Right *

*Some of the English may have jeered at James I; but in the reign of his son, Charles I, tempers grew shorter, and the relations between king and Parliament became grim. As Parliament tried to assert its authority in matters not traditionally its business, Charles refused to budge from a position which he believed right. But in 1628 he was obliged to accept Parliament's "Petition of Right" in order to gain from Parliament the revenues with which to finance his government.*

To the King's Most Excellent Majesty.

. . . Whereas it is declared and enacted by a statute made in the time of the reign of King Edward that no tallage or aid shall be laid or levied by the King or his heirs in this realm, without the goodwill and assent of the Archbishops, Bishops, Earls, Barons, Knights, Burgesses, and other freemen of the commonality of this realm: and by authority of Parliament holden in the five and twentieth year of the reign of King Edward the Third, it is declared and enacted, that from thenceforth no person shall be compelled to make any loans to the King against his will. . . .

Yet nevertheless, of late divers commissions directed to sundry Commissioners in several counties with instructions have issued, by means whereof your people have been in divers places assembled, and required to lend certain sums of money unto your Majesty, and many of them upon their refusal . . . become bound to make appearance and give attendance before your Privy Council, and in other places, and others of them have been therefore imprisoned, confined, and sundry other ways molested and disquieted. . . .

And where also by the statute called, "The Great Charter of the Liberties of England" [Magna Carta], it is declared and enacted, that no freeman may be taken or imprisoned . . . or be outlawed or exiled; or in any manner destroyed, but by the lawful judgment of his peers, or by the law of the land: . . .

Nevertheless, against the tenor of the said statutes, and other the good laws and statutes of your realm, to that end provided, divers of your subjects have of late been imprisoned without any cause showed, and when for their deliverance they were brought before your Justices, by your Majesty's writs of Habeas Corpus, there to undergo and receive as the

* "The Petition of Right," *Old South Leaflets*, No. 23.

Court should order, and their keepers commanded to certify the causes of their detainer; no cause was certified, but that they were detained by your Majesty's special command, signified by the Lords of your Privy Council, and yet were returned back to several prisons, without being charged with anything to which they might make answer according to the law:

And whereas of late great companies of soldiers and mariners have been dispersed into divers counties of the realm, and the inhabitants against their wills have been compelled to receive them into their houses, and there to suffer them to sojourn, against the laws and customs of this realm. . . .

They do therefore humbly pray your Most Excellent Majesty, that no man hereafter be compelled to make or yield any gift, loan, benevolence, tax, or such like charge, without common consent by Act of Parliament; and that none be called to make answer, or take such oath, or to give attendance, or be confined, or otherwise molested or disquieted concerning the same, or for refusal thereof; and that no freeman, in any such manner as is before-mentioned, be imprisoned or detained; and that your Majesty will be pleased to remove the said soldiers and mariners, and that your people may not be so burdened in time to come; . . .

## Parliament Defies the King *

> Charles I refused to go beyond the Petition of Right in meeting the demands of Parliament. In 1629 he ordered Parliament to adjourn; but Parliament angrily defied him, as we read below. Charles nonetheless had his way, and for eleven years ruled without Parliamentary aid.

Upon Monday the second of March, as soone as praiers were ended, the Speaker went into the chaire, and delivered the Kinges command for the adjournment of the Howse untill Tewsday sevenight following, being the tenth of March.

The Howse made him answere, that it was not the office of a Speaker to deliver any such command unto them, but for the adjórnement of the

* Elizabeth Kendall, *Source-Book of English History*, New York, The Macmillan Company, 1900.

Howse it did properly belong unto themselves, and after they had uttered some thinges they thought fitt to be spoken of, they would sattisfie the King.

The Speaker tould them, he had an expresse command from his Majestie that as soone as he had delivered his message he should rise, and upon that left the chaire, but was by force drawne to it againe. . . .

The King, hearing that the Howse continued to sitt (notwithstanding his command for the adjornement thereof) sent a messinger for the Serjant with his mase, which being taken from the table there cann be noe further proceeding; but the key of the dore was taken from the Serjant and delivered to Sir Miles Hubert to keepe, who, after he had receaved the same, put the serjant out of the Howse, leaving his mase behind him, and then locked the dore. After this, the King sent Mr. Maxwell (the usher of the black rodd) for the dissolucion of the Parliament; but being informed that neither he nor his message would be receaved by the Howse, the King grewe into much rage and passion, and sent for the Captaine of the Pentioners and Guard to force the dore; but the rising of the Howse prevented the danger and ill consequence that might have followed.

### Civil War in England *

> More than a decade after the Petition of Right, religious issues combined with political ones to shake the authority of Charles I. The king's problems were complicated by difficulties with Ireland and Scotland. By 1642 Parliamentary armies with a large Puritan following were in open rebellion against the king's "Cavalier" forces. A Puritan account of events in the autumn of 1642 is a reminder that this was the period when the religious fervor of the Reformation had reached its height.

1642. October the 23rd, being the Lord's day in the forenoon, both the Armies met in the midway between *Banbury* and *Stratford-upon-Avon*. And they had a very hot skirmish, their ordnance playing very hot from

* Nehemiah Wallington, *Historical Notices*, vol. 2, London, Richard Bentley, 1869.

twelve o'clock till three in the afternoon, and made a great slaughter, and then the main forces joined battle, both horse and foot, and had a furious skirmish on both sides, which continued all that day.

But that which I would take notice of is God's great mercy and providence, which was seen to his poor despised children, that although the enemy came traitorously and suddenly upon them, and unexpectedly, and four of our regiments falling from us, and our soldiers being a company of despised unexperienced youths, and never using to lie in the fields on the cold ground before the enemy, they being strong, old, experienced soldiers. But herein we see God's great mercy, for all that to give us the victory; for, as I hear, that the slaughter in all was five thousand five hundred and seventeen; but ten of the enemies' side were slain to one of ours. And observe God's wonderful works, for those that were slain of our side were most of them run away; but those that stood most valiantly to it, they were most preserved; so that you may see the Lord stands for them that stand for Him.

If I could but relate how admirably the hand of providence ordered our artillery and bullets for the destruction of the enemy, when a piece of ordnance was shot off, what a lane was made in their army; but when the enemy shot their ordnance against us, O how did God guide the bullets (as I wrote afore at *Southam*) that some fell down before them, some grazed along, some bullets went over their heads, and some, one side of them. Oh how seldom or never almost were they hurt that stood valiant to it, by their bullets; You would stand and wonder. . . .

Again, consider one wonderful work of our God more; which is, that many of our youths that went forth were weakly, and sickly, some with the king's evil, some with agues, and some with the toothache, which their parents and friends were in great care and grief for; yet, when they have lain days and nights in the wet and cold fields, which one should think should make a well body sick, much more to increase their misery and pain that were ill, yet they have testified that their pain hath left them, and never better in all their lives.

This is the Lord's doing, and it is marvellous in my eyes.

I did forget to write this remarkable passage, how the King's army shot off thirty pieces of ordnance and killed not passing four of our men; and the first time we shot, we made a lane among them cutting off two of their colours.

*November* the 5th, being *Saturday*, that treacherous, cruel, and bloody fight was at *Brentford*, where the enemy took Captain *Lilburn* away prisoner. But how the great God and Lord of Hosts did preserve us, and gave us at last the victory, that they were glad to steal and run away. But of this I do intend to write more at large in my book, called "The wonderful working God, or, The God-working wonders."

About the latter end of *December*, at Twyford, three miles from *Reading*, the Cavaliering Rebels set upon some of the Parliament Army, and they perceiving the wind against our Army, and a water mill being by them, they set that on fire, to the intent that the wind might blow the smoke, and so smother in our Armies, that so they might have the victory over them. But mark the wonderful works of the Lord, which hath the command of the winds; that at the very time when the mill began to smoke, our God commanded the wind and smoke, to turn back in the faces of His and our enemies so that fourscore of our Army beat three troops of their Dragooneers, and two men of us, through God's help, slew sixteen of the rebels, and not one of us, our Army, was killed; no, nor hurt, that I could hear of; but made the rest of our enemies to run away.

This also cometh from the Lord of Hosts which is wonderful in counsel, and excellent in works.—*Isaia.* xxviii. 29.


## The Trial of King Charles I *

BULSTRODE WHITELOCK

> *In 1648 Parliament, victorious over the king, came under the control of a radical minority group. The king was subjected to a "trial" and sentenced to death. His execution, the first in which a reigning king died at the hands of revolutionaries, horrified most Englishmen; to many, Charles the Martyr became a saint. We read of the king's trial.*

*January 20, 1648.* The Lord President in a short speech acquainted the King with the cause of his being brought there, in order to be tried, upon a Charge against him, by the Commons of England, which was to be read, and his Majesty to give his answer. . . . He was charged under the name of Charles Stuart, King of England, as guilty of all the blood

* Bulstrode Whitelock, *Memorials of the English Affairs*, London, Printed for Nathaniel Ponder, at the Sign of the Peacock, in the Poultry, near the Church, 1682.

that had been shed . . . that he had been present in arms against the Parliament, and other particulars very large.

The King smiled at the reading of his Charge, and after it was read, demanded of the President, by what Lawful Authority he was brought thither. He was answered, "In the name of the Commons of England." He [the King] replyed, he saw no lords there which should make a Parliament . . . ; and urged that the Kingdom of England was hereditary and not successive, and that he should betray his trust, if he acknowledged or made answer to them, for he was not convinced that they were a lawful authority. After he had been often demanded to answer and refused, he was remanded to St. James's, and the High Court adjourned. . . .

*January 22, 1648*. The President [again] required the King to answer to the Charge against him by the Commons of England, of High Treason, etc. The King said . . . that a King cannot be tried by any Superior Jurisdiction on Earth. But, he said, it was not on his case alone that he stood for, but the freedom of all the People of England, for if power without Law, may make, or alter Law, no subject can be safe for his life, or anything that he calls his own.

PRESIDENT. "Sir, I must interrupt you . . . that what you do is not agreeable to the proceedings of any Court, you appear as a prisoner before this Court, and are not to dispute their Authority, but to give a punctual answer to the Charge."

KING. "Sir . . . the Commons of England was never a Court of Law. I would know how they came to be so!"

PRESIDENT. "Sir, you are not permitted to go on in that speech and these discourses."

Then the Clerk of the Court read this aloud: Charles Stuart King of England, you have been accused on the behalf of the People of England, of High Treason, and other crimes, the Court have determined, that you ought to answer the same.

KING. "I will answer the same, so soon as I know by what Authority you do this."

PRESIDENT. "If this be all that you will say, then Gentlemen, you that brought the Prisoner here, take charge of him back again."

KING. "I do require that I may give my reasons, why I do not answer, and give me time for that."

PRESIDENT. " 'Tis not for Prisoners to require."

KING. "Prisoners; Sir, I am not an Ordinary Prisoner."

PRESIDENT. "The Court already affirmed their jurisdiction; if you will not answer we shall give order to record your default."

KING. "You have not heard my reason yet."

PRESIDENT. "Sergeant, take away the Prisoner."

KING. "Sir, remember that the King is not required to give his reasons for the Liberty and freedom of all his subjects."

PRESIDENT. "Sir, you are not to have Liberty to use this language, how great a friend you have been to the Laws and Liberties of the People, let all England and the world judge. . . ."

[The King was removed from the Court.]

*January 23, 1648.* Mr. Coke, Solicitor General, moved, "That whereas the Prisoner, instead of giving answer to the charges against him, did still dispute the Authority of the Court, then according to Law if a prisoner shall stand in contempt, and shall not give a plea, Guilty or Not Guilty . . . that therefore speedy judgment be pronounced against him."

PRESIDENT. "Sir, in plain terms . . . you are to give your positive, and final answer in plain English, whether you are guilty or not guilty, of these Treasons laid to your Charge."

KING. After a little pause. "When I was here yesterday, I desired to speak for the Liberties of the people of England, I was interrupted; I desire to know whether I may speak freely or not."

PRESIDENT. "Sir, You have had the resolution of the Court, upon the question . . . answer your Charge."

KING. "For the Charge, I value it not a rush, it is the Liberty of the People of England, that I stand for; for me to acknowledge a new Court, that I never heard of before; I that am your King, that should be an example to all the People of England to uphold justice, to maintain old Laws. . . . You spoke very well the first day that I came here . . . of the obligations that I had laid upon me by God, to maintain the Liberty of my People; the same obligation you spoke of, I do acknowledge, to God, that I owe to Him and to my People, to defend as much as in me the Ancient Laws. Therefore until I may know that this [Court] is not against the fundamental Laws of the Kingdom . . . I can put no particular answer. . . ."

PRESIDENT. "Sir, this is the third time you have publicly disavowed this Court and put an affront upon it; but how far you have preserved the Liberties of the People, your actions have spoke it; but truly Sir, mens intentions ought to be known by their actions; you have written your meaning in bloody characters throughout the Kingdom. . . ."

[The President then adjourned the Court.]

*January 27, 1648.* The President made a long speech of the Kings misgovernment, and that by Law, Kings were accountable to their People, and to the Law, which was their Superior, and he instanced several Kings, who had been deposed, and imprisoned by their subjects, especially in the Kings native country [Scotland], where, of one hundred and nine Kings, most were deposed, imprisoned, or proceeded against for misgovernment. . . .

After this the Clerk was commanded to read the sentence, which recited the Charge, and the several crimes of which he had been found guilty.

For all of which Treasons and crimes, the Court did adjudge, that he the said Charles Stuart, as a tyrant, traitor, murderer, and public enemy, shall be put to death by the severing of his head from his body.


## Cromwell Dissolves Parliament *

EDMUND LUDLOW

> *After the execution of Charles I, the victors experimented with a form of government called a "commonwealth," with neither king nor a House of Lords. Out of the chaos emerged a state more dictatorial than that of the Stuart kings, based on military control in the hands of Oliver Cromwell. Whether called "king" or "lord protector" (Cromwell's title), it was clear that absolutism was still the pattern of the seventeenth century. Edmund Ludlow describes Cromwell's treatment of Parliament in 1653.*

. . . Calling to Major-General Harrison, who was on the other side of the House, to come to him, he told him, that he judged the Parliament ripe for a dissolution, and this to be the time of doing it. The Major-

* Elizabeth Kendall, *Source-Book of English History,* New York, The Macmillan Co., 1900.

General answered, as he since told me; "Sir, the work is very great and dangerous, therefore I desire you seriously to consider of it before you engaged in it." "You say well," replied the General [Cromwell], and thereupon sat still for about a quarter of an hour; and then the question for passing the Bill being to be put, he said again to Major-General Harrison, "this is the time I must do it;" and suddenly standing up, made a speech, wherein he loaded the Parliament with the vilest reproaches, charging them not to have a heart to do any thing for the publick good, to have espoused the corrupt interest of Presbytery and the lawyers, who were the supporters of tyranny and oppression, accusing them of an intention to perpetuate themselves in power, had they not been forced to the passing of this Act, which he affirmed they designed never to observe, and thereupon told them, that the Lord had done with them, and had chosen other instruments for the carrying on his work that were more worthy. This he spoke with so much passion and discomposure of mind, as if he had been distracted. Sir Peter Wentworth stood up to answer him, and said, that this was the first time that ever he had heard such unbecoming language given to the Parliament, and that it was the more horrid in that it came from their servant, and their servant whom they had so highly trusted and obliged: but as he was going on, the General stept into the midst of the House, where continuing his distracted language, he said, "Come, come, I will put an end to your prating;" then walking up and down the House like a mad-man, and kicking the ground with his feet, he cried out, "You are no Parliament, I say you are no Parliament; I will put an end to your sitting; call them in, call them in:" whereupon the serjeant attending the Parliament opened the doors, and Lieutenant-Colonel Worsley with two files of musqueteers entered the House; which Sir Henry Vane observing from his place, said aloud, "This is not honest, yea it is against morality and common honesty." Then Cromwell fell a railing at him, crying out with a loud voice, "O Sir Henry Vane, Sir Henry Vane, the Lord deliver me from Sir Henry Vane." Then looking upon one of the members, he said, "There sits a drunkard," and giving much reviling language to others, he commanded the mace to be taken away, saying, "What shall we do with this bauble? here, take it away." Having brought all into this disorder, Major-General Harrison went to the Speaker as he sat in the chair, and told him, that seeing things were reduced to this pass, it would not be convenient for him to remain there. The Speaker answered, that he would not come down unless he were forced. "Sir," said Harrison, "I will lend you my hand;" and thereupon putting his hand within his, the Speaker came down. Then Cromwell applied himself to the members of the House. . . . "It's you that have forced me to this, for I have sought the Lord night and day, that he would rather slay me than put me upon the doing of this work."


## Stuart Restoration in England *

JOHN EVELYN

> *Oliver Cromwell had won respect for England abroad, but Englishmen at home had grumbled at Puritan restrictions. On his death in 1658, the government was entrusted to his son Richard, who—to the surprise of nobody—had no taste for power and retained it only long enough for arrangements to be made by the army to recall the Stuarts to the throne. The shortness of "Dick's" rule was summarized in the equally brief jingle*
>
> > *A, B, C,*
> > *Tumbledown D.*
>
> *While "Tumbledown Dick" departed into happy exile, London rejoiced in the homecoming of King Charles II. John Evelyn recalls the day.*

[May] 29th. This day his Majestie Charles the Second came to London after a sad and long exile and calamitous suffering both of the King and Church, being 17 yeares. This was also his birth-day, and with a triumph of above 20,000 horse and foote, brandishing their swords and shouting with inexpressible joy; the wayes strew'd with flowers, the bells ringing, the streetes hung with tapissry, fountaines running with wine; the Maior, Aldermen, and all the Companies in their liveries, chaines of gold, and banners; Lords and Nobles clad in cloth of silver, gold, and velvet; the windowes and balconies all set with ladies; trumpets, music, and myriads of people flocking, even so far as from Rochester, so as they were seven houres in passing the citty, even from 2 in ye afternoone till 9 at night.

I stood in the Strand and beheld it, and bless'd God. And all this was done without one drop of bloud shed, and by that very army which

* William Bray, ed., *Diary of John Evelyn*, vol. 2, New York, Charles Scribner's Sons, 1906.

rebell'd against him; but it was ye Lord's doing, for such a restauration was never mention'd in any history antient or modern, since the returne of the Jews from the Babylonish capitivity; nor so joyfull a day and so bright ever seene in this nation, this hapning when to expect or effect it was past all human policy. . . .

## The Surrender of New Amsterdam *

> In the seventeenth-century rivalry between the Netherlands and England, the Dutch continued their advance in the East Indies, but permitted New Netherland in America to fall into British hands. Peter Stuyvesant, the last Dutch governor of New Netherland, tried to lay the blame for the loss on the Dutch West India Company. The company's answer to the charges follows.

TO THE HONORABLE MIGHTY LORDS, THEIR HIGH MIGHTINESSES' DEPUTIES FOR THE AFFAIRS OF THE WEST INDIA COMPANY

. . . First taking up the Want of provisions: The Company will once more, in good faith, plead ignorance of there having been an insufficient supply of provisions, since it cannot imagine that, in a country so productive as New Netherland, any scarcity should exist in a year of such abundance as that of 1664. . . .

. . . Further, that there is not the least foundation for what he sets forth both generally and particularly in his Defence, viz.: that he had not timely notice of the designs which the English, and especially the aforesaid frigates might have had against New Netherland, and that the Company had, on the contrary, as he gives out, informed him, from this place, that the English had no intention to use violence against New Netherland. For, it is true and certain that, in order that he might victual the place and fort of New Amsterdam and keep it victualed, the aforesaid Stuyvesant was warned time enough from here and from New England, of the apparent difficulties between this State and the English, and, more particularly, of the equipment and approach of the aforesaid frigates; . . .

* F. B. O'Callaghan, ed., *Documents Relative to the Colonial History of the State of New York*, vol. 2, Albany, 1858.

Secondly. Herewith falls the excuse he makes, that the farmers were constrained by the English not to convey any grain into the fort, and that the said English had everywhere cut off the communication, so that grain could not be conveyed across the river; for, having been warned in time, they ought not to have waited the arrival of the frigates . . . to provide themselves with grain. . . .

Want of ammunition being represented as the second fundamental cause of the surrender of the aforesaid fort, city and Province of New Netherland, the abovenamed Company will also, in good faith, plead ignorance of that want; yea, will, on the contrary, assert that it is informed for certain that, if there had not been a sufficient supply in store, a very considerable quantity of gunpowder would be found among the Burghers, and particularly at Fort Orange and the Colonie Renslaers Wyck among the traders; . . .

. . . The third point of his defence—the Unwillingness of the Burghers to defend the city—since all the world sufficiently knows what zeal they had exhibited to protect their property; working with all their might at the defence of the place, until the want of provisions and ammunition was instilled into their minds by the government, and the enemy's strength represented to be much greater than it was in fact, and, moreover, security for their private property had been given by the English, in case of surrender; and finally, until the two frigates passed the fort unobstructed, when their courage began to fail and the idea of surrender gained ground, on perceiving the intention of the government after it had permitted the aforesaid frigates to pass freely the fort unimpeded; although, under all circumstances, it is sufficiently shown in the Observations aforesaid, that the unwillingness of the Burghers to fight, cannot be any excuse for him, inasmuch as it was his duty to defend the fort. . . .

The fourth point was: that they had no hope of relief. This is spread out so broad, as if, for this reason alone, the place ought not to be defended. On this point the Company will merely persist in what is stated in its Observations, and accordingly submit, that it could not know what the aforesaid Director also might say if no relief should arrive. In all cases, he was not at liberty to surrender such a place without striking a blow, especially so long as it was not really attacked; for, as regards relief, they did not know what help would arrive from Fatherland, because the Company's last letters had assured them of immediate assistance or a settlement of the Boundary. Consequently, the one or the other being to happen, he ought not to have adopted so rash a resolution. . . .

# The Glorious Revolution *

John Evelyn

> *Whether or not people would accept royal absolutism seems to have depended heavily on the manner in which it was applied. England permitted much to Elizabeth, tolerated James I, beheaded Charles I, loved Charles II, and drove James II into exile. James was forced to leave England largely because of his Catholic faith and because of the birth of a Catholic heir to the throne. John Evelyn's diary gives us a day-by-day account of James's downfall and the coming of the Dutch prince, William III of Orange.*

*May 18, 1688.* The King injoyning the ministers to read his Declaration for giving liberty of conscience (as it were styl'd) in all the churches of England, this evening six Bishops . . . in the name of all the rest of the Bishops, came to his Majesty to petition him that he would not impose the reading of it to the several congregations within their dioceses. . . . The King was so far incens'd at this address, that he with threatening expressions commanded them to obey him in reading it at their perils, and so dismiss'd them. . . .

*June 8.* This day the Archbishop of Canterbury, with the Bishops of Ely, Chichester, St. Asaph, Bristol, Peterborough, and Bath and Willis, were sent from the Privy Council prisoners to the Tower . . . on their not reading the declaration for liberty of conscience; . . . The concern of the people for them was wonderfull, infinite crowds on their knees begging their blessing, and praying for them as they pass'd out of the barge along the Tower-wharfe. . . .

*June 10.* A *young Prince* borne, which will cause disputes. . . . About two o'clock we heard the Tower ordnance discharg'd, and the bells ringing for the birth of the Prince of Wales. . . .

*June 29.* They [the Bishops] appeared; the trial lasted from nine in the morning to past six in the evening, when the Jury retired to consider of their verdict. . . . They were acquitted. When this was heard, there was greate rejoicing; and there was a lane of people from the King's Bench to the water side, on their knees, as the Bishops pass'd. . . .

* William Bray, ed., *Diary of John Evelyn*, vol. 3, New York, Charles Scribner's Sons, 1906.

*August 10.* Dr. Tenison now told me there would suddenly be some great thing discover'd. This was the Prince of Orange intending to come over. . . .

*August 23.* . . . The Dutch make extraordinary preparations both at sea and land. . . . The Popish Irish soldiers commit many murders and insults; the whole nation disaffected. . . .

*September 18.* I went to London, where I found the Court in the utmost consternation on report of the Prince of Orange's landing, which put White-hall into so panic of feare, that I could hardly believe it possible to find such a change. . . .

*October 7.* Hourly expectation of the Prince of Orange's invasion. . . . [The king] in the mean time called over 500 Irish, and 4000 Scots, and continued to remove Protestants and put in Papists at Portsmouth and other places of trust, and retained the Jesuits about him, increasing the universal discontent. It brought people to so desperate a passe, that they seem'd passionately to long for and desire the landing of that Prince whom they look'd on to be their deliverer from Popish tyranny. . . .

*October 14.* The King's birth-day. No gunns' from the Tower as usual. . . . The wind which has been hitherto west, was east all this day. Wonderfull expectation of the Dutch fleet. Public prayers order'd to be read in the churches against invasion.

*October 28.* A tumult in London on the rabble demolishing a Popish chapel that had been set up in the Citty. . . .

*October 31.* My birth-day, being 68th year of my age. O blessed Lord, grant that as I grow in yeares, so may I improve in grace! Be Thou my protector this following year, and preserve me and mine from the dangers and greate confusions that threaten a sad revolution to this sinfull nation! . . .

*November 5.* I went to London; heard the newes of the Prince having landed . . . coming with a fleete of neere 700 saile. . . . This put the King and Court into greate consternation; they were now employ'd in forming an army to stop their further progresse. . . .

*November 14.* The Prince increases every day in force. Several Lords go in to him. . . . The Citty of London in disorder; . . . The Queen prepares to go to Portsmouth for safety. . . .

*December 2. . . .* Plymouth declar'd for the Prince. Bath, York, Hull, Bristol, and all the eminent nobility and persons of quality through England, declare for the Protestant religion and laws, and go to meete the Prince. . . .

*December 13.* The King flies to sea, puts in at Faversham for ballast; is rudely treated by the people; comes back to White-hall. The Prince of Orange is advanc'd to Windsor, is invited by the King to St. James's, the messanger sent was the Earle of Faversham, the General of the forces, who going without trumpet or passeport is detain'd prisoner by the Prince, who accepts the invitation, but requires his Majesty to retire to some distant place, that his owne guards may be quarter'd about the Palace and Citty. . . .

*December 17.* That night was a Council; his Majesty refuses to assent to all the proposals; goes away again to Rochester.

*December 18.* I saw the King take barge to Gravesend at 12 o'clock—a sad sight! The Prince comes to St. James and fills White-hall with Dutch guards.

### England's Bill of Rights *

> *When William III and Mary II took the throne—the only instance in English history of a king and queen both reigning at the same time—Parliament required them to subscribe to the "Bill of Rights," which restricted their authority. England, in this act, again outdistanced Europe in political development by limiting the power of monarchs; elsewhere, absolutism continued for another century. We read some of the articles of the Bill of Rights.*

1. That the pretended power of suspending of laws, or the execution of laws, by regal authority, without consent of Parliament, is illegal.

4. That levying money for or to the use of the Crown by pretence and prerogative, without grant of Parliament, for longer time or in other manner than the same is or shall be granted, is illegal.

* University of Pennsylvania, *Translations and Reprints from the Original Sources of European History,* vol. 1, no. 6, Philadelphia, 1897.

5. That it is the right of the subjects to petition the King, and all commitments and prosecutions for such petitioning are illegal.

6. That the raising or keeping a standing army within the kingdom in time of peace, unless it be with consent of Parliament, is against law.

7. That the subjects which are Protestants may have arms for their defence suitable to their conditions, and as allowed by law.

8. That election of members of Parliament ought to be free.

9. That the freedom of speech, and debates or proceedings in Parliament, ought not to be impeached or questioned in any court or place out of Parliament.

10. That excessive bail ought not to be required, nor excessive fines imposed; nor cruel and unusual punishments inflicted.

13. And that for redress of all grievances, and for the amending, strengthening, and preserving of the laws, Parliament ought to be held frequently.

## Peter the Great *

JOHN PERRY

> In Russia, royal absolutism continued to flourish as it had in the days of Ivan the Terrible. Peter I reigned from 1682 to 1725. Having visited western Europe and studied its ways for himself, he determined to modernize and Europeanize his country, against much resistance by the nobility, the church, and the people. Among his techniques of breaking the power of tradition were building of a new capital (St. Petersburg, today Leningrad) on the western border of Russia; forcing the upper classes to wear western styles of dress; and taxing heavily anyone who wished to look old-fashioned by wearing a beard. Peter's efforts to modernize Russia are described by John Perry, an English engineer, who in 1712 wrote an account of his fourteen years in Russia.

* John Perry, The State of Russia under the Present Czar. Reprinted from Seven Britons in Imperial Russia, edited by Peter Putnam, by permission of Princeton University Press. Copyright, 1952 by Princeton University Press, London, Geoffrey Cumberlege, Oxford University Press.

It had been the manner of the Russes, like the Patriarchs of old, to wear long beards hanging down upon their bosoms, which they comb'd out with pride, and kept smooth and fine, without one hair to be diminish'd. . . . The Czar, therefore, to reform this foolish custom, and to make them look like other Europeans, ordered a tax to be laid, on all gentlemen, merchants, and others of his subjects (excepting the priests and common peasants, or slaves) that they should each of them pay a hundred rubles per annum, for the wearing of their beards, and that even the common people should pay a copeck at the entrance of the gates of any of the towns or cities of Russia. . . .

It is most certain, that the Russes had a kind of religious respect and veneration for their beards; and so much the more, because they differed herein from strangers, which was back'd by the humours of the priests . . . and which nothing but the absolute authority of the Czar, and the terror of having them (in his merry humour) pull'd out by the roots, or could ever have prevailed with the Russes to have parted with their beards. On this occasion there were letters drop'd about the streets, sealed and directed to His Czarish Majesty, which charged him with tyranny and heathenism. . . .

About this time the Czar came down to Veronize, where I was then on service, and a great many of my men that had worn their beards all their lives, were now obliged to part with them, amongst which, one of the first that I met with just coming from the hands of the barber, was an old Russ carpenter that had been with me at Camishinka, who was a very good workman with his hatchet, and whom I always had a friendship for. I jested a little with him on this occasion, telling him that he was become a young man, and asked him what he had done with his beard? Upon which he put his hand in his bosom and pull'd it out, and shew'd it to me: farther telling me, that when he came home, he would lay it up to have it put in his coffin and buried along with him, that he might be able to give an account of it to St. Nicholas, when he came to the other world; and that all his brothers (meaning his fellow-workmen, who had been shaved that day) had taken the same care. . . .

The Czar . . . gave orders that all his boyars and people whatsoever, that came near his court, and that were in his pay should . . . equip themselves with handsome cloathes made after the English fashion. . . . And next he commanded, that a pattern of cloathes of the English fashion should be hung up at all the gates of the city of Mosco, and that publication should be made, that all persons (excepting the common peasants who brought goods and provisions into the city) should make their cloathes according to the said patterns; and that whosoever should disobey the said orders, and should be found passing any of the gates of the city in their long habits, should . . . have their coats cut off just even with the ground, so much as it was longer than to touch the ground when they kneeled down, of which there were many hundreds of coats that were cut accordingly; . . . and soon broke the custom of their wearing long coats, especially in places near Mosco, and those other towns wherever the Czar came. . . .

. . . Among some other causes, one of the chief which makes the generality of the nobility at present uneasy, is, that the Czar obliges them against their will, to come and live at Petersburgh, with their wives and their families, where they are oblig'd to build new houses for themselves, and where all manner of provisions are usually three or four times as dear, and forage for their horses, etc. at least six or eight times as dear as it is at Mosco; which happens from the small quantity which the countrey thereabouts produces, being more than two thirds woods and bogs; and not only the nobility, but merchants and tradesmen of all sorts, are oblig'd to go and live there, and to trade with such things as they are order'd, which crowd of people enhances the price of provisions, and makes a scarcity for those men who are absolutely necessary to live there, on account of the land and sea service, and in carrying on those buildings and works which the Czar has already, and farther designs to make there. Whereas in Mosco, all the lords and men of distinction, have not only very large buildings within the city, but also their countrey seats and villages, where they have their fishponds, their gardens, with plenty of several sorts of fruit and places of pleasure; but Petersburgh, which lies in the latitude of 60 degrees and 15 minutes north, is too cold to produce these things. Besides, Mosco is the native place which the Russes are fond of, and where they have their friends and acquaintance about them; their villages are near, and their provision comes easy and cheap to them, which is brought by their slaves.

As for the Czar, he is a great lover of the water, and entirely delights in ships and boats, and in sailing. . . . But his lords have no relish nor pleasure in those things, and though they seemingly complement the Czar whenever he talks to them of the beauties and delights of Petersburgh; yet when they get together by themselves, they complain and say that there are tears and water enough at Petersburgh, but they pray God to send them to live again at Mosco.

# Catherine II Becomes Mistress of Russia *

> *Catherine II of Russia, German by birth, wife of Tsar Peter III, in 1762 overthrew her husband and became absolute mistress of Russia. Within a week her deposed husband died, an event about which there were conflicting versions and opinions, as we see first in Catherine's own account and then in that of a French diplomat.*

Peter III had lost the small share of senses which naturally belonged to him. . . .

On the occasion of the celebration of peace with the King of Prussia, after having publicly insulted me at table, he gave, in the evening, an order for my arrest. My uncle, Prince George, had the order retracted, and it was only from this time that I listened to the proposals which had been made to me since the death of the Empress Elizabeth. It was intended to seize him in his room, and imprison him. . . . The minds of the guards were prepared, and, towards the end, some thirty or forty officers and nearly ten thousand men were in the secret. In this number there was not a single traitor during the space of three weeks. . . . A report was spread on the 27th that I had been arrested. The soldiers became excited; one of our officers quieted them. Then came a soldier to a captain, named Pacik, the head of a party, and told him that I was certainly lost. Pacik assured him that he had just heard from me. The man, still alarmed for my safety, went to another officer and told him the same story. This person was not in the secret; terrified at learning that an officer had dismissed the man without arresting him, he went to the major; the latter had Pacik arrested, and sent, during the night, a report of the arrest to Oranienbaum. Instantly the whole regiment was in commotion, and our conspirators in alarm. It was resolved . . . to bring me into the city. . . .

. . . At six o'clock on the morning of the 28th, Alexis Orloff entered my room, awoke me, and said very quietly, "It is time to get up; everything is prepared for proclaiming you." I asked for details. He replied, *"Pacik has been arrested."* I no longer hesitated, but dressed hastily . . . and entered the carriage which he had brought with him. . . .

. . . I went to the new Winter Palace, where the synod and senate had assembled. The manifesto and oath were drawn up in haste. Thence I descended, and made, on foot, the inspection of the troops; there were

* Alexander Herzen, ed., *Memoirs of Catherine II*, New York, D. Appleton and Company, 1859.

more than fourteen thousand men, guards and country regiments. The instant I appeared the air was rent with shouts of joy, which were caught up and repeated by an innumerable multitude. I then proceeded to the old Winter Palace, to take the necessary measures for completing our work. There a council was held, and it was determined that I should go at the head of the troops to Peterhoff, where Peter III was to dine. . . . Then came the Chancellor Voronzoff to reprove me for having left Peterhoff. He was led to the church to swear fealty to me; that was my answer. Next came Prince Troubetzkoy and Count Alexander Schouvaloff, also from Peterhoff: they came to assure themselves of the fidelity of the regiments, and put me to death. They also were quietly led away to take the oath.

Having despatched all our couriers, and taken all our precautions, I dressed, about ten o'clock at night, in the uniform of the guards, and had myself proclaimed Colonel amid acclamations of inexpressible enthusiasm. I mounted on horseback, and we left behind us only a small detachment from every regiment for the protection of my son, who remained in the city.

Thus I set out at the head of the troops, and we marched all night towards Peterhoff. . . .

Peter III renounced the empire at Oranienbaum, in full liberty. . . . After this, I placed the deposed Emperor under the command of Alexis Orloff, with four chosen officers, and a detachment of quiet and sober men . . . while decent and comfortable apartments were prepared for him at Schlusselburg, and relays of horses placed on the road. But it pleased God to dispose otherwise. Terror had brought on a dysentery, which continued for three days, and stopped on the fourth. He drank to excess on that day, for he had everything he wanted except his liberty. . . . The hemorrhoidal cholic again came on, accompanied by delirium; he was two days in this condition, which was followed by excessive weakness, and, notwithstanding the efforts of the physicians, he at last sunk, demanding a Lutheran clergyman. I was afraid the officers might have poisoned him, so much was he hated. I had him opened, but not a trace of poison could be discovered. . . .

### Narrative of the French Charge D'Affaires, Beranger *

The death of the late Emperor, a week after the catastrophe, rivets the attention of most people here. It is declared quite publickly that it is the

* R. Nisbett Bain, *Peter III, Emperor of Russia*, Westminster, Archibald Constable & Co. Ltd, 1902.

natural result of the despair caused by his deposition, but in secret people say that they don't believe this at all, but that he was poisoned. I cannot speak affirmatively, my Lord, as to this, but I have everything which might justify the most violent suspicions.

Certain persons, who saw Peter III. at the moment of his departure from Peterhof, assure me that he was composed and in good health; that this Prince, having little genius or sensibility, had never been the prey of any grief, and that the colic with which he is said often to have been attacked was an idea invented to account for his end.

It is even said, my Lord, that this Prince dined as usual on the day of his death, and that on rising from table he was attacked by very sharp and violent pains and that he himself said he was going to die. . . . It is said, my Lord, that the Empress did not know of the death of Peter III. till twenty-four hours afterwards. The tidings were conveyed to her while she was at table. She [then] went into a side chamber with two or three of her confidants. She has only appeared in public a very little since then and has forgotten nothing whereby she may impress her Court with the grief and affliction which this event has caused her. . . .

. . . I do not suppose that the heart of the Princess is so atrocious that she could have had a hand in the death of the Czar; but inasmuch as the most profound mystery will, in all probability, for ever conceal from public knowledge the real author of the horrible crime, the Empress who profits directly by it will always be the object of odious suspicions.

So many people, many of them bad characters overwhelmed with debt and of no reputation, contributed to bring about this Revolution, that it is very probable that one of them may have committed this outrage without the participation of this Princess, in order either to provide for his own personal safety, or perhaps in the belief that he would thereby win her favour. . . .

## A Foreigner's Impressions of Moscow *

WILLIAM COXE

> Although Peter the Great had built St. Petersburg as Russia's window on the Baltic and gateway to the west, Moscow

* William Coxe, *Travels into Poland, Russia, Sweden and Denmark*, vols. 1 & 3, London, Printed for T. Cadell, in the Strand, 1792.

*remained a vital core of Russian life. Here an English
traveler found much less westernization in 1772 than he
had been led to expect he would find.*

*August 30, 1772.* Our approach to Moscow was first announced about
the distance of six miles by some spires. . . . About two or three miles
further we ascended an height, from whence a most superb prospect of
the vast city burst upon our sight. It lay in the form of a crescent, and
stretched to a prodigious extent; while innumerable churches, towers,
gilded spires and domes . . . formed a most splendid appearance, yet
strangely contrasted by an intermixture of numberless wooden hovels. . . .

I was astonished at the immensity and variety of Moscow. A city so
irregular, so uncommon, so extraordinary, and so contrasted, had never
before claimed my astonishment. . . . Wretched hovels are blended with
large palaces; cottages of one story stand next to the most superb and
stately mansions. . . . Numerous churches presented themselves in every
quarter built in a peculiar style of architecture. . . . In a word, some parts
of this vast city have the appearance of a desert, other quarters, of a
populous town; some of a contemptible village, others of a great capital.

Moscow may be considered as a town built upon the Asiatic model,
but gradually becoming more and more European; exhibiting in its present
state a motley mixture of discordant architecture. . . .

Much has been written concerning the great civilization which Peter I.
introduced into this country; that he obliged the people to relinquish their
beards, and their national dress; that he naturalized the arts and sciences;
that he disciplined his army, and created a navy; and that he made a
total change throughout each part of his extensive empire. We may
readily allow the truth of this with respect to his improvements in the
discipline of his army and the creation of a navy. . . . But the pompous
accounts of the total change he effected in the national manners, seem to
have been the mere echoes of foreigners, who have never visited the
country. . . . For though a nation, when compared with itself at a former
period, may have had a rapid progress towards improvement, if put in
competition with the refinements of other nations, seems scarcely to exist.
. . . I must own I was astonished at the barbarism in which the bulk of
the people still continue. I am ready to allow that the principal nobles
are civilized, and as refined in their entertainments and mode of living as
those of other European countries. But there is a wide difference between
polishing a nation, and polishing a few individuals. . . .

# A Royal Absolutist in Prussia *

## FREDERICK THE GREAT

*In the eighteenth century King Frederick II of Prussia (1740–1786) was Europe's foremost example of an "enlightened despot," governing his people according to some of the more advanced ideas of the time. Frederick shows us that enlightened despotism was a full-time occupation, calling for untiring energy and attention to endless details.*

### ON PRIVATE POLICY.

A prince must show only the better side of his character: that is to what you must apply yourself in good earnest, my dear nephew. When I was the Prince Royal, I was a very poor soldier: I liked my own comfort and convenience, good cheer, and good wine. . . .

When I became a king, I appeared to be a soldier, a philosopher, and a poet. I ate coarse bread like my soldiers, drank very little wine in the presence of my subjects. . . .

### ABOUT MY TRAVELLING.

I always walk without any escort; and, day and night, I go on my way without any military display. My suite is not numerous, but very select; my carriage is quite plain in appearance, but it is perfectly easy and commodious, so that I sleep in it as comfortably as in my bed.

I appear to pay very little attention to my manner of living: a footman, a cook, and a pastry-cook are all the servants I require to wait upon me. I order my dinner myself: and that is not the worst thing I do, because I know all about the country where I am travelling; and I ask for the best game, fish, or meats which it affords.

When I arrive at a place, I appear tired, and I show myself to the crowd in a great-coat and an uncombed wig. These things are trifles which often produce strange impressions. . . .

In all that I say, I always appear to think of nothing but my subjects' happiness. I ask questions of noblemen, tradesmen, and workmen, and I converse with them on the least topics.

You must have heard as well as myself, my dear nephew, the flattering remarks of those good people: remember the man who said I must be

* Frederic II, *The Hohenzollern Doctrine and Maxims*, Boston, Crosby & Damrell, 1870.

very kind to give myself so much trouble after such a long and wearisome war. And remember, also, the one who pitied me from the bottom of his heart on seeing my threadbare overcoat, and the small dishes served up at my table. The poor man was not aware that I had a nice coat underneath; and he thought people could not live if they had not a whole ham or a quarter of veal for dinner.

## The Reviewing of my Troops.

Before reviewing a regiment, I take care to read the names of all the officers and sergeants; and I commit to memory three or four of them, with the name of the company to which they belong.

I take care to be strictly informed of the little wrongs and abuses committed by the captains, and I allow the soldiers to complain to me personally.

The hour appointed for the review arrives. I start from my quarters: very soon a crowd surrounds me, and I do not allow any one to disperse it. I talk with the man who stands nearest to me, and who makes the best answers to my questions.

When I have reached the regiment, I make it manœuvre. I pass through the ranks slowly, and talk to every captain: when I am opposite those whose names I have remembered, I call them out, as well as their lieutenants and sergeants; and that gives me the appearance of having a good deal of memory and reflection. . . .

By thus passing reviews, I become thoroughly acquainted with my troops; and, when I find an officer who answers all my questions clearly and straightforwardly, I put his name on my list, so that I may remember him when opportunity requires.

To this day, every one believes that the great love I have for my subjects induces me to visit the different parts of my kingdom as often as I can. I let every one remain under that impression, although this is not my real motive. The fact is, I am obliged to act thus; and here is the reason why.

My government is a despotic one; consequently, he who rules over the kingdom has the exclusive charge of it. If I did not travel over my States, my governors would take my place, and would gradually dispense with the principles of obedience, to adopt only those of independence. Besides, as my orders cannot be otherwise than imperious and peremptory, those who represent me would assume the same tyrannical tone; whilst, by occasionally travelling through my kingdom, I have the means of discovering the abuse which they make of the power that I have delegated to them, and of recalling to their duty and admonishing those who might be tempted to depart from it. Add to those reasons that of making my subjects believe that I come into their country to listen to their complaints, and to relieve them from their troubles.

## Divided Germany *

CASPAR RIESBECK

*In spite of the continued growth of Prussian strength under Frederick The Great and his predecessors, Germany remained divided in the eighteenth century. Caspar Riesbeck, traveling along the Rhine during the year 1780, observed the economic effects of disunity.*

Nothing displays the constitution of the German empire in a better light, than the navigation of the Rhine. Every prince, so far as his domain on the banks reaches, considers the ships that go by as the vessels of foreigners, and loads them, without distinction, with almost intolerable taxes. They do not in the least consider, whether the commodities which pass by are the produce of Germany or other countries, and whether the empire will gain or lose by them. On the contrary, some of the articles exported from Germany, such as wine, wood, &c. have greater taxes laid upon them, in proportion to their intrinsic value, than any foreign ware. Flourishing as the banks of the Rhine now are, they would be still much richer if they belonged only to one master, and were governed according to the principles of a sound policy; as things now are, the exports of the country are visibly cramped by the numerous custom-house duties, so as to make it almost incredible how navigation can be so great as it is.

In the twelfth and thirteenth centuries, as Germany was approaching near to the anarchy in which it in fact still continues, the princes of the Rhine . . . compelled the emperor to give them so many customs as to make every city a custom-house: originally all the customs belonged to

* Caspar Riesbeck, "Travels Through Germany," in John Pinkerton, ed., *A General Collection of the Best and Most Interesting Voyages and Travels*, vol. 6, Philadelphia, Kimber and Conrad, 1812.

the emperors; but their want of men, money, and other services compelled them to part with most of them to purchase friends. Whilst the anarchy lasted, every one took by force what was not given him by free will; and at the peace, they found means to preserve themselves in the possession of what they had stole. . . .

In the small district between Mentz and Coblentz, which, with the windings of the river, hardly make twenty-seven miles, you don't pay less than nine tolls. Between Holland and Coblentz there are at least sixteen. . . .

## A Scene in Parliament *

CHARLES P. MORITZ

> In the minds of liberals throughout Europe, the British Parliament represented the best form of government yet devised. By modern standards, however, it had its limitations: personal wealth was needed to become a member, and Parliament represented only the landed upper classes of Britain. A young German who visited the House of Commons in 1782 wrote home, "I have been to the Parliament House and . . . had I seen nothing else in England but this, I should have thought my journey thither amply rewarded." We read his description.

The first time I went up this small stair-case, and had reached the rails, I saw a very genteel man in black standing there. I accosted him without any introduction, and I asked him whether I might be allowed to go into the gallery. He told me that I must be introduced by a member, or else I could not get admission there. Now, as I had not the honour to be acquainted with a member, I was under the mortifying necessity of retreating, and again going down stairs, as I did, much chagrined. And now, as I was sullenly marching back, I heard something said about a bottle of wine, which seemed to be addressed to me. I could not conceive

---

* Charles P. Moritz, "Travels, Chiefly on Foot, Through Several Parts of England in 1782," in John Pinkerton, ed., *A General Collection of the Best and Most Interesting Voyages and Travels, in All Parts of the World*, vol. 2, Philadelphia, Kimber and Conrad, 1810.

what it could mean, till I got home, when my obliging landlady told me, I should have given the well-dressed man half-a-crown or a couple of shillings for a bottle of wine. Happy in this information, I went again the next day; when the same man who before had sent me away, after I had given him only two shillings, very politely opened the door for me, and himself recommended me to a good seat in the gallery.

And thus I now, for the first time, saw the whole of the British nation assembled in its representatives, in rather a mean-looking building, that not a little resembles a chapel. The Speaker, an elderly man, with an enormous wig, with two knotted kind of tresses, or curls behind, in a black cloak, his hat on his head, sat opposite to me on a lofty chair; which was not unlike a small pulpit, save only that in the front of this there was no reading desk. Before the Speaker's chair stands a table, which looks like an altar; and at this there sit two men, called clerks, dressed in black, with black cloaks. . . .

All round on the sides of the house, under the gallery, are benches for the members, covered with green cloth, always one above the other, like our choirs in churches; in order that he who is speaking may see over those who sit before him. The seats in the gallery are on the same plan. The members of parliament keep their hats on, but the spectators in the gallery are uncovered.

The members of the House of Commons have nothing particular in their dress; they even come into the house in their great coats, and with boots and spurs. It is not at all uncommon to see a member lying stretched out on one of the benches while others are debating. Some crack nuts, others eat oranges, or whatever else is in season. There is no end to their going in and out; and as often as any one wishes to go out, he places himself before the Speaker, and makes him his bow, as if, like a school-boy, he asked his tutor's permission.

Those who speak, seem to deliver themselves with but little, perhaps not always with even a decorous, gravity. All that is necessary, is to stand up in your place, take off your hat, turn to the Speaker (to whom all the speeches are addressed) to hold your hat and stick in one hand, and with the other to make any such motions as you fancy necessary to accompany your speech.

If it happens that a member rises who is but a bad speaker; or if what he says is generally deemed not sufficiently interesting, so much noise is made, and such bursts of laughter are raised, that the member who is speaking can scarcely distinguish his own words. This must needs be a distressing situation; and it seems then to be particularly laughable, when the Speaker in his chair, like a tutor in a school, again and again endeavours to restore order, which he does by calling out, to order, to order; apparently often without much attention being paid to it.

On the contrary, when a favourite member, and one who speaks well and to the purpose, rises, the most perfect silence reigns; and his friends and admirers, one after another, make their approbation known by calling out, hear him; which is often repeated by the whole house at once; and in this way so much noise is often made, that the Speaker is frequently interrupted. . . .

The first day that I was at the House of Commons, an English gentleman who sat next to me in the gallery, very obligingly pointed out to me the principal members, such as Fox, Burke, Rigby, &c. all of whom I heard speak. The debate happened to be, whether, besides being made a peer, any other specific reward should be bestowed by the nation on their gallant admiral Rodney. . . .

Fox was sitting to the right of the speaker, not far from the table on which the gilt sceptre lay. He now took his place so near it that he could reach it with his hand, and, thus placed, he gave it many a violent and hearty thump, either to aid, or to shew the energy with which he spoke. . . . It is impossible for me to describe with what fire and persuasive eloquence he spoke, and how the speaker in the chair incessantly nodded approbation from beneath his solemn wig; and innumerable voices incessantly called out, hear him! hear him! and when there was the least sign that he intended to leave off speaking, they no less vociferously exclaimed, go on; and so he continued to speak in this manner for nearly two hours. . . .

The little less than downright open abuse and the many really rude things which the members said to each other, struck me much. For example, when one has finished, another rises, and immediately taxes with absurdity all that the right honourable gentleman (for with this title the members of the House of Commons always honour each other) had just advanced. It would indeed be contrary to the rules of the house, flatly to tell each other that what they have spoken is false, or even foolish; instead of this, they turn themselves, as usual, to the Speaker, and so, whilst their address is directed to him, they fancy they violate neither the rules of parliament, nor those of good breeding and decorum, whilst they utter the most cutting personal sarcasms against the member, or the measure they oppose.

# Purchase of Parliamentary Seats in Britain *

LORD CHESTERFIELD, SAMUEL ROMILLY

*Royal absolutism had been checked in Britain by the rise of Parliamentary power, but this did not mean that democracy had arrived in the eighteenth century. The House of Lords was composed only of titled nobles, while the House of Commons was made up of relatives or dependents of the nobles and of men wealthy enough to purchase a seat from one of the boroughs, which sold their votes to the highest bidder. We read Lord Chesterfield's letter of 1767 regretting that he cannot buy his son a seat in the House of Commons. The situation had not improved forty years later, as we see in Sir Samuel Romilly's letter of 1807.*

. . . I desired to secure you a seat in the new Parliament . . . and I spoke to a borough-jobber, and offered five-and-twenty hundred pounds for a secure seat in Parliament; but he laughed at my offer, and said, That there was no such thing as a borough to be had now; for that the rich East and West Indians had secured them all, at the rate of three thousand pounds at least; but many at four thousand; and two or three, that he knew, at five thousand. This, I confess, has vexed me a good deal. . . .

I shall procure myself a seat in the new Parliament, unless I find that it will cost so large a sum, as, in the state of my family, it would be very imprudent for me to devote to such an object, which I find is very likely to be the case. Tierney, who manages this business for the friends of the late administration, assures me that he can hear of no seats to be disposed of. After a Parliament which has lived little more than four months, one would naturally suppose, that those seats which are regularly sold by the proprietors of them would be very cheap; they are, however, in fact, sold now at a higher price than was ever given for them before. Tierney tells me that he has offered 10,000*l.* for the two seats of Westbury, the property of the late Lord Abingdon, and which are to be made the most of by trustees for creditors, and has met with a refusal. . . .

\* First excerpt from Philip Dormer Stanhope, Earl of Chesterfield, *Letters to His Son*, London, J. Dodsley, 1774; second from Sir Samuel Romilly, *Memoirs*, vol. 2, London, John Murray, 1840.

This buying of seats is detestable; and yet it is almost the only way in which one in my situation, who is resolved to be an independent man, can get into Parliament. To come in by a popular election, in the present state of the representation, is quite impossible; to be placed there by some great lord, and to vote as he shall direct, is to be in a state of complete dependence; and nothing hardly remains but to owe a seat to the sacrifice of a part of one's fortune. It is true that many men who buy seats, do it as a matter of pecuniary speculation, as a profitable way of employing their money: they carry on a political trade; they buy their seats, and sell their votes. For myself, I can truly say that, by giving money for a seat, I shall make a sacrifice of my private property, merely that I may be enabled to serve the public. I know what danger there is of men's disguising from themselves the real motives of their actions; but it really does appear to me that it is from this motive alone that I act.


## A Sailor's Life *

Tobias Smollett

*The eighteenth century race between France and England for overseas possessions made the quality of their seamen a matter of great importance—which, however, was unrecognized by the governments of the time. Conditions of the sailors' lives at sea were so terrible that crews had to be made up by press gangs seizing men ashore. Tobias Smollett, who served as ship's doctor on several warships, and describes conditions of about 1750 in his novel* Roderick Random. *The experiences that the hero, Roderick, describes were typical of the time.*

As I crossed Tower-wharf, a squat tawny fellow, with a hanger by his side, and a cudgel in his hand, came up to me, calling: "Yo, ho! brother, you must come along with me!" As I did not like his appearance, instead of answering his salutation, I quickened my pace, in hope of ridding myself of his company; upon which he whistled aloud, and immediately another sailor appeared before me, who laid hold of me by the collar, and began to

* T. Smollett, *Roderick Random,* as quoted in Charles W. Colby, *Selections from the Sources of English History,* New York, Longmans, Green, & Co., 1905.

drag me along . . . ; and, after an obstinate engagement, in which I received a large wound on my head, and another on my left cheek, I was disarmed, taken prisoner, and carried on board a pressing tender, where, after being pinioned like a malefactor, I was thrust down into the hold among a parcel of miserable wretches, the sight of whom well nigh distracted me. As the commanding officer had not humanity enough to order my wounds to be dressed, and I could not use my own hands, I desired one of my fellow-captives, who was unfettered, to take a handkerchief out of my pocket, and tie it round my head to stop the bleeding. He pulled out my handkerchief, 'tis true, but, instead of applying it to the use for which I designed it, went to the grating of the hatchway, and, with astonishing composure, sold it before my face to a bumboat woman, then on board, for a quart of gin, with which he treated my companions, regardless of my circumstances and entreaties.

I complained bitterly of this robbery to the midshipman on deck, telling him at the same time that, unless my hurts were dressed, I should bleed to death. But compassion was a weakness of which no man could justly accuse this person, who, squirting a mouthful of dissolved tobacco upon me, through the gratings, told me "I was a mutinous dog, and that I might die and be d——d.". . .

[Roderick was eventually brought to his quarters.] We descended by divers' ladders to a space as dark as a dungeon, which I understood was immersed several feet under water, being immediately above the hold. I had no sooner approached this dismal gulf, than my nose was saluted with an intolerable stench of putrefied cheese and rancid butter, that issued from an apartment at the foot of the ladder, resembling a chandler's shop, where, by the faint glimmering of a candle, I could perceive a man with a pale meagre countenance, sitting behind a kind of desk, having spectacles on his nose, and a pen in his hand. This (I learned of Mr. Thomson) was the ship's steward, who sat there to distribute provision to the several messes, and to mark what each received. He therefore presented my name to him, and desired that I might be entered in his mess; then, taking a light in his hand, conducted me to the place of his residence, which was a square of about six feet, surrounded with the medicine chest, that of the first mate, his own, and a board, by way of table, fastened to the after powder-room: it was also inclosed with canvas nailed round to the beams of the ship, to screen us from the cold. . . .

The surgeon grinned approbation, and, taking the list, began to examine the complaints of each, as they could crawl to the place appointed. The first who came under his cognizance was a poor fellow just freed of a fever, which had weakened him so much, that he could hardly stand. Mr. Mackshane (for that was the doctor's name) having felt his pulse, protested he was as well as any man in the world; and the captain delivered him over to the boatswain's mate, with orders that he should receive a round dozen at the gang-way immediately, for counterfeiting himself sick; but before the discipline could be executed, the man dropt down on the deck, and had well nigh perished under the hands of the executioner. . . .

The third complained of a pleuritic stitch, and spitting of blood; for which Doctor Mackshane prescribed exercise at the pump . . . : but whether this was improper for one in his situation, or that it was used to excess, I know not; for in less than half an hour he was suffocated with a deluge of blood that issued from his lungs. . . . It would be tedious and disagreeable to describe the fate of every miserable object that suffered by the inhumanity and ignorance of the captain and surgeon. . . .

Some gave up the ghost in the presence of their inspectors; and others, who were ordered to their duty, languished a few days at work among their fellows, and then departed without any ceremony. On the whole, the number of the sick was reduced to less than a dozen.


## *Civilian Travel By Sea* *

GOTTLIEB MITTELBERGER

> *While civilians were not subject to the lash and other brutalities inflicted on sailors, the crossing of the Atlantic offered such hardships as to daunt any but the boldest, most desperate, or most adventurous. The ordeal of travel shows how earnestly migrants must have wanted to escape from Europe to a new life overseas. A German schoolteacher coming to Pennsylvania in 1750 describes the ocean crossing.*

When the ships have . . . weighed their anchors . . . the real misery begins with the long voyage. For from there the ships, unless they have good wind, must often sail 8, 9, 10 to 12 weeks before they reach Philadelphia. But even with the best wind the voyage lasts 7 weeks.

* *Gottlieb Mittelberger's Journey to Pennsylvania*, Philadelphia, Jon. Jos. McVey, 1898 (translated by Carl Theo. Eben).

But during the voyage there is on board these ships terrible misery, stench, fumes, horror, vomiting, many kinds of sea-sickness, fever, dysentery, headache, heat, constipation, boils, scurvy, cancer, mouth-rot, and the like, all of which come from old and sharply salted food and meat, also from very bad and foul water, so that many die miserably.

Add to this want of provisions, hunger, thirst, frost, heat, dampness, anxiety, want, afflictions . . . [also] the lice abound so frightfully, especially on sick people, that they can be scraped off the body. The misery reaches the climax when a gale rages for 2 or 3 nights and days, so that every one believes that the ship will go to the bottom with all human beings on board. In such a visitation the people cry and pray most piteously. . . .

Among the healthy, impatience sometimes grows so great and cruel that one curses the other, or himself and the day of his birth, and sometimes come near killing each other. Misery and malice join each other, so that they cheat and rob one another. One always reproaches the other with having persuaded him to undertake the journey. Frequently children cry out against their parents, husbands against their wives and wives against their husbands, brothers and sisters, friends and acquaintances against each other. But most against the soul-traffickers.

Many sigh and cry: "Oh, that I were at home again, and if I had to lie in my pig-sty!" Or they say: "O God, if I only had a piece of good bread, or a good fresh drop of water." Many people whimper, sigh and cry piteously for their homes; most of them get home-sick. Many hundred people necessarily die and perish in such misery, and must be cast into the sea, which drives their relatives, or those who persuaded them to undertake the journey, to such despair that it is almost impossible to pacify and console them. In a word, the sighing and crying and lamenting on board the ship continues night and day, so as to cause the hearts even of the most hardened to bleed when they hear it. . . .

Children from 1 to 7 years rarely survive the voyage; and many a time parents are compelled to see their children miserably suffer and die from hunger, thirst and sickness, and then to see them cast into the water. I witnessed such misery in no less than 32 children in our ship, all of whom were thrown into the sea. The parents grieve all the more since their children find no resting-place in the earth, but are devoured by the monsters of the sea. It is a notable fact that children, who have not yet had the measles or small-pocks, generally get them on board the ship, and mostly die of them.

Many other accidents happen on board these ships, especially by falling, whereby people are often made cripples and can never be set right again. Some have also fallen into the ocean. . . .

At length, when, after a long and tedious voyage, the ships come in sight of land, so that the promontories can be seen, which the people were so eager and anxious to see, all creep from below on deck to see the land from afar, and they weep for joy, and pray and sing, thanking and praising God. The sight of the land makes the people on board the ship, especially the sick and the half dead, alive again, so that their hearts leap within them; they shout and rejoice, and are content to bear their misery in patience, in the hope that they may soon reach the land in safety. But alas!

When the ships have landed at Philadelphia after their long voyage, no one is permitted to leave them except those who pay for their passage or can give good security; the others, who cannot pay, must remain on board the ships till they are purchased, and are released from the ships by their purchasers. The sick always fare the worst, for the healthy are naturally preferred and purchased first; and so the sick and wretched must often remain on board in front of the city for 2 or 3 weeks, and frequently die, whereas many a one, if he could pay his debt and were permitted to leave the ship immediately, might recover and remain alive.

## *The Black Hole of Calcutta* *

ROBERT ORME

> *Five great periods of war in the eighteenth century involved European states and their holdings in Asia and America. In these wars, Britain and France were always on opposing sides. While each of the wars involved the rise and decline of nations within Europe, they also reflected overseas competition for trade and colonial bases. In India France began the training of "sepoys" (native Indians) in European methods of warfare. The incident of the death of the British garrison in the "Black Hole of Calcutta" served to arouse British determination to extend their own Indian efforts.*

* Robert Orme, *History of the Military Transactions of the British Nation in Indostan from the Year 1775*, vol. 2, London, John Nourse, 1778 (adapted).

. . . Before all were within, the room was so thronged, that the last entered with difficulty. The guard immediately closed and locked the door; confining 146 persons in a room not 20 feet square, with only two small windows, and these obstructed by the veranda.

It was the hottest season of the year; and the night uncommonly sultry even at this season. The excessive pressure as soon as the door was shut, convinced the prisoners that it was impossible to live through the night in this horrible confinement; and violent attempts were immediately made to force the door; but without effect, for it opened inward: on which many began to give a loose to rage. Mr. Holwell, who had placed himself at one of the windows, exhorted them to remain composed both in body and mind, as the only means of surviving the night, and his remonstrances produced a short interval of quiet; . . .

. . . Every minute had increased their sufferings. The first effect of their confinement was a profuse and continued sweat, which soon produced intolerable thirst . . . with difficulty of breathing little short of suffocation. Various means were tried to obtain more room and air. . . . Attempts were again made to force the door, which, failing as before, redoubled their rage: but the thirst increasing, nothing but water! water! became soon after the general cry. The good Jemautdar [an elderly guard] immediately ordered some skins of water to be brought to the windows: but, instead of relief, his benevolence became a more dreadful cause of destruction; for the sight of the water threw every one into such excessive agitation and ravings, that, unable to resist this violent impulse of nature, none could wait to be regularly served, but each with the utmost ferocity battled against those who were likely to get it before him; and in these conflicts many were either pressed to death by the efforts of others, or suffocated by their own. . . . Before midnight, all who were alive and had not partaken of the air at the windows, were either in a lethargic stupefaction, or raving with delirium. Every kind of invective and abuse was uttered, in hopes of provoking the guard to put an end to their miseries, by firing into the dungeon; and whilst some were blaspheming their creator . . . heaven was implored by others with wild incoherent prayers; until the weaker, exhausted by these agitations, at length laid down quietly, and expired. . . . Those who still survived in the inward part of the dungeon . . . made a last effort to obtain air, by endeavouring to scramble over the heads of those who stood between them and the windows; where the utmost strength of every one was employed for two hours, either in maintaining his own ground, or in endeavouring to get that of which others were in possession. . . . [At long last the sun rose.] The survivors then at the window, finding that their intreaties could not prevail on the guard to open the door, it occurred to Mr. Cooke, the secretary of the council, that Mr. Holwell, if alive, might have more influence to obtain their relief; and two of the company undertaking the search, discovered him, having still some signs of life; but when they brought him towards the window, every one refused to quit his place, excepting Captain Mills, who with rare generosity offered to resign his; . . . He had scarcely begun to recover his senses, before an officer, sent by the Nabob, came and enquired if the English chief survived; and soon after the same man returned with an order to open the prison. The dead were so thronged, and the survivors had so little strength remaining, that they were employed near half an hour in removing the bodies which lay against the door, before they could clear a passage to go out one at a time; when of one hundred and forty-six who went in, no more than twenty-three came out alive. . . .

## British Optimism *

ROBERT CLIVE

> *The refusal of Britons to be daunted by reverses such as that at Calcutta is reflected in the letter of Robert Clive, who was to become Britain's greatest empire builder in India.*

HONOURABLE GENTLEMEN,

From many hands you will hear of the capture of Calcutta by the Moors, and the chain of misfortunes and losses which have happened to the Company in particular, and to the nation in general. . . .

Upon this melancholy occasion, the Governor and council thought proper to summon me to this place. . . . I am now upon the point of embarking on board His Majesty's squadron, with a fair body of Euro-

* John Malcolm, *The Life of Robert, Lord Clive*, vol. 1, London, John Murray, 1836.

peans, full of spirit and resentment for the insults and barbarities inflicted on so many British subjects.

I flatter myself that this expedition will not end with the taking of Calcutta only; and that the Company's estate in those parts will be settled in a better and more lasting condition than ever. There is less reason to apprehend a check from the Nabob's forces, than from the nature of the climate and country. The news of a war . . . expected between France and England may likewise interfere with the success of this expedition: however, should that happen, and hostilities be committed in India, I hope we shall be able to dispossess the French. . . .

I have a true sense of my duty to my country and the Company; and I beg to assure you, that nothing shall be wanting, on my part, to answer the ends of an undertaking on which so very much depends. . . .

R. CLIVE

Fort St. George, 11th Oct., 1756

## France Loses Canada *

JOHN KNOX

*Each of the great eighteenth-century wars involved America as well as Europe and Asia. Toward the end of the Seven Years War (called "The French and Indian War" by the British colonials), Quebec fell to the British General Wolfe. Britain's retention of Canada at the close of the war released the British colonials from their long-standing fear of France, and seventeen years later they allied themselves with their former enemy as the American Revolution widened into yet another all-European conflict. We hear Captain John Knox's report of the battle of Quebec in 1759.*

Sept. 11, 1759. Great preparations are making throughout the fleet and army to surprise the enemy, and compel them to decide the fate of Quebec by a battle. All the long-boats below the town are to be filled with seamen, marines, and such detachments as can be spared from Points Levi and

* Captain John Knox, "Historical Journal of the Campaigns in North America for the Years 1757, 1758, 1759, and 1760," *Old South Leaflets,* No. 73.

Orleans, in order to make a feint off Beauport and the Point de Lest, and endeavor to engross the attention of the Sieur de Montcalm, while the army are to force a descent on this side of the town. . . .

THURSDAY, Sept. 13, 1759. Before daybreak this morning we made a descent upon the north shore, about half a quarter of a mile to the eastward of Sillery; . . . . This was a great surprise on the enemy, who from the natural strength of the place did not suspect, and consequently were not prepared against so bold an attempt. The chain of sentries which they had posted along the summit of the heights galled us a little, and picked off several men and some officers before our light infantry got up to dislodge them. This grand enterprise was conducted and executed with great good order and discretion. As fast as we landed, the boats put off for re-enforcements, and the troops formed with much regularity. . . . We lost no time here, but clambered up one of the steepest precipices that can be conceived, being almost a perpendicular, and of an incredible height. . . . We then faced to the right, and marched toward the town by files till we came to the Plains of Abraham, an even piece of ground which Mr. Wolfe had made choice of, while we stood forming upon the hill. Weather showery. About six o'clock the enemy first made their appearance upon the heights between us and the town, whereupon we halted and wheeled to the right, thereby forming the line of battle. . . . About ten o'clock the enemy began to advance briskly in three columns, with loud shouts . . . until they came within forty yards, which our troops withstood with the greatest intrepidity and firmness, still reserving their fire and paying the strictest obedience to their officers. This uncommon steadiness, together with the havoc which the grape-shot from our field-pieces made among them, threw them into some disorder, and was most critically maintained by a well-timed, regular, and heavy discharge of our small arms, such as they could no longer oppose. Hereupon they gave way, and fled with precipitation, so that by the time the cloud of smoke was vanished our men were again loaded, and, profiting by the advantage we had over them, pursued them almost to the gates of the town and the bridge over the little river, re-doubling our fire with great eagerness, making many officers and men prisoners. The weather cleared up, with a comfortably warm sunshine. . . . The officers who are prisoners say that Quebec will surrender in a few days. . . . Thus has our late renowned commander by his superior eminence in the art of war, . . . made a conquest of this fertile, healthy, and hitherto formidable country, with a handful of troops only, in spite of the political schemes and most vigorous efforts of the famous Montcalm, and many other officers of rank and experience at the head of an army considerably more numerous. . . .

When . . . Montcalm being answered that his wound was mortal, he calmly replied, "he was glad of it." His Excellency then demanded "whether he could survive it long, and how long." He was told, "About a dozen hours, perhaps more, . . ." "So much the better," rejoined the eminent warrior; "I am happy I shall not live to see the surrender of Quebec". . . . Some time before this greatman departed we are assured he paid us this compliment: "Since it was my misfortune to be discomfited, and mortally wounded, it is a consolation to me to be vanquished by so brave and generous an enemy. . . ."

After our late worthy general of renowned memory was carried off wounded to the rear of the front line, he desired those who were about him to lay him down. . . . One of them cried, "They run, see how they run!" "Who runs?" demanded our hero with great earnestness like a person roused from sleep. The officer answered: "The enemy sir. . . ." Thereupon the general rejoined: *"Go, one of you, my lads, to Colonel Burton—; tell him to march Webb's regiment with all speed down to Charles River, to cut off the retreat of the fugitives from the bridge."* Then, turning on his side, he added, *"Now, God be praised, I will die in peace!"* and thus expired.

## Despot or Citizen King?

George III

> George III, king of the United Kingdom of Great Britain and king of Hanover, had no desire to be an absolutist in the style common on the continent, but rather sought to work within the system established by the Glorious Revolution of 1689. For a time he enjoyed wide popularity among Americans, who saw him as their defender against the growth of Parliamentary authority. But when it became clear that he could not (or would not) support the colonies against Parliament, his popularity vanished, and he was attacked in America as an intolerable despot. George III speaks to us at the beginning and again at the end of the American Revolution.

## George III Decides to Fight *

. . . Step by step the demands of America have risen: independence is their object; that certainly is one which every man not willing to sacrifice every object to a *momentary* and inglorious peace must concurr with me in thinking that this country can never submit to: should America succeed in that, the West Indies must follow them, not independence, but must for its own interest be dependent on North America. Ireland would soon follow the same plan and be a separate state; then this island would be reduced to itself, and soon would be a poor island indeed, for, reduced in her trade, merchants would retire with their wealth to climates more to their advantage, and shoals of manufacturers would leave this country for the new empire. These self-evident consequences are not worse than what can arise should the Almighty permit every event to turn out to our disadvantage; consequently this country has but one sensible, one great line to follow, the being ever ready to make peace when to be obtained without submitting to terms that in their consequence must annihilate this empire, and with firmness to make every effort to deserve success.

## A Confession of Defeat **

My Lords and Gentlemen;

Since the close of the last session, I have employed my whole time in that care and attention which the important and critical conjecture of affairs required of me.

I lost no time in giving the necessary orders to prohibit the further prosecution of offensive war upon the continent of North America. Adopting, as my inclination will always lead me to do, with decision and effects, whatever I collect to be the sense of my parliament and my people; I have pointed all my views and measures as well in Europe as in North America, to an entire and cordial reconciliation with those colonies.

Finding it indispensable to the attainment of this object, I did not hesitate to go the full length of the powers vested in me, and offered to declare them free and independent states, by an article to be inserted in the treaty of peace. Provisional articles are agreed upon, to take effect whenever terms of peace shall be finally settled with the court of France.

In thus admitting their separation from the crown of these kingdoms, I have sacrificed every consideration of my own, to the wishes and opinion

---

* W. Bodham Donne, ed., *The Correspondence of King George the Third with Lord North,* vol. 2, London, John Murray, 1867.
** Elizabeth Kendall, *Source-Book of English History,* New York, The Macmillan Co., 1900.

of my people. I make it my humble and earnest prayer to Almighty God, that Great Britain may not feel the evils which might result from so great a dismemberment of the empire; and, that America may be free from those calamities, which have formerly proved in the mother country how essential monarchy is to the enjoyment of constitutional liberty. Religion—language—interest—affections may, and I hope will yet prove a bond of permanent union between the two countries: to this end, neither attention nor disposition on my part, shall be wanting. . . .

## A Political Theory against Royal Absolutism *

JOHN LOCKE

> *Writing in 1690, when absolutism was triumphant everywhere except in his own England, John Locke sought to justify the Glorious Revolution that had recently overthrown a king and established the right of Parliament to share in the government. Locke held that all men have "natural rights" to life, liberty, and property and that government exists to protect these rights. Should a government attempt to take these rights away, men were justified in changing it. Parts of the American Declaration of Independence are based directly on Locke, and no other writer has been so often quoted by spokesmen for democracy.*

Men being . . . by Nature all free, equal, and independent, no one can be put out of his estate and subjected to the political power of another without his own consent, which is done by agreeing with other men, to join and unite into a Community, for their comfortable, safe and peaceable living one amongst another. . . .

When any number of men have by the consent of every individual, made a Community, they have thereby made that Community one body, with a power to act as one body, which is only by the will and determination of the majority. . . .

And thus every man, by consenting with others to make one body politic under one Government, puts himself under an obligation to every one of that Society, to submit to the determination of the majority. . . .

* John Locke, *Two Treatises of Government*, London, Awnsham and John Churchill, 1698.

But though men when they enter into Society, give up the equality, liberty, and executive power they had . . . , into the hands of the Society, to be . . . disposed of by the legislative, as the good of the Society shall require; yet . . . [they do so] only with an intention in every one the better to preserve himself, his liberty and property; . . . [and therefore] the power of the Society, or legislative, constituted by them, can never be supposed to extend farther than the common good. . . .

The great end of men's entering into Society being the enjoyment of their properties in peace and safety, and the great instrument and means of that being the laws established in that Society: the first and fundamental positive law of all Commonwealths is the establishing of the legislative power. The first and fundamental law, which is to govern even the Legislative itself, is the preservation of the Society, and (as far as will consist with the public good) of every person in it. This legislative is not only the supreme power of the Commonwealth, but sacred and unalterable in the hands where the community have once placed it; nor can any edict of anybody else, in what form soever conceived, or by what power soever backed, have the force and obligation of a law, . . . [unless it has] its sanction from that legislative which the public has chosen and appointed. . . .

As usurpation is the exercise of power which another has a right to; so tyranny is the exercise of power beyond right, which nobody can have a right to. And this is making use of the power any one has in his hands; not for the good of those who are under it, but for his own private separate advantage. . . .

Wherever law ends, tyranny begins, if the law be transgressed to another's harm; and whosoever in authority exceeds the power given him by the law and makes use of the force he has under his command . . . which the law allows not, ceases in that to be a magistrate, and [since he is] acting without authority, may be opposed.

## The Separation of Powers *

CHARLES DE MONTESQUIEU

> *Absolute power in the hands of kings had been checked in England, whose example was now being studied by thought-*

* Montesquieu, *The Spirit of Laws,* vol. 1, Cincinnati, Robert Clarke & Co., 1873.

*ful people elsewhere in Europe. In 1748 Charles de Montesquieu, a French nobleman, renewed the attack on absolutism in* The Spirit of Laws. *Recognizing that one person's freedom must not be so great that he can take away the freedom of someone else, Montesquieu proposed a system of "separation of powers" in which individual liberty would be guaranteed by a system of checks and balances.*

Liberty is a right of doing whatever the laws permit; and if a citizen could do what they forbid, he would be no longer possessed of liberty, because all his fellow citizens would have the same power. . . .

To prevent this abuse, it is necessary from the very nature of things, [that] power should be a check to power. A government may be so constituted, as no man shall be compelled to do things to which the law does not oblige him, nor forced to abstain from things which the law permits. . . .

In every government there are three sorts of power: the legislative; the executive, in respect to things dependent on the law of nations; and the judiciary, in regard to matters that depend on the civil law. . . .

When the legislative and executive powers are united in the same person, or in the same body of magistrates, there can be no liberty; because apprehensions may arise, lest the same monarch or senate should enact tyrannical laws, to execute them in a tyrannical manner.

Again, there is no liberty, if the judiciary power be not separated from the legislative and executive. Were it joined with the legislative, the life and liberty of the subject would be exposed to arbitrary control; for the judge would be then the legislator. Were it joined to the executive power, the judge might behave with violence and oppression.

## Natural Science Moves Ahead *

BENJAMIN FRANKLIN

*Benjamin Franklin was typical of numbers of Europeans and Americans of the eighteenth century in his lively interest in*

* Albert Henry Smyth, ed., *The Writings of Benjamin Franklin,* vol. 3, New York, The Macmillan Company, 1905.

*everything in the world around him. An example was his curiosity about a toy which was invented in Europe in 1745, by which electrical sparks were generated in a jar of fluid. Franklin's experiments led him to discover the fluid quality of electricity, its positive and negative currents, and that it was identical with lightning. Fortunately he was not electrocuted in playing with lightning and lived to write the following letter.*

As frequent mention is made in public papers from *Europe* of the success of the *Philadelphia* experiment for drawing the electric fire from clouds by means of pointed rods of iron erected on high buildings, &c., it may be agreeable to the curious to be informed, that the same experiment has succeeded in *Philadelphia*, though made in a different and more easy manner, which is as follows:

Make a small cross of two light strips of cedar, the arms so long as to reach to the four corners of a large thin silk handkerchief when extended; tie the corners of the handkerchief to the extremities of the cross, so you have the body of a kite; which being properly accommodated with a tail, loop, and string, will rise in the air, like those made of paper; but this being of silk, is fitter to bear the wet and wind of a thunder-gust without tearing. To the top of the upright stick of the cross is to be fixed a very sharp-pointed wire, rising a foot or more above the wood. To the end of the twine, next the hand, is to be tied a silk ribbon, and where the silk and twine join, a key may be fastened. This kite is to be raised when a thunder-gust appears to be coming on, and the person who holds the string must stand within a door or window, or under some cover, so that the silk ribbon may not be wet; and care must be taken that the twine does not touch the frame of the door or window. As soon as any of the thunder-clouds come over the kite, the pointed wire will draw the electric fire from them, and the kite, with all the twine, will be electrified, and the loose filaments of the twine will stand out every way, and be attracted by an approaching finger. And when the rain has wet the kite and twine, so that it can conduct the electric fire freely, you will find it stream out plentifully from the key on the approach of your knuckle. At this key the phial may be charged; and from electric fire thus obtained, spirits may be kindled, and all the other electric experiments be performed, which are usually done by the help of a rubbed glass globe or tube, and thereby the sameness of the electric matter with that of lightning completely demonstrated.

# The Future Progress of Mankind *

JEAN ANTOINE NICOLAS DE CONDORCET

> *Condorcet (1743–1794) was a French mathematician, phi-*
> *losopher, and political leader whose faith in human progress*
> *was typical of the optimistic views of the eighteenth-century*
> *philosophes. He summed up his attitude in the book* The
> Progress of the Human Mind, *in which he traces the devel-*
> *opment of mankind and predicts that the final stage—the*
> *perfection of man—will soon arrive.*

If man can predict, almost with certainty, those appearances of which
he understands the laws; if, even when the laws are unknown to him,
experience of the past enables him to foresee, with considerable probability,
future appearances; why should we suppose it a chimercial [unrealistic]
undertaking to delineate [outline] with some degree of truth, the picture of
the future destiny of mankind from the results of history? The only foundation of faith in the natural sciences is the principle, that the general laws,
known or unknown, which regulate the phenomena of the universe, are
regular and constant; and why should this principle, applicable to the
other operations of nature, be less true when applied to the development
of the intellectual and moral faculties of man? . . .

. . . Will not men be continually verging towards that state, in which
all will possess the requisite [necessary] knowledge for conducting themselves in the common affairs of life by their own reason, and of maintaining
that reason uncontaminated by prejudices; in which they will understand
their rights, and exercise them according to their opinion and their conscience; in which all will be able, by the development of their faculties, to
procure the certain means of providing for their wants; lastly, in which
folly and wretchedness will be accidents, happening only now and then,
and not be the habitual lot of a considerable portion of society? . . .

. . . We shall find the strongest reasons to believe, from past experience, from observation of the progress which the sciences and civilization
have hitherto made, and from the analysis of the march of human understanding, and the development of its faculties, that nature has fixed no
limits on our hopes. . . .

* Jean Antoine Nicolas de Condorcet, "The Progress of the Human Mind," *Introduction to Contemporary Civilization in the West*, New York, Columbia University
Press, 1947, pp. 868–869, 876.

# Index

Authors and source documents are indicated by page references in *italics*.